Dear Reader:

The book you are about to read is the latest bestseller from
the St. Martin's True Crime Library, the imprint *The New
York Times* calls "the leader in true crime!" Each month,
we offer you a fascinating account of the latest, most
sensational crime that has captured the national attention. St. Martin's is the publisher of John Glatt's riveting
and horrifying SECRETS IN THE CELLAR, which shines a
light on the man who shocked the world when it was revealed that he had kept his daughter locked in his hidden
basement for 24 years. In the Edgar-nominated WRITTEN IN
BLOOD, Diane Fanning looks at Michael Petersen, a Marine-
turned-novelist found guilty of beating his wife to death and
pushing her down the stairs of their home—only to reveal
another similar death from his past. In the book you now
hold, A SOCIALITE SCORNED, award-winning author Kerrie
Droban examines a dramatic case of money and murder.

St. Martin's True Crime Library gives you the stories behind
the headlines. Our authors take you right to the scene of the
crime and into the minds of the most notorious murderers
to show you what really makes them tick. St. Martin's True
Crime Library paperbacks are better than the most terrifying thriller, because it's all true! The next time you want a
crackling good read, make sure it's got the St. Martin's True
Crime Library logo on the spine—you'll be up all night!

Charles E. Spicer, Jr.
Executive Editor, St. Martin's True Crime Library

A SOCIALITE SCORNED

THE MURDER OF A TUCSON HIGH-ROLLER

Kerrie Droban

St. Martin's Paperbacks

A SOCIALITE SCORNED

Copyright © 2012 by Kerrie Droban.

For information address St. Martin's Press, 175 Fifth Avenue, New York, NY 10010.

ISBN: 978-0-312-54125-5

Printed in the United States of America

St. Martin's Paperbacks edition / February 2012

St. Martin's Paperbacks are published by St. Martin's Press, 175 Fifth Avenue, New York, NY 10010.

10 9 8 7 6 5 4 3 2 1

"There are no secrets in life, just hidden truths that lie beneath the surface."
—Jeff Lindsay

CONTENTS

AUTHOR'S NOTE

Tucson, Arizona, situated just one hour from the Mexican border, surrounded by cactus forests, impressive mountain ranges, and evergreen sky islands, always seemed a quirky and *safe* place to live. Even reputed retired mobsters settled in Tucson without hassle and the desert-dwelling Tohono O'odham tribe (meaning "People of the Desert") still sold their intricate and beautiful hand-woven basketry they called "man in the maze" in kiosks along the main streets. Hollywood producers, enamored with the Wild West, regularly scripted gunfights at the Old Tucson Studios, a rough-and-tumble cowboy town lined with old saloons, candy shops, and novelty stores that stood in stark contrast to the crumbled Spanish 1797 mission San Xavier del Bac framed against the Tucson skyline.

Gary Triano's bombing rippled through this quiet community like a shock wave as people tried to comprehend the idea of total annihilation, much less rational motive. Gary's case, which took nearly a decade to solve and another two years to litigate, revealed a tale as dark as any murder-for-hire plot with an unusual and perplexing twist: Gary's purported killers left behind a "treasure trove" of information for this author that not only provided marvelous insight into their criminal pathology but also revealed the complexity involved in investigating a bombing. Ironically, Gary's alleged coconspirators' attention to detail, as a way to *conceal* their reputed activity, actually led to their dramatic exposure and made writing this book an author's dream.

The documentation available to reconstruct the crime, alleged conspiracy and relationship between Pamela Phillips and Ron Young, was extraordinary. Aided in large part by the cooperation of the Pima County Sheriff's Department, I had access literally to a warehouse of evidence. The room, stacked from floor to ceiling with boxes of materials pertaining to the Triano investigation, contained graphic crime scene photographs, hundreds of hours of interviews with potential suspects (many of whom were discarded early in the investigation as red herrings), thousands of pages of police reports, volumes of financial records, bomb debris, search warrants and countless recordings of conversations between Ron Young and Pamela Phillips, select portions of which are memorialized nearly verbatim in some passages and reconstructed in others, consistent, in some instances, with the prosecution's theory of what transpired. Additionally, I pored through more than 11,000 e-mails between the pair that underscored their general paranoia, the terms of their financial agreement, and the proverbial prison each created.

My narrative is based on hundreds of hours of research of public documents, trial accounts, interviews, and news sources. The dialogue included herein came from e-mail correspondence between Ron Young and Pamela Phillips, recordings, police interviews, trial proceedings, police affidavits, court documents, and news accounts. Every attempt has been made to present the story in the order that it occurred. However, a few events are presented out of chronological sequence for easier reading and understanding of the facts of this complicated case.

Many people facilitated this complex investigation, but Detective James Gamber assumed the lead (and the burden) of solving this murder. By making him the central character in this story I do not mean to imply that he did all of the work and it is not my intention to diminish in any way the fine efforts of the other individuals who helped bring this case to justice. I was blessed to have the generous ear of retired Detective James Gamber and several other investigators and officials in the Pima County Sheriff's Department and Pima County Attorney's Office whose interviews with me contributed greatly to the details in this book and enriched an already powerful story.

Gary Triano's bombing intrigued me on so many levels: the perverse relationships between the players, the dark portraits that emerged, and the uncompromising spirit of a law enforcement community that refused to give up even after the case went cold. In writing this book, I not only wanted to applaud that dedication—to seek justice—but also to *learn* from that truth. Maybe, in the end, we all wish the truth *was* fiction. It might be more palatable. Imagination is a kind of frontier without borders or restrictions; but with true evil, at least we *hope* there is definition, limit and some moral barometer. We search for explanation, excuse, and even justification. And if we don't find any then we look for motivation, for clues in a person's childhood, for that toxic cocktail that transformed them into a monster, for brutal figures who influenced them, used them, abused them, and ultimately erased what made them human. And if we don't find *those* factors, then we're left with the untenable hypothesis that there really are natural-born killers.

PROLOGUE: THE MURDER

"You could lose something important today."
— Gary Triano's horoscope, November 1, 1996

Tucson, Arizona
1996

Tucson, Arizona, a dusty desert town nestled in the Sonoran Desert, celebrates November 1 in the ancient Aztec tradition called Día de los Muertos, or Day of the Dead. Mexican children parade through the streets wearing skulls and masks called *calacas*. They spin trance-like behind white horses adorned with marigold wreaths. Little girls dressed in ruffles, red ribbons trailing through their dark braids, smile as they eat sugar skulls of their dead relatives. They lick the names stenciled in icing on the foreheads. Some skulls they keep as trophies, speared and grinning in the wind on long bamboo rods.

A bride and groom twirl passed the crowd. They dress in shredded sheets and share a bouquet of dead roses. A shock of white hair sprouts from the bride's mask: an old woman already, content to be in a "dead marriage" and live "happily ever after." The couple smile at each other through papier-mâché masks and head to the cemetery on the hill. They drape stone crosses with marigold vines, bloodred geraniums, gold beads, and votive candles. Then they kneel to pray. Death, the Aztecs believed, was not the end of life but its continuation.

Life was the nightmare. Only in death did people truly awaken.

On another hill, in an affluent Tucson neighborhood, Gary Triano, land developer and real estate mogul, eagerly anticipated his own celebration, his fifty-third birthday. After completing a round of golf at the Westin La Paloma Country Club, he slipped his impressive six-foot-two-inch, 241-pound frame into his borrowed 1989 maroon Lincoln Town Car and dangled his keys in the ignition. He waved good-bye to his golf partner and spotted a curious blue canvas bag propped on his passenger seat. His fingers skimmed the wood cigar-box-like container.

The blast that immediately followed blew open his skull, split apart his forehead, and exposed a bridge of bone. Metal from the explosion flew into his brain. His hair singed and his eyes ruptured. His right hand, except for his pinky, blew off, and rocketed with the windshield and other car parts, up to two hundred yards into the resort's swimming pool. Gary's right arm was severed above the elbow. Shards split open his thick abdomen and cut his liver in half. The hands on his dial-less gold Movado watch stopped at 5:38 p.m.

At first the scene held witnesses spellbound. Their gorgeous sunset displaced unexpectedly by "a ten-foot-tall dark funnel cloud with mushroom." Debris scattered around the car. The roof was peeled completely off. Glass from the blown-out windows littered the ground and nearby cactus. The outer shell of the passenger door lay bowed in the parking lot. Then, as if a button had been pressed, people sprang to action. The scene near Sunshine Boulevard erupted in pandemonium as victims, struck by flying shrapnel, dropped their tennis rackets on the court mid-game and fled to "safe" rooms inside the resort. Other guests huddled in the Desert Garden and Roadrunner lounges, fearing a "terrorist attack."

Bathers from the swimming pool, still dripping in their swimsuits and with towels wrapped around their waists, gathered in the lobby. Others drove their golf carts off the course, heading to the nearby streets. Diners left their half-eaten meals on plates. Bloody steak juice dripped off tablecloths. Kitchen staff scrambled to shut off burners and faucets. Some guests stood transfixed or plastered their faces to the dome glass windows of the resort. The roar of ambulances and fire trucks punctuated the surprise. Passing motorists described "a flash of light," "a pillar of smoke," and "a distinct smell of burning carpet."

One breathless victim injured in the blast said "a large windstorm pushed through [his] car and [he] was covered in glass." As he was raced to the hospital, his maroon minivan buzzed in the parking lot, the keys still in the ignition. The air smelled like gunpowder. Metal fragments spiraled over the treetops. Papers littered the ground like confetti.

Dr. Samuel Butman, an off-duty University of Arizona cardiologist, one of the first to arrive on the scene following the explosion, actually attempted CPR. "There was little blood. The body looked pale, so pale it almost blended into the light-colored upholstery of the Lincoln Town Car," he said as fresh fire flared from beneath the dash. A cook from the resort joined the doctor on the curb and hosed the blaze with his fire extinguisher. "We were in shock," he reported later, still dressed in his apron and chef's toque hat, his face sweaty and flush from the heat. He smelled of burnt cinnamon and flesh. "It never occurred to us that there might be a second explosion." The vehicle smoldered and made a sound like a "stuck horn," witnesses described. "I remember the sunset, a gorgeous fiery glow on the horizon and then a metallic bang as if a helicopter had crashed into a building," one said.

"Everyone was a potential witness and we didn't have enough manpower to contain them all," a resort employee later remarked. Some hotel staff tempered the stricken crowd but most joined them in their panic. "We were like chickens," said a man who shook his head in disbelief, his thick accent still noticeable through his stutter. "Just like chickens." His face blanched. He was all of twenty-three and wore a tag that labeled him "Security." He looked skittish as a rabbit. The resort boasted recreation and relaxation; lush, well-manicured golf courses; sparkling play pools with man-made waterfalls and fake boulders; and pretty umbrella drinks. Guests experienced events through aquarium-like windows while they dined. Surrounding streets had names like Sunrise Drive and Skyline Drive. Guests paid a premium for bland, predictable beauty they could understand. Horror did not compute. Plumes of black smoke and officers dressed in raid gear, with Kevlar helmets and long shotguns, shocked their very core. This was not their world.

"An event like that," one woman said hugging her little boy close to her chest, "it just changes you. I will always have this memory now. One minute the man's playing golf with friends, the next, he's just . . . gone." She snapped her fingers in disbelief. "No one deserves to die like that."

Agents from the Bureau of Alcohol, Tobacco, Firearms and Explosives' (ATF) enforcement unit streamed out of their vans, armored in black helmets and raid vests. Bomb-sniffing dogs spilled onto the paved walkways. Banquet employees, still dressed in their black slacks, gray jackets, and bow ties, gave the scene an eerie feel of a funeral. First responders Pima County Sheriff's deputies corralled the witnesses inside the club, took preliminary statements, and returned to the smoking car two hours later. Pima County sheriff Clarence Dupnik and his wife arrived, wearing grim masks of calm and control. But the slight tremor in the sheriff's right hand betrayed his composure. He grabbed a subordinate's flashlight and walked over to the car to view

Gary's battered body. No one stopped him. No one was concerned that he might mess with trace evidence or leave with something important. It was not every day that a politician identified the body of a friend and a personality so charismatic at times he overshadowed the sheriff. As police would later learn "people *knew* Gary Triano, or they knew of him. He died the way he lived . . . explosive."

Amidst a transformed black sky, detectives from the Pima County sheriff's homicide and bomb squad divisions and the Tucson Police Department bomb squad parked askew on the streets, cordoned off the scene with bright yellow police tape, and collected bomb components, car parts, and human tissue. And as darkness fell over the parking lot, lamps and flashlights lit up the scene in a ghostly glow. A crowd of onlookers paled on the grassy knolls. Shock slid behind their eyes. More guests huddled inside the hotel. A pall of apprehension hung in the air. The country club was a place for "members." They all *looked* like they belonged.

Pima County deputy sheriff Detective James Gamber had been a homicide detective for a mere six months before being dispatched to the bombing. Still, he was pretty certain even a seasoned detective had never been to a scene like *this*. He had already worked a full shift by the time he received the callout, already steeped in paperwork from other cases. He was behind on reports and discovery requests from prosecutors. This one promised to be an administrative nightmare, and Thanksgiving loomed just weeks ahead. He had been looking forward to a quiet Friday evening and an uneventful weekend until his sergeant's voice crackled over the line: "There's been an explosion."

The detective had never heard of Gary Triano. He had no knowledge yet that the victim had purportedly left behind a legacy of enemies and had "made a career out of being the most hated man in Tucson." All Gamber cared

about at that moment was sifting through the hundred or
so potential witnesses at the scene to learn who might have
had motive to plan, build, and execute a bomb. As uniforms
roped off the exits and main parking lot and secured the
guests' cars for processing, Gamber listened intently to a
child's account of the explosion.

The sixth grader from Estrella Middle School described
"a two-door sedan pull[ing] away from the parking lot with
its left rear window covered by a garbage bag." Another
woman countered that the car was a 1970s faded blue Monte
Carlo with gray primer patches "possibly driven by a Hispanic male." A third witness shook his head: "It was a green
Jeep Wagoneer, I'm sure of it." No, it was a gold Mercedes
driven by "a blond guy with glasses" who "held something
dangling in his hands." Other witnesses described a guy
"walking off like a zombie" heading to his Trans Am;
toward "late-model vehicles" that were "blue in color," "the
kind you would not ordinarily see in a country club parking
lot"; toward a burgundy Isuzu Trooper LS parked askew
near the victim's flaming hulk of a car. So far he had varied
descriptions of cars. No faces. *What was he supposed to
do with that?*

Some of the resort staff, eager to offer a clue, a lead,
recounted strange phone calls they had received "just minutes after the explosion": a disembodied female voice asking about Gary's "accident" before news media could even
broadcast the explosion. The voice was most concerned
whether Gary had survived. A male had called, too, several times, days before the explosion to confirm Gary's tee
time. No one had caught the caller's name.

In the glow of lamps and flashlights, at two in the morning, Gamber walked the crime scene with his partner,
Sergeant Keith St. John. Crowds huddled in the main parking lot. Red wigwags flashed like strobes over the scene,
briefly lighting up the second parking lot and dark tunnels
that opened like portals to another dimension. No one had

bothered to guard the exits. Gamber's gaze spanned the rows and rows of empty striped parking spaces. And his gut told him no one had seen the bomber. No one he interviewed had anything to do with the explosion. His *real* killer had just disappeared.

Fatigue settled over Gamber's bones. Residual smoke from the bomb clogged his lungs. His head ached. The chilly November air bit into his cheeks as he listened, recorded, and nodded to story after story. Some blended facts. Some embellished details. Others were more reserved. Some just wanted an audience. Some used the exposure as a forum to offer public opinion about the life and death of Gary Triano. Meanwhile, the clock ticked.

PART I

CHAPTER ONE:
HAPPILY EVER AFTER

"The nightmare is in your mind."
—Ron Young to Pam Phillips

Pamela Phillips, a striking blond commercial real estate agent, noticed Gary long before he ever saw her. Newly divorced from her first husband, a prominent Tucson attorney who eventually succumbed to cancer, Pam worked for the esteemed brokerage firm of Grubb & Ellis and had a reputation as being ruthless, unscrupulous, and cold. She crashed Gary's parties, sipped champagne casually alongside his first wife, Mary Cram, and fixed Gary with her stunning crystal-blue gaze. Pam worked the crowd like an electric bolt, abrupt, charged, and at times shocking. She mentioned frequently, like punctuation at the end of a sentence, that her net worth was a cool two million and she was looking for a partner. Gary.

She liked that he had earned substantial revenue through Indian gaming casinos.

And a few months later, in 1986, Gary ended his first marriage with a short phone call to his wife while she and their two children, Heather and Brian, vacationed in Europe. Although their connection crackled, Gary's message reverberated loud and clear. He had found a distraction and was totally "smitten" by Pam. They had everything in common—not just potent sexual passion but a *real* love . . .

of money. Gary divorced Mary quickly and without flare, generously deeding Mary his cemetery property, the Tucson Memorial Gardens, in their divorce settlement. Mary could not have realized then the irony in Gary's gesture; eventually she would bury his remains in that garden.

At Pam and Gary's wedding, Pam radiated happiness. Gary basked in her glow and together they seemed the perfect couple. Theirs was an expensive black-tie affair on a yacht at sunset in San Diego. Ocean water shimmered around them. Gary towered over his new bride, his arm draped protectively around her slim waist. She adorned him well. Dressed in a white southern-belle gown with puffed sleeves, a white lace rose in her fitted embroidered cap, and a delicate single strand of pearls around her slender neck. She beamed for the camera, but there was something forced in her expression, like an artificial sweetener with a bitter aftertaste. Still, she had never looked more beautiful nor Gary more polished in his shiny tails, crisp white shirt, bow tie, and perfectly lacquered hair. They made a stunning portrait.

David Bean, the couple's wedding photographer, captured the newlyweds in a series of posed images: Gary seated, legs crossed next to a floor-length mirror, red velvet draped behind him, his lips curled in a half smile, his dark eyes expectant, as if waiting for the camera flash, Pam holding a champagne glass, toasting her good future, her reflection distorted in the golden liquid. Bean snapped the newlyweds in a rare photo together as they prepared to slice their cream-laced wedding cake. The crowd audibly gasped as Gary playfully pressed the butcher knife to his new bride's throat.

They created the perfect illusion of happiness. The couple purchased a home in Tucson's affluent Skyline Country Club, a community nestled in the foothills of the Catalina Mountains overlooking Sabino Canyon and the Westin La Paloma golf resort. The view from their balcony dazzled with white city lights and bruised horizons. They drove twin Jaguars, attended social events with Donald Trump and Marla Maples, and jetted to Trump's Mar-a-Lago* estate† in Palm Beach before Trump donated the property to President Carter and it became known as "Florida's White House."

Trump's mansion, situated between the ocean and Lake Worth, once rested on jungle-type undergrowth and swampy grounds before it evolved into the "Jewel of Palm Beach." The hurricane-resistant structure is anchored by concrete and steel to a coral reef comprising twenty acres of perfectly landscaped lawns dotted with sculptures of monkeys, parrots, and other assorted wildlife. Pam, wrapped in a gauzy white sundress and delicate straw hat, stood barefoot in the seventy-five-foot tower that overlooked the main house, reminiscent of a Mediterranean villa. Lake wind smacked her cheeks. Water lapped against the Dorian stone embedded with seashells and fossils—"imported from Genoa, Italy," Gary enlightened her. Walls and arches encased her; the day fell around her like fine mist.

"It's perfect here, isn't it?" said Marla, joining her in the tower, looking like Pam's twin. She squeezed Pam's elbow affectionately. Her skin glistened in the afterglow of seaweed and mud treatments from the Trump Spa. She wore a white linen sheath, slim white heels, and a tasteful strand of pearls. Her bloodred lips bloomed against her white canvas.

Pam smiled. "The place is timeless." *Perfect, like Marla, impossibly lovely.* Marla twittered about the five-course dinner she anticipated sharing with Pam and Gary in the Gold and White ballroom with its ornate ceilings and crystal

* Latin for "Sea to Lake."
† Marjorie Merriweather Post (then Mrs. E. F. Hutton) opened the estate in 1927 when it became apparent that she was to be the dowager queen of Palm Beach.

chandeliers in the style of Louis XIV. Later, as Pam clicked across the black-and-white marble imported from an old castle in Cuba, Marla stood to greet her at the dining room table. She wore a chic Carolina Herrera column gown tastefully adorned with $2 million Tiffany diamonds. Donald beamed at her as if she were a gorgeous jewel.

Gary squeezed Pam's hand beneath the table. She caught her reflection in the gold-bordered plates. Hers was a dirty beauty, brassy like patina on wood. Gary ordered their dinner from a menu with no prices, each course accompanied by a different bottle of wine. Pam lost track of the dishes, the exotic aromas. The wine made her tipsy and when she laughed, her voice sounded like ice clinking against crystal. Their lives were foil, a bright sheen on the outside, but inside, terribly dull. Gary and Pam's honeymoon was over far too soon.

"Gary never paid me for the photographs," David Bean recalled. "But he *did* invite me to dinner several weeks after their wedding as a token of his appreciation. I expected an occasion. Wine, good food, pleasant company, and lively conversation. It wasn't like that at Gary's residence. They had a glass dinner table. Two thin panels that rose from the floor. We looked see-through. Pam and Gary sat on opposite ends of the giant table like chess pieces. A king and queen approaching checkmate. There was no conversation, just the click of forks scraped against china. It was a little uncomfortable. While I sipped my wine, my first course still steaming on the plate, I looked up and the two of them had already devoured their food."

Bean shook his head. "Then I got the tour of their house. I remember one room in particular was filled with bronze statues, all Native American heads of Gary. And there were strange paintings that reminded me of Jackson Pollock. Gary's nose dripped off the canvas, his long face pulled like a scream; disembodied parts of him floated in white space."

The white space crept into Pam's bright world. She didn't *know* Gary before she married him. She fell in love with his *image*. He boasted a net worth of $800,000 annually from Indian bingo halls and slot-machine parlors in Arizona and California. She accompanied him while he hosted Donald Trump at a University of Arizona football game, donated money to charities, and briefly ran for the Tucson City Council. And yet, he was embroiled in litigation: she would later learn about seventy-four lawsuits involving failed business and real estate investments. She knew Gary could be irascible, having once sued Pan American World Airways because he was dissatisfied with his $4,410 first-class seat, but she had no idea he owed his first wife, Mary Cram, $1.8 million in business debts and loans, a Tucson attorney $91,476 in legal fees, his own mother $68,000 in loans and a Bally's health and fitness club $30,000 in past due membership costs.

But that wasn't the worst of it. Shortly after their wedding, while Pam was pregnant with the couple's first son, Trevor, Gary invited her to consult with a bankruptcy attorney. As she listened to the soothing sounds of waterfalls and rain piped over the speakers, the rose-colored walls closed in around her. Gary's hand over her fist was cold and clammy. Her heart flapped against her chest like a riot of wings. A familiar helplessness enveloped her, nearly paralyzing her. Images of her childhood flashed in her mind's eye: her mother's death when Pam was fourteen; her father's wilted form filling his brown suit like a rotten banana, stinking of alcohol; the echoes of his boots on bare tile, his muttering late at night as he peeled potatoes in the sink, chilling Pam to her very core.

Now Pam was about to lose another home.

Gary agreed to pay for the Skyline property by promising the investor land in neighboring Cochise County. Instead, Gary repurchased the acreage and kept the $650,000 in proceeds for himself. He insisted he was entitled: the

Skyline house was infested with poisonous "kissing bugs."
A judge disagreed and ordered Gary to reimburse the investor $681,197 plus $17,000 in attorney's fees. The Skyline
house was seized and sold at auction to satisfy the judgment.

After that, Pam became cautious with her finances. She
maintained separate bank accounts and loaned Gary money
for his investments. She recorded every transaction on a
promissory note. She provided the down payment for their
next investment, Woodland property, and populated the
land with farm animals, including a potbellied pig. The
place had a long, winding driveway, a pool, and tennis
courts. But even as her money dwindled, Gary placated her
with lavish gifts, buying her gold watches and expensive
port on a whim, and when she protested he simply laughed,
dismissing her with a wave of his hand and willing her to
believe that everything was going to be all right.

"Pretense was a way of life," Pam explained. Her fingers
trailed the long column of her throat. "To the outside world
we never *looked* like we struggled. We'd be in a restaurant
and Gary would tip the waitress a hundred bucks because
he liked the way the young lady smiled. Meanwhile we
owed creditors thousands of dollars. I stashed $2 million
markers in my cocktail purse in Las Vegas, knowing it was
all bluff. Once, at a New Year's Eve party, Gary bought
cocktails for the entire staff." Their applause resounded in
Pam's ears like a giant wave crashing on the shore. And
when the tide receded, she washed up with the debris. Pam
suggested she contribute to help ease the family finances.

"But Gary never wanted me to work," she advised police later in one of her initial interviews. "How would that
look?" Gary demanded to know her plans, wanted to control the finances, and smothered her with attention.

"He called constantly," one of Pam's friends recalled.
"All hours of the day and night. Even when Pam wasn't
home, there would be four and five telephone messages

from Gary waiting for her return. And they'd all sound the same. You know, 'It's me. I know you're there. Pick up the phone.' Or 'Me again.' Or he'd say something like 'Just calling to let you know I'm watching you.' By their very nature, the messages he left were themselves intimidating."

But Pam minimized his calls, pretending not to register his veiled threats, mistaking his control for concern while all the while bracing for the inevitable, the violence.

She recalled the first episode in vivid detail: An early winter morning turned leaden and the temperature dropped to a chilly fifty degrees. Freezing rain fell. Cactus stalks glistened in a beard of ice. Pam arrived home ten minutes late from a shopping trip with girlfriends. The sight of Gary at the front door filled her with dread. She dropped her Macy's bags on the bar. The house resounded with her children's laughter. Gary's penetrating gaze bore into the back of her head like a brand. She faced him. She thought he studied her as if she were an insect he contemplated smashing with the heel of his boot. The girlfriends scattered like exotic birds into the street.

"Where've you been?"

Pam bristled at his question, all too familiar with his pattern: interrogation first, then anger, then condescension, as if she were a child scolded by her father. She pointed to the shopping bags. Gary turned up the volume on the television. A commercial vibrated through the room. He flipped up the radio switch. Violins collided with feedback. The moment took on an unreal cast, the tenor of a film noir. Then, in a rush of movement, Gary shoved Pam into the bedroom and locked the door. He dropped the wooden blinds. Shadows climbed the walls. The veins in Gary's neck bulged. Without warning, he pounced on Pam and pressed his thick hands to her throat. White spots popped behind Pam's eyes. The room spun. She buckled beneath him like a rag doll. Gary crushed her spine into the iron bed frame. Pain tore through her. A scream died in the back of her throat.

Gary loosened his grip. Pam curled to her knees, crawled to the door, a mirage she could not reach. But Gary was on top of her. He punched her head with his fist, buried her nose into the carpet. Her temple throbbed with the impact. Sounds reverberated around her, dull, distant, like a fuzzy recording.

He gathered her curls in his hand, lowered his lips to her ear, and whispered, "Don't be late again."

Pam never reported Gary to the police. The next morning she brushed makeup on her throat to cover the bruises, the obvious handprints. She still looked fine, though the light behind her skin had darkened to coals. She patted her cheeks, still puffy with fresh tears. She had divorced her first husband after he became ill with cancer. Once a handsome attorney with impeccable taste, he obsessed over dark patches of skin in their bathroom and embodied her worst fear: helplessness. Ill, he became an invalid. She vowed not to become *that*.

Days passed without incident. Neither she nor Gary spoke of the assault. And then one night Gary stumbled home drunk. He plopped on their living room couch. Pam trembled in the archway. She heard the click of Gary's revolver as he spun the cylinder in the dark. He had stashed an arsenal of weapons in their house, including a rifle. But Pam fixated on the flash of chrome and the clicks. One. Two. Three. He pointed the gun at her. Click. She forgot to breathe.

"I'm thinking about killing you and then turning the gun on myself," he laughed.

"He had a cruel streak," Pam insisted. "Mr. Life of the Party, jovial . . . Everyone thought he was a pleasant, happy guy. But there was something scary about him . . . I don't know . . ." Her voice faded, as if there were more to the story she couldn't share. The next morning the phone shrilled at five o'clock. Pam had barely slept. She overheard Gary's conversation, his voice forceful and low between sips of coffee. Curious, she padded to the doorway, cinching her robe tight. Gary curled the telephone cord in his fingers. Sunlight streamed through their expensive white curtains. Gary looked up, crossed his legs, and gave his wife a wink. Calmly, he replaced the receiver to the cradle. He adjusted his tie at his neck. His next words chilled her.

"He's done, finished. One phone call and he's gone, just like that." He snapped his fingers.

And yet, Pam insisted Gary often suppressed news coverage that he had any associations with organized crime.

"The name 'Triano,'" she said, "is actually Spanish in origin, not Italian, but that detail never stopped him from exploiting his possible connections. In Las Vegas everyone knew him as 'Mr. T.,' you know . . . It was the illusion that mattered."

Gary often flew to Las Vegas in his chartered Learjet, portraying a man with Mafia connections and serious money like a character straight out of a Hollywood movie. Duped officials gave Gary an expensive suite in Las Vegas. He flashed wads of cash in the casinos, betting and losing Pam's money while Pam fumed quietly in the wings.

The illusion quickly soured behind closed doors. As Gary's violence toward her escalated, Pam became even more dependent on Gary.

"Sure, I fantasized about leaving him, but then I thought: How would I actually *do* that? I mean, where would I go, how would I *live*? He was the center of attention. He made me feel like I was nothing, and after a while I believed I *was* nothing . . . *became* nothing."

"When he looked at her, his gaze seemed to drift past her, as if he was seeing someone who wasn't there," one of her friends confirmed.

Later in their marriage, Gary grew paranoid after investing

in a riverboat casino in Macau, China. "I heard it was a pretty horrible place, rampant with drugs and prostitution," Pam remarked. "Not the kind of people who messed around. Gary screwed them over."

And Pam no longer felt safe in her own home. "Gary slept with a loaded gun, his finger always on the trigger."

She spent most nights awake fully dressed. Moonlight spilled across their sheets. Her heart drummed in her chest. Wind rattled their bedroom window. Thoughts of her children swirled in her head and terror replaced depression. How would she protect them if something happened to Gary or, worse, if something happened to *her*?

Then one night, as exhaustion gave way to restless sleep, Pam startled awake. Panic shot through her. She felt pressure at her temple. Gary never said a word, just held the gun to her head and stared at her in the darkness with the cold, penetrating gaze of a shark.

The next morning Pam stood barefoot at the bathroom sink with a swirl brush in her hand. She wore panties and a T-shirt.

"Without provocation, he shoved me into the porcelain bowl, pressed my face into the chrome faucet, and stripped me naked so that I stood raw and exposed." Gary hurled a mobile phone at the bridge of her nose. Blood trickled into the corners of Pam's eyes, but she didn't blink. She resisted the urge to cry. She stared at Gary, forcing him to see what he had done. His beautiful wife was now damaged. He panted, sweat pooling above his brows.

"He looked crazed, really crazed," Pam recalled. "I mean, like foaming white at the mouth."

"What are your plans today?" he barked.

"Nothing," Pam whispered. "I am . . . nothing."

The phone shrilled, sometimes twenty times in the span of three hours. Gary's presence filled the dark house as Pam curled up in their king-size bed, knees to her chest, white satin sheets bunched at her throat. She focused on the clock. Two in the morning. The calls had started at noon. He'd wanted to know what she was doing for lunch. Her answer didn't matter. If she said she was out, he'd arrive unannounced at the door. If she said she was home, he'd cruise through the street.

Her children froze in the arch of her bedroom door.

"Who's calling, Mom?" her daughter's plaintive voice tore through the stillness. They climbed into Pam's bed, forming perfect lumps on the pillows, and inhaled sharply with each piercing ring. Pam watched the windows for movement, for shadows in the sagebrush—for Gary. Her heart raced with expectation.

"The real nightmare is in your mind," she recalled later, during her first police interview. "Checking beneath pillows for a loaded gun . . . waiting for something to snap the tension."

Relief finally came in the form of a *real* death threat. "Another of Gary's business deals," Pam explained. Gary had borrowed capital from a group of Mexican investors and provided his partner's land in Sabino Canyon as collateral. Gary also personally guaranteed the $2 million. He claimed he had personal connections. But when Gary's partner filed for bankruptcy and the Mexicans lost their collateral, they came after Gary for the money.

"Of course, Gary didn't have it," Pam said. "So they sued him for fraud."

And then one night, while Pam settled into her couch with a book, the phone rang. Her heart raced and she felt the familiar dizziness return. She picked up the receiver and a man with a thick Hispanic accent spoke on the other end. He was an attorney for the Mexicans.

"It's real simple," the man breathed. "One minute you'll be there, the next . . . you won't, if you don't make good on this."

The dial tone buzzed in her ear. She closed the book, turned off the lamp, and sat alone in the darkness, listening intently for the bullet.

Gary promised to work out the details. He promised to honor his word. *This time.* The Mexicans dropped the fraud suit.

"And I filed for divorce," Pam said.

CHAPTER TWO:
THE DIVORCE

October 1993

Pam insisted her divorce proceeding was a quick sixty-day affair. The media described it as a "bitter custody battle" that spanned years of hostilities and revolved around money. Pam locked Gary out of the Woodland property and sought the first of three restraining orders against him, citing his use of offensive language, threats, and harassment. She feared he would sabotage the sale of the home she'd purchased for them with her money. Pam insisted he had threatened to plant cocaine in the bedsheets.

"I started to think *I* was the crazy one, can you imagine?" Pam told officers later.

And when she finally did sell the property for a net profit of $300,000, she pocketed the proceeds.

"She felt entitled," her close friend Joy Bancroft explained. "After all, Gary was only ordered to pay her $200 monthly in child support. How was she supposed to live on that?"

Pam had reason to panic. In 1994, Gary filed for Chapter 11 bankruptcy reorganization. He listed assets of $1.36 million and debts of nearly $26.8 million. And Gary insisted that the $100,000 he earned from performing "consulting work" for the Victor Fears Trust constituted expenses, not income. That same month, the divorced couple pressed charges against each other three times. Pam accused Gary of abusing substances, mixing his cocktails with antidepressants; of stalking her; of threatening their children with retribution. She filed numerous orders of protection. And she threatened friends of Gary's with bodily harm if they allied themselves too closely with him.

"He made me so nuts," Pam stated. She recalled that once she doused Gary with water in the superior court hallway. She stood trembling across from him and tossed the empty bottle into the trash. He turned to face her, his hair and suit jacket soaked. She heard nothing but her own ragged breath. And then Gary broke the silence with hysterical laughter.

"What did I tell you?" He slapped his lawyer on the shoulder, motioned for a deputy to approach, and pressed assault charges against Pam.

"I'll kill you," Pam seethed, and the veins in her neck corded. "I'll kill you."

The judge ultimately increased Gary's monthly child support payments to $1,055.

"It was strange," a friend who had attended the hearing observed. "Pam always had impeccable fashion sense, but that day in court I hardly recognized her. She looked matronly dressed in a long gray skirt and high-necked ruffled blouse. She pulled back her curls in a severe bun and wore chunky sensible heels as if she wanted to blunt her sensuality, as if she thought it were somehow inappropriate for the venue, as if she were suddenly, inexplicably . . . herself?"

"We thought Pam was being premature with the divorce," the friend's husband chimed in. " 'Gary loves you,' we told her. But she fixed us with cold flat eyes and replied, 'Gary loves me too much.' "

Part of a detective's job is to process information into different filters, compartmentalize incidents, interpret remarks and perceived threats, and record observations until clues emerge and form a more cohesive portrait. Pam, the well-dressed socialite, had different personas. The fact that she had arrived for court frumpy and unkempt might have been a sympathy ploy, a profound manipulation, or evidence of something darker still . . . a glimpse into mental illness?

In late fall of 1994, Pam carefully planned her escape to Aspen, Colorado, with her two young children. She plotted with her broker to have her Woodland house in Tucson sell for "a bargain," a scheme that coincided with Gary's vacation to Mexico. With the house proceeds in hand, Pam rented a Ford Explorer Eddie Bauer and drove "madly" through the night to a rental property the couple owned on Snowbunny Lane. She felt significant. And at least for a short while she had money.

The tiny duplex had just two bedrooms, space enough for her longtime nanny, Samantha Stubbs, and the few belongings Pam had shoved into suitcases. Pam left her front door unlocked. Powder snow sparkled on the windowsill. Her dentist neighbor, hidden beneath layers of wool, propped his skis against his house and smacked excess snow from his mittens and cap. A frigid hush fell around Pam and her teeth chattered—not from cold but from fear. She moved away from the window, startled at the sight of another neighbor, an old man with a shock of white hair, seated naked and cross-legged in a yoga position in his living room. She lay on her cool white sheets, curled her knees to her chest, and listened to her heart beat in heavy percussion: no income, no job, and no future.

"She probably felt like an impostor," a friend remarked. "Here she was living in this wealthy zip code, pretending to be okay, and really she teetered on the brink of oblivion."

But Pam wasn't alone. Within days of her arrival in Aspen she heard Gary's voice bark on her answering machine, sometimes two or three times in succession, then hang up. He demanded to speak to his children, insisted he "just wanted to hear their voices." When Pam bothered to answer, she scolded him, "It's midnight, Gary, the children are asleep" or "eating dinner" or "unable to talk" or "taking their baths" or "unavailable." Her responses sounded rehearsed, tired, rote, and they incensed Gary. After a while, Pam enlisted third parties—nannies, acquaintances, and friends—to answer the phone: "We're sorry, Gary, try again later."

Finally, tired of the hourly disruptions, Pam relented. She could be reasonable if pressed. She allowed Gary exactly one hour—between 6:00 and 7:00 each evening—to reach his children. But when he did, she hovered nearby and tapped on her watch. Sometimes static crackled over the line and Gary pretended he was calling from exotic locales like the Caribbean or China while all the while the caller ID flashed a Tucson area code.

"I don't know who he was trying to impress," Pam told police later. "It was strange, part of his deception."

Pam eventually tired of the illusion, and two months later she changed her mind again. She accused Gary of not following the rules. *Her* rules. Frustrated, Gary chartered a single-engine plane to fly from Tucson to Aspen to collect his kids for visitation. But Pam feared for her children's safety in the mountainous terrain.

"I'm not allowing our children to fly in blizzard conditions through the Rockies." Pam stood at her open window and released a sharp breath, creating a cloud that dissipated quickly into the afternoon light, gauzy and dim. In one letter Pam drafted to her lawyer, Douglas Clark, she wrote: "I have made it clear I cannot permit the children to be transported from Aspen in a rented single-engine piston plane especially piloted by Gary. It is wintertime. The airport is surrounded by 12,000 foot mountains . . . in addition because Gary's state of mind was determined to be less than rational at the hearing in May and since he has repeatedly violated Judge Maxwell's protective order, his piloting such a plane with the children is naturally unacceptable."

Gary tried again in the few weeks before Christmas. He landed his plane in a white meadow near the town. Electric blue lights glowed on the trees and lampposts. Wreaths adorned windows and doors. Snowflakes lingered in Gary's hair. Pam's friend, Anna, met Gary near the plane. She had no children with her. She zipped her leather jacket, tucked her black ponytail into the fur collar, and said, "Pam's changed her mind, Gary, sorry."

More than the terrain and the weather conditions, rumors swirled about Gary's failing health. Pam heard he suffered from prostate cancer, that he had dizzy spells. She worried he might be too feeble to land the plane. Undeterred, Gary proposed that Pam meet him in Denver with the children. But the day before Gary planned to depart, Pam faxed him a cancellation note. She suggested that Gary plan ahead next time, maybe consult with a travel agent rather than require her on short notice to drive ten hours round-trip to and from Denver.

By January 1995, Gary had had enough. He filed a *pro per* petition for contempt in the Pima County Superior Court. He claimed to have exhausted nearly $17,000 monthly in visitation costs alone. But Judge Margaret Maxwell was less than sympathetic and wrote in a subsequent minute entry that she did not find the amount he had listed inappropriate.

On the rare occasions Pam *did* allow the children to visit Gary in Tucson, Gary once discovered a kissing bug crawling around in the children's suitcases.

"They're bloodsuckers, also known as little assassins," Robin Gardner, Gary's former girlfriend, advised. "They bite the lips of their sleeping victims. Gary was allergic to them. He could have died." But more than a fatal insect bite, Gary voiced concerns to his friends that Pam's threats had become more pronounced and he worried that some-one was stalking him.

"He never identified anyone in particular; it was just a feeling he had, a foreboding," Robin said. "Once Gary flew his private airplane back from Aspen to Tucson and he noticed a second aircraft following him. It made him nervous enough that he landed in the White Mountains and stayed at a cabin in Greer, Arizona.

"He grew increasingly paranoid about Pam's phone calls, said they had an eerie quality to them that made him uncomfortable, so much so that he thought it wise to cancel their life insurance; but the company insisted Pam owned the policy, and because she faithfully paid the premium each month, Seaboard Life had no authority to terminate his ownership," she added.

While Gary's anxiety mounted, Pam, too, worried. She had nightmares that her children had disappeared into thin clouds and she couldn't find them. In her visions she saw Gary wander into town armed with shotguns, aiming to hunt her down. She'd heard from his daughter, Heather, that Gary kept a shrine to his children in the Tucson home he shared with his business partner, Richard Hickey. The room brimmed with bright furniture, toys, and accessories. The walls fluttered with poems he wrote for them. Their crayon drawings littered the desk inside. Stuffed animals hung from the ceiling on a dismembered broomstick. Dust collected on their tails.

"Gary loved our kids," Pam admitted to her friend Joy. "He would have done anything for them . . . *anything*."

If it wasn't for the kids, I'd be dead by now.

His children corroborated Gary's fierce attachment to them. Heather, Gary's daughter from his first marriage, called her father daily, and even went so far as to tease him that he was her stalker.

"He planned my wedding in Venice when I was just twelve," Heather recalled wistfully. "He joked that he would arrange to have my marriage presided over by the pope. He made me dance with him" in the dark without music, two souls holding hands with their shadows. He traveled with a bodyguard. Gary called at all hours of the night, hoping to tell his children he loved them. He carefully chose his words, like a poet, mindful of the rhythm and white spaces, the invisible breaths between beats.

CHAPTER THREE:
MONEY, MONEY, MONEY

"With money, you can buy blood but not life."
                                        —Ancient Chinese proverb

While Pam insisted she worried about her children's safety, her friend Joy Bancroft fretted about Pam's increasingly fragile financial stability.

"It was an almost daily topic of conversation," Joy recalled. "We reserved 'big' conversations for the meadow near my home. We'd pack a bottle of wine, a baguette with a hunk of cheese, and spread out a blanket on the grass."

Joy hoped the fresh mountain air might calm her friend, but Pam's hands trembled on the stem of the wineglass. As she studied her reflection in the Beaujolais, she'd complain, "I just don't know what I'm going to do, how I'm going to live: children are so . . . expensive."

Joy offered to buy them horseback riding lessons: "I was the children's godmother, after all. How could I say no?"

"I'm really struggling," Pam said the next time they met in the meadow. She bunched the blanket around her ankles and took a sip of wine. "You know I can't repay you. Gary hasn't coughed up anything at all. I just don't know how I'm supposed to make it up here." Pam's eyes misted. She bit her lower lip and whispered desperately, "I might have to move."

Joy bought the children new clothes. She insisted Pam park her moving van in front of her garage to save on storage costs. The truck contained thousands of dollars in antique furniture and expensive statues. Pam sold some pieces at cost, not because she needed the money, but because she'd "rather have the cash than hunks of bronze."

"They were reliefs of Gary's head," Joy supplied.

Pam's fire sale several months before Gary's death was a red flag for Detective Gamber. Cold, calculated, and just a little desperate, Pam fit the profile of a killer, but the detective needed more than mere instinct. Sifting through moral fiber was hardly an exact science. And while hatred often motivated homicide, Pam had sold the bronze reliefs for money, not vindication. She had no interest in deflating Gary's ego. The distinction was chilling and sociopathic but, the detective reasoned, evidence of nothing.

"She held an interest in Potrero, a parcel of land she and several partners had invested in, located near San Diego," Joy told the detective later.

"If I could just sell it, I'd have two to three million in the bank," Pam lamented time and again, though the property was embroiled in litigation.

But her voice held a desperate quality. She teetered on the edge of a cliff with no imminent rescue as her money dwindled. Joy loaned Pam $60,000, convinced if she did not give Pam the money she would default on the loan and forfeit her interest in the investment.

One morning, Pam announced to Joy almost breathlessly, "Samantha had to go."

But the sacrifice was short-lived. She replaced her nanny with several substitute nannies. Some were seasonal: there for the winter and gone in the summer months. She hired a local ski bum, someone Joy had recommended. A live-in blond, sculpted, with a vibrant white smile.

"She was distraught over the boy's attitude," Joy confirmed. "She paid him $200 a month plus odd jobs she arranged for him with friends. He changed my winter tires once. He seemed like a decent enough kid until he borrowed my car, played pool, drank, and wrecked my lawn. Pam fired him and they quarreled over money. She refused to pay him."

Pam hired another live-in nanny, a man named Kevin. She interviewed him for forty-five minutes. She conducted no background check, never inquired about his past or his plans. He never met the children.

"I found it so bizarre you know . . . it being my first time in Aspen and me a black person . . . and right away she says, 'Yeah you're hired.'" Kevin slept in the garage while Pam left almost nightly for appointments and social events at billionaire clubs.

"I was Mr. Nanny, there to do the laundry, polish the floor, and basically, you know . . . keep the kids invisible," Kevin said. He left when the snow melted, and Samantha returned for short intervals.

Pam seemed particularly distracted one day. The meadow glistened with fresh dew. A hawk circled the sky. Crisp autumn wind bit into Pam's cheeks. Pam poured the wine and tore off a corner of bread. Joy offered Pam a slab of soft goat cheese.

"You're a bad influence," Pam laughed, and gave in to temptation. "I need to cut back." Her voice trembled and Joy would later remark that she noticed a shadow darken her friend's face—a flicker of sadness or fear—"but it passed over her so quickly."

"How long have we known each other?" Pam asked.

"A long time."

"A lifetime." Pam nodded; it was a conversation that slowly stitched itself into the fabric of their relationship, a moment that transformed everything that came afterward.

"Pam spoke of a life insurance policy she owned with

Gary. She said the monthly payments were exorbitant. She needed to eliminate unnecessary expenses. It seemed like such a foolish idea to cancel the policy," Joy remarked later to Detective Gamber.

"Gary took it out in 1992, when tensions between us were at their worst," Pam said, averting her gaze. She fixated on a twig near the blanket and snapped it in half. "He declared me the beneficiary of a $2 million policy." Pam rolled her eyes as if the idea was absurd.

Joy assumed the payments temporarily until Pam could get on her feet or Gary became financially responsible.

"It was the least I could do to help out a friend," she insisted. "I never really questioned why Pam owned the policy, or why *she* was listed as the beneficiary and not her children. I just did what I was asked to do." Joy's payments were late a few times. And on the night of Gary's murder, Joy had forgotten to pay the premium entirely.

But, as detectives later learned, *Pam* hadn't forgotten. In fact, she made the final payment on the night of her ex-husband's murder, scrambled to meet the deadline before Seaboard Life Insurance canceled the policy altogether for delinquency. The money posted on November 6, 1996. On November 15, 1996, Pam made a claim for Gary's death.

The picture Pam painted for the detective was of a woman besieged by an abusive husband who had relentlessly stalked and threatened her the last couple of years and unlawfully withheld child support and spousal maintenance. The detective heard at least a half dozen times about Gary's veiled threats and harassing phone calls in the middle of the night. It sounded as if she had been living in hell. She appeared to be helpless, financially destitute in Aspen, waiting for the elusive rescue. And yet, she spoke with deliberate calm and appeared rational in the silences even as she informed the detective that under no circumstances would she submit to a polygraph.

"Have you ever had one?" Gamber hedged.

"Well, you know first of all I just feel very . . . I don't know if I appear shaky to you, but I feel shaky . . . I had [an] experience with a polygraph once. I mean, the polygrapher asked me a question that I didn't lie on and it went, like, you know, I mean, it indicated that I lied and I didn't lie. I mean, I didn't have, you know, an affair on my first husband . . . maybe it's just me but . . . I mean, it's unreliable . . ."

The detective stared at her. He noted the slackness in her jaw. Her very posture was limp, her narrow shoulders dragged down . . . by the impact of Gary's violent death or the burden of guilt?

He spoke at last: "I'll be honest with you. It's Investigation 101. If a person refuses a polygraph, that's the person I look hardest at, you know what I'm saying?"

"I'm not the one that did it. I'm not guilty." She folded her hands in her lap, shredding a piece of Kleenex. She stared at the detective. She didn't blink. "I'm not the one who would ever go after Gary. I mean, he's the father of my children. You know, I mean, even if he did things that I could have gotten him in trouble for, which there were definitely things, definitely . . . I would leave. I wouldn't even do that. I mean, why would I want to, you know . . . There's no way. You know, um, so . . . no."

Blotchy red marks traveled the length of her neck. Words tumbled out of her recklessly. Too many details, too many clichés, too much forced affection for Gary. Suddenly, Pam looked small and pale.

Gamber cleared his throat. "There are people who categorize you this way: the minute Gary started going downhill in his business . . ."

"Oh, I hate this." Pam rolled her eyes, suddenly agitated by the accusation. "I know where this is going."

"You dumped him."

He let the statement linger between them like smoke. Her deep-blue eyes had lost all light. They looked older than her thirty-five years. She looked at him stoically, almost hopelessly.

"Did Gary have any enemies that you know of?" the detective asked, switching gears, knowing the rich made enemies often unaware. Over the years Gary had made business deals with people who believed they were jilted or entitled and who made idle threats against him. But Gary didn't run scared. He had always considered himself fully capable of defending himself; he'd thought himself invincible. Still, Gary's business partner and an assortment of close friends noticed that in the last few weeks of his life he was jumpy and tense—not at all like himself. He began to carry a gun, enlist bodyguards, and even part his hair differently.

Pam's voice dropped to a conspiratorial whisper. "He had many enemies." Gary's death, she insisted, had everything to do with his *life*.

Gamber pursued that notion for a while. In Gary's case it wasn't so much a matter of finding *a* suspect but of finding the *right* suspect and eliminating red herrings. His mind flashed to the dark exposed tunnels at the country club for golf carts to pass more easily between holes, the escape routes no one had guarded, no one had explored, because they seemed too far removed from the crime scene.

He began with Gary's closest friends, Kola and Ron, who had arranged to meet Gary at his favorite bar the night he was murdered. They had convinced him it would be a quiet affair, dinner and cocktails. They hoped to brighten his dark mood. He had learned that his children, Lois and Trevor, had inexplicably canceled their weekend plans and he wouldn't see them for his birthday after all.

"He acted more paranoid than usual," Kola said. "He thought he might have a stalker. He worried about his former wife's associations. Gary started carrying a gun."

Kola and Gary's latest girlfriend, Dawn, had planned a surprise party for him. Pam would later insist to police that she was "so grateful" to Dawn for never having called her children to participate. "They would have been right there, you know . . . ," Pam's voice trailed off.

But in fact Gamber learned that Heather, Gary's daughter by his first wife, *had* reached Pam and invited her half siblings.

"They were supposed to be there," Heather insisted.

Gary's closest friends and family huddled in the dark of Gary's apartment. Streamers blew from the blades of a ceiling fan. Each guest held a clump of confetti in one hand and a full wineglass in the other. Muffled giggles punctuated the silence. The whole room waited to exhale. Each guest had received Kola's handwritten invitation elegantly scrawled with the words: "Come celebrate! We're going to roast Gary!"

Heather never made it to her father's party.

She was running late. She stopped to type up her father's favorite poem, "If—" by Rudyard Kipling." The first lines eerily resonated Gary's fate, as if his life were over already:

If you could do it all again, if you could set aside your flaws . . .

Gary's niece Melissa never made it, either. She waited with her fiancé at the Tucson Medical Center. He had broken his nose in a bar brawl. Still dressed in his Halloween costume, he looked every bit a real firefighter. She received the call about Gary's murder, and just as she moved through the revolving doors of the hospital entrance, several people injured from the explosion were wheeled passed her in a white blur. At first Melissa thought it was a joke, part of Gary's "surprise." Heather choked back sobs. "We don't know anything," she managed. Melissa called the golf resort and spoke to the bartender.

"Has my uncle been there?" Melissa asked urgently.

"I'm so sorry. I'm so sorry," the man responded, and Melissa hung up the phone.

Joy described the bombing as a JFK moment. Late for a dinner fund-raiser, an elegant affair she could not postpone, she fiddled with her diamond studded earrings when the phone shrilled. Debating whether to let it ring, she relented, cradled the receiver between her shoulder and chin, and heard Pam's hysterical voice over the line.

"I couldn't understand a word she said," Joy relayed to the detective, but nonetheless, Joy promised Pam she would drop by later, after the children were asleep. But all through dinner Joy's nerves were rattled. She had known Pam many years; they used to be ski instructors together. She couldn't recall a time when Pam had dissolved so completely. Joy had a terrible sense of foreboding; she sensed that this was more than a financial crisis. She couldn't wait for the fund-raiser to end.

She hurried to Pam's duplex and found the door ajar. Pam was rocking in a fetal position on the couch, dressed in cornflower-blue pajamas. Balled Kleenex surrounded her. The television flickered on mute. An empty bottle of wine sat on the coffee table. Pam looked wilted. Her blond hair hung loose around her shoulders. At the sight of Joy, Pam hiccupped with relief and burst into fresh tears. "What happened?" Joy asked, ready to comfort her friend.

Pam sobbed. "You missed October's life insurance payment."

"What *happened*?" Joy repeated, still confused.

"Gary's dead." Pam blinked at her friend, as if that detail were obvious. "He's in pieces, unidentifiable." Those specifics chilled Joy as she realized no news accounts had yet reported on Gary's condition. Pam had far bigger problems. She called Seaboard Life that night and negotiated an overnight payment. *Thank God* the company had a thirty-day grace period.

"Pam was shaking," Joy recalled, "literally shaking. She worried about being destitute. With Gary's death there would be no more child support. No income—period." Joy glossed over that fact, seemingly forgetting that Pam had never had income *anyway*.

"You'll be okay," Joy consoled her, already thinking of the money she planned to give Pam "until she got on her feet."

"Really?" Pam blinked. "Do you *really* think I'll be okay?"

"Absolutely." Joy hugged Pam, who exhaled like a deflating balloon.

Pam's former nanny, Kevin, happened to be visiting his parents in Tucson when he first heard the news of Gary's bombing on television. He called Pam immediately.

"I just can't believe it," Kevin stuttered. His thoughts raced. Snippets of the broadcast droned in the background. A sheen of perspiration coated his face. He paced his living room. Words tumbled out of his mouth.

"Yeah, I know: shocking," Pam said calmly. She sounded as if she had food in her mouth. "I missed the October payment on Gary's life insurance policy. But it's taken care of now. The FBI has already talked to me." Kevin detected no tremor in her voice, no tears. He felt chilled when he hung up the phone and even more numb when he later learned from the FBI that they had *never* contacted Pam.

Preliminary interviews helped Gamber form a useful victim profile. Apparently everyone knew Gary never locked his house, left his keys in his ignition, and habitually played golf at the Westin La Paloma resort. By contrast, a detective never lived by routine. Patterns revealed predictability. Habits signaled easy prey. Gary was either extremely naïve or dangerously arrogant. Maybe he was a little of both? The man, according to his niece, confided his darkest thoughts in the women he dated. Maybe he thought they were safe, fungible and distracting. But if "everyone" knew, every invited guest who failed to show suddenly became a "person of interest."

Melissa described how her uncle's prominent lawyer, Bob Hirsh, invited her to lunch later that week. "Very hush-hush," Melissa recalled. "He ushered me outside to a patio table and ordered us water and lime. He removed his cowboy hat, placed it on the table, steepled his fingers, and whispered, 'I think Pam did it.' No apology, no hesitation. Just unequivocal: 'Pam did it.' He later elaborated. Pam had contacted him shortly before Gary's death to inquire about her felon brother, whom Hirsh had once represented. She wondered if Hirsh had heard from him. Last she knew, her brother had fled to Mexico to continue his cocaine dealing."

Pam would insist to police she had only one brother, an airline pilot who worked for Federal Express. "I *think* that's the only brother I have," she said, but then relented. "I might have another brother. I'm just not sure he's alive."

Melissa named a list of shady characters authorities should consider, including a business associate of Gary's, with whom he lived following his divorce, who had been involved in drug dealings. But she quickly added that the bombing seemed personal and twisted, something only a witch would contemplate. But Pam's actions in the months preceding the murder—pawning Gary's coveted golf clubs for pennies and stealing Gary's bottles of aged wine from his cellar and spilling the contents into her swimming pool—were understandable, under the circumstances. She fit the criteria of the scorned, embittered divorcée. However, Gary, who had apparently never been paranoid before, suddenly trusted no one. And in the months before his murder, he tape-recorded his conversations, dictated notes of particularly compelling phrases, and began to interpret dialogue as having certain stressors. For a man who prided himself on veneer, his shell noticeably began to crack.

Detective Gamber and his partner, Sergeant Keith St. John, interviewed Gary's former girlfriend, Robin Gardner, at her kitchen table. After the bombing, she had relocated to a sleepy Virginia suburb. The television flickered in the living room. The front screen door banged shut like a cough in deep summer. She offered them a plate of ginger-snaps. Gamber politely refused, though all he'd had to eat in the last eight hours was a bag of pretzels on the plane. He removed a notebook and pen from the lapel of his jacket. He wrote down everything—details, observations, thoughts, questions—to refresh his memory later, though he was fairly certain he'd remember Robin.

His partner, Keith St. John, sounded like sandpaper as he sat on the edge of his seat, his clothes too crisp, as if he'd just removed them from plastic wrap. Not a crease in them. He smiled politely at Robin, unable to mask the hard glint in his eyes. He and Gamber had a routine and roles they played, and though they'd only been partners for a short time, they'd shared dark laughs in foul-smelling jail cells, tense revelations, and the most intimate moments of their lives.

Police partners were closer than married couples ever would be or hoped to be. Gamber and St. John enjoyed an instant trust born of circumstances and experience, a fierce attachment that demanded focus. They learned to process horror and compartmentalize grief. Emotion was a luxury most cops could not afford. Some laymen misinterpreted a cop's steely resolve as arrogance when actually it was a survival mechanism. Walls formed a protective shield. Vulnerability was weakness; every cop instinctively knew the life he chose would forever change him, and not necessarily for the better.

Robin chewed thoughtfully on a cookie and recalled for the detectives the first time she noticed Gary "frazzled": "We had pulled into a gas station, let the engine idle. It was close to dusk and an eerie stillness surrounded us. Sweat soaked Gary's shirt. A gun protruded from his waistband. He broke down, just sobbed, his head bowed on the steer-ing wheel. He really loved Pam, but *she* had fallen out of

love with him. 'She loved someone extremely rich,' he repeated. 'I'm not the same person.' He sounded desperate,
like he needed to *be* that person again, not because he
wanted to be rich, but because he feared being poor might
kill him."

Now, *that* detail meant something. If money defined
Gary's identity, what might Gary do to preserve his image?
More importantly, what might others do to destroy it? So far,
the women in Gary's life featured prominently. They were
his closest confidantes, seemingly disarming, too young and
impressionable, safe. He probably never imagined any would
betray him. He seduced them with money. He could afford to
be vulnerable with them.

"Did he elaborate?" Gamber asked, intrigued by Robin's theory that Gary *feared* poverty. Was Gary a textbook
example of the anxiety disorder known as chrematopho-
bia, the fear of having too little or too much money? Even
the smell of crisp dollar bills could trigger flu-like symp-
toms in its victims.

"You know how a caterpillar becomes a butterfly?"
Robin asked rhetorically. "Gary *was* a butterfly who became
a caterpillar, slowly disappearing into his dark cocoon." She
moved to the window, leaned against the sill, and looked
out, her arms wrapped tightly around her body. Gamber
noticed the loose skin on the back of her hands, the short,
practical nails, the way she clenched and unclenched her
fists. She and Pam had opposite coloring; while both women
were attractive, Pam exuded coldness, a brittle outer mask
that left Gamber feeling hollow. Robin was softer, more real
somehow. She looked less . . . *damaged*. But looks could be
deceiving.

Robin described an incident in which Gary, after meeting a business associate for dinner, caught a late film. The
mostly empty theater usually provided respite for Gary,
but this night a stranger entered the dark space and sat directly behind him. He carried a backpack and had trouble

squeezing into the seat. He shifted behind Gary, his presence unsettling. Gary fixated on the man's quick breaths,
as if the stranger had just been running. Gary stopped eating his popcorn, placed the half-eaten bag on the floor.
The music in the film matched the hammering in his chest.
And as the credits rolled across the giant screen, Gary
rose, stumbled to the aisle and caught the man's hard stare.
Gary exited into a side street. Rain smacked against his
cheeks. He fumbled with his keys. He heard footsteps behind him and he quickened his pace. He reached his car,
shakily opened the door, and slid inside. The man watched
him from the shadows, toying with a thread from his backpack.

Gamber dutifully scribbled in his notebook. He listened
intently to Robin's story: deflection or truth? Had Gary really been stalked by a shadowy figure with a backpack,
or . . . He studied Robin with a critical eye. She was attractive, young, unskilled, a single mother and waitress struggling through the night shift. Exactly the kind of woman
Gary would have desired. Except that she had carried
Gary's child.

Robin blanched at the memory. "Yes, it was the beginning of the end for us."

"Why's that?" His phone vibrated in his pocket, but he
didn't answer it.

"It was a difficult pregnancy." Robin shifted uncomfortably and smiled, a small, amused turning up of the corner
of her mouth. She pulled at a loose thread in her blouse.
Her boots clicked on the kitchen tile. She offered Gamber a
glass of lemonade. He remained seated, a strategy he hoped
would encourage Robin to relax enough to share. The detective wasn't certain yet whether he was in the presence of
a cold-blooded killer or another victim.

"Difficult physically?" he pressed. The kitchen where
they were interviewing Robin was too warm. Cherries
popped from the wallpaper. His elbow stuck to the vinyl

checkered tablecloth. His partner munched quietly on gingersnaps.

"Physically, emotionally, both." Robin let out a heavy sigh. She closed the refrigerator door with her hip and poured lemonade over ice.

"Gary encouraged me to have an abortion, insisted at first that the baby wasn't his. He didn't want a new family, couldn't afford a new baby. I had already lost *nine* children. Doctors put me on prednisone. Gary warned me not to take the medicine. He tape-recorded our conversations and promised to marry me if I aborted. He taunted me with other women while I was pregnant. Then he put me in touch with Pam and it was sort of like sending a fly into a spider's mouth."

Robin cracked open a window. The smell of rain rushed in.

"She offered me a solution to my 'problem,' said she knew of potential adoptive parents for my unborn child, as if I would ever consider such an idea. Pam insisted it would be fine; after all, Gary's mom had put *him* in an orphanage a few times. She was trying to be sympathetic. She came across as just . . . crazy." Robin wiped her mouth with the back of her hand.

"Did Gary's actions make *you* a little crazy?" Gamber prompted when they had reached a lull in conversation.

Robin smothered a smile and wagged a finger at Gamber.

"I know what you're thinking. I came from poverty, *Coal Miner's Daughter*, and Gary spent $10,000 on luggage and $20,000 on *drapes*. And I carried his child." She sued Gary for paternity. "I'll admit I harassed him," she said. After her daughter's birth, Gary paid her child support and rent. "He took good care of us and he didn't have to . . . not really. He filed for bankruptcy but he had hidden assets. Like the car he drove the night he was killed, he put in Richard Hickey's name. He may have had his own reasons for doing things for other people, but the day he died . . .

I've just never seen anything quite so cruel. People he called his *friends* behaved like vultures. They stripped his house bare, peeled pictures off his walls. It was like Gary was really *gone*, like he never existed. Like he wasn't *supposed* to ever exist, you know?"

Gamber let that remark slide. He was immensely talented at reading people, at judging their veracity by the way they shifted their bodies, averted their gazes, cleared their throats, gulped, coughed, breathed, smoked, drank. Robin's body spoke plainly: Gary's death made her uncomfortable, not sad, not regretful, but wary. She wasn't fooled by the detective's calm, congenial demeanor. She knew they had flown a great distance for answers. St. John finished the plate of cookies. He wiped his hands calmly with a napkin. He thanked her politely. They were delicious, he said. Gamber imagined his partner's composure unnerved Robin; he studied her movements like a panther watches its prey, his hazel eyes gold chips flickering bright and then dim as Robin spoke.

Gamber pulled a cassette tape from his briefcase. "I'd like to play you a recording." Robin swallowed the remaining lemonade and placed it in the sink. The detective rewound the tape. In the bright yellow kitchen, her shrill threats echoed: *"You'll pay someday, you'll pay."*

The column of Robin's neck bloomed splotchy red.

"You left that message on Gary's answering machine," Gamber offered.

"I was hormonal," she explained and laughed nervously. Her hands fluttered to her throat.

"Did you ever mention Gary's other girlfriends to Pam?"

"He had several," Robin volunteered. She stared at the ceiling as if trying to settle on a number. "I might have mentioned one, Taylor. He dated her while I was pregnant. She had been involved with a drug dealer and drove a ratty car. I might have shared where Taylor lived. I just couldn't believe Gary chose *her* over me, you know?"

Gamber's eyes were grainy from lack of sleep and he had hours to go as he methodically preserved the bright yellow kitchen in his mind, searching for details that were out of place, for anything that might constitute a clue.

"You called Pam after the bombing?" Gamber cleared his throat.

"I spoke to her maybe sixty seconds and hung up."

"Why?"

"I had a bad feeling about her. She sounded so ... cold."

But cases weren't made on bad *feelings*. They were made on hard evidence. That Robin might have been a scorned woman who harassed Gary relentlessly for child support— even humiliated him once by forcing him to empty his pockets of cash while standing in her doorway—did not necessarily make her a killer. After all, she had commiserated with Pam in the months before Gary's murder and, by her own admission, had participated in "male bashing." She had stalked Gary during the weeks before she delivered and, in a fit of jealous rage, had hurled his girlfriend's latest birthday present—a glass vase of flowers—at his head. But one detail nagged at Gamber's conscience. Robin did not benefit from Gary's death. And, she insisted, Gary ultimately treated her well, supported her as if she were his concubine. She would not have wanted that arrangement to end. Still, Robin had no solid alibi for the afternoon of Gary's murder.

CHAPTER FOUR:
LOOSE ENDS

Detective Gamber approached every homicide investigation the way a hunter tracks his prey. He searched for clues in the bushes, patches of trampled grass, scraped rocks, and broken cactus needles. He watched his lone buck in the clearing, its black eyes alert and expectant, its hide sweaty and damp, as if it had been galloping just paces ahead of its hunter. He retraced his steps, hoping to catch the beast off guard. Gamber arranged to interview Pam again. He had several follow-up questions. He had his target: the homicide. Now he needed a bullet to hit the bull's-eye.

Pam insisted that her divorce lawyer, Doug Clark, be present for her second police interview on November 10, 1996, just nine days after the bombing.

"We have this issue of this life insurance policy," Gamber began, once again taking a seat so that he spoke to Pam on her level.

Pam nodded sympathetically, wanting to be helpful. But her gaze had an unsettling intensity. She wore a sapphire-blue blouse that precisely matched her eyes. Gold earrings skimmed her shoulders; a masculine ring adorned her pinky. She looked fresh-faced, her makeup subdued but elegant. Not the appearance of a grieving widow.

"I just got a copy of it. So . . . might not even be an issue, we'll see here, but, uh . . ."

"It better be an issue," her lawyer interjected. He wrapped his arm protectively around Pam's shoulders. His striped suit bunched at the collar.

"Gary's the one that took this out," Pam said flatly. "Before he ever did a bankruptcy or was thinking about a bankruptcy. He, uh, felt that it was, uh, important that I have something."

"Is this the only policy that you're aware of? Is there another policy?"

"Um . . . you know what, I had another one. I think I've got it somewhere, I just couldn't find it right away, so I called and got another one."

Gamber stared at her, allowing the fumbling to continue. He moved his gaze from Pam to Mr. Clark, noting the stunning contrasts. Pam, not surprisingly, had chosen an unremarkable-looking man with a forgettable face devoid of expression, easy prey for a beautiful woman. A person could look right through him. Gamber was accustomed to being lied to. Everybody lied to the cops, even the innocent.

"Well, you . . . you mean another insurance company, another . . . ," Mr. Clark stuttered. Sweat pooled beneath his armpits.

"Correct." Gamber waited a beat and said for clarification. "Another separate insurance policy."

"Oh, I'm just thinking of the . . . this thingy. Um . . . I don't think so. I mean I don't know. I don't know. I mean, you might . . . you'll be able to tell me. I mean, I don't know." Pam's face betrayed a slight drift of annoyance.

"Okay. So, to the best of your knowledge, this is the only one?" Gamber repeated.

"Right. Right. You know he had a different one before that. Different company." Pam said, again providing too much information.

"And you don't remember the name of that company?"

"I don't . . ."

"Or if it's in effect?

"Well, it wouldn't be in effect because if I wasn't paying on it it wouldn't be in effect . . . so . . ." her voice trailed off. She looked at her attorney for guidance.

"Okay," Gamber nodded. "But this one did get paid on . . ."

"That's in question too," Mr. Clark remarked. "That's a problem. Apparently the premium was due October fifth and was not paid. When I found out it wasn't paid, I told Pam to pay the premium immediately."

"This was after Gary's death?"

"Uh, this is on November fifth. Pam overnighted to the company and they got it on November sixth. There's a thirty-one-day grace period in the policy."

"Okay."

"But October has thirty-one days in it, so I guess theoretically they could make a claim that that payment was not made within the thirty-one-day grace period."

"Okay, now, your specialty is in bankruptcy, right?" Gamber asked, changing topics.

"No. Our *firm* specializes in bankruptcy." Clark said.

"'Cause one question in my mind, and maybe you have some insight into this: Would part of the bankruptcy, would the creditors . . . would this policy be an asset . . ."

"No. This is all Pam's. This is one hundred percent Pam's money."

Gamber's partner, Sergeant Keith St. John, pursued the life insurance issue. The information he discovered corroborated Pam's statements. Gary obtained the policy in 1992; his children, Lois and Trevor, were the beneficiaries, but any proceeds were to be distributed to Pam as their trustee until the children reached majority. When Gary could no longer make the premium payments, Pam assumed the responsibility. And in 1995 she appointed her friend Joy to take over the payments until Gary's death. But it wasn't enough that Pam benefited from Gary's life insurance policy—and if ever a woman had a right to be bitter and resentful toward her ex-husband, it was Pam. According to her, Gary had abused her relentlessly, left her destitute with two children, and had the nerve to declare bankruptcy. But would Pam resort to murder? *Could* she orchestrate a bomb—from Aspen, no less—and detonate it in public, in broad daylight, in the presence of hundreds of spectators? Witnesses insisted Pam detested Gary *that much*. Gary's family members, convinced that they had all but handed Gamber a blueprint for murder, were annoyed that he failed to arrest her immediately.

Gamber wished it were that classically simple. But there was nothing inherently suspicious about a life insurance policy. A bombing evoked such complexity, a Mafia execution-style assassination that signaled payback, like a "gangland calling card"; but none of the government agencies consulted could confirm that Gary's death was mob inspired. The media spun tales that Tucson's notorious crime family, the Bonannos, had orchestrated the professional hit. And Gamber wasted precious days dispelling that dead end and other rumored mob connections. Even Gary's associates who had notorious surnames like Castellano* needed to be eliminated.

The suspect list read like a rap sheet and smaller players, like Gary's golf partner, Ruben Lopez, who failed to show as planned on the day of Gary's murder, suddenly became interesting. Witnesses claimed he rushed to Gary's

---

* Constantino "Paul" Castellano, headed the New York Gambino crime family. He was shot to death in New York City on December 16, 1985.

aid following the explosion, held a cell phone in his hand, but insisted his "fingers fumbled on the buttons"; he could not dial 911. Instead he yelled to Gary "Hang in there!" and later mumbled "Those bastards killed Gary" loud enough for bystanders to catch. His words took on an obscure meaning: *Which* bastards had killed him? Had the golf buddy made a general proclamation, or did he have useful information about Gary's murder? Or did he just voice the popular consensus that *everyone* apparently wished Gary dead? The task of sifting through layers of meaning to uncover a kernel of truth fell almost exclusively on the case agent. Gamber dictated which leads to pursue, which to discard. Early on, the investigation led him to the dusty border town of Nogales, Mexico, to interview a disgruntled detainee, a fugitive from Syracuse, New York, wanted on bomb possession charges. But even as bomb units and canines scoured the kiosks of bruised fruit, wax-wrapped chocolates, and metal sheds winking with silver jewelry, Gamber couldn't shake the chilling feeling that Gary's *real* killer watched him from close range the way a sniper steadies his scope.

Eager to play out that theory, the detective attended Gary's funeral services held at St. Thomas the Apostle Catholic Church in Tucson,* hoping that the victim's murderer lurked among the more than two hundred friends and relatives who slid into pews, ducked in the bushes, and worried they might become the bomber's next targets. Many killers attended their victim's funerals; it was a way for them to relish the results of their handiwork and also to keep abreast of their hunters. Gamber looked for someone out of place, someone in the shadows, someone who feigned too much emotion or too little. He had known col-

---

* Authorities allowed Triano's body to be cremated, didn't preserve his bodily fluids, and lost or misplaced metal fragments retrieved from the body.

leagues of his to note important details on such occasions, like red Converse sneakers on a mourner that matched the muddy shoe prints found near a windowsill at a murder scene. But Gamber registered only grief-stricken faces, genuine shock in their expressions, and a trepidation that mirrored the tension of victims who had survived a natural disaster and were uncertain of the future, wary of their luck, worried they might become a target.

As friends and acquaintances described Gary as a "spiritual poet" and a man who appreciated fine art and bronze portraits of himself, explosive-detecting dogs sniffed the church for bombs and several off-duty sherriff's deputies and plainclothes detectives stood guard beneath stained-glass panels of Jesus bleeding from the cross.

Photographers snapped pictures and filmed the mourners as they entered the sanctuary. Father Todd O'Leary led the group in prayers, hymns, and eulogies, imploring the crowd that "only truth sets us free." Former television anchorman Vic Caputo read a statement from Gary's oldest daughter, Heather, that began, "My father, my friend,' and went on to describe him as "the most amazing man [she'd] ever known." Longtime businessman James Sellers described Gary as a gentle, caring father and trusted business associate who "represent[ed] different things to each of us . . . a golf or tennis partner, business partner and, in better times, both a borrower and a lender." Sellers recalled Gary's passion for writing song lyrics and poetry. Dr. Charles Fina, a Tucson orthopedic surgeon, tearfully addressed the crowd: "Gary had a tremendous zest for life. That was his greatest legacy."

Robin Gardner watched the services from her locked car. Pam Phillips didn't attend at all. Neither did Gary's children, Trevor and Lois. Instead, Pam sent family "photos." She never called Gary's other children with condolences. She never sent flowers or a card.

"That doesn't make her a killer," Gamber insisted. "It makes her cold."

"A loose end," St. John confirmed.

The case had so many. But in a simultaneous federal and state task force investigation, it was easy to blame false starts on "cultural conflicts," turf wars between agencies, disinformation, and overwrought media reports. The Pima County sheriff, an elected official who believed his loyalties lay with his constituents, spoke openly and often to reporters without regard to leaks or exposure. While the federal agents remained tight-lipped about their findings, focusing on the technical aspects of the case, the sheriff expounded, possibly incensing Gary's oldest daughter, Heather, to question the pace of the investigation.

Months passed and still the Pima County Sheriff's Department had arrested no one. Gamber cradled the phone against his ear and absorbed the near exhaustion in Heather's voice. She was only twenty-six and he was certain she had stopped sleeping, afraid that if she did, she might miss an important clue. Gamber dreaded her phone calls, her rants like mantras in his head. He sympathized with her helplessness, and as the weeks turned into months, he reminded himself why he had embarked on a law enforcement career at all.

In college he had studied civil engineering, a practical goal that left him hollow. He chose a profession that mocked formal education; and yet, death investigations demanded analytical skills and critical thinking. College should have been a prerequisite to police work. He might have garnered more sympathy from his own administration. Instead, his bosses—mere "street monkeys"—pressured him to produce, produce, produce, yet most had never worked a homicide investigation and had no comprehension of the magnitude of paperwork involved in Gary's case. They cared about statistics and closure. As participant bystanders, they wanted daily progress reports. And when Gamber couldn't deliver fast enough, frustration mounted.

But you like police work, the continuing investigation, the follow-through . . .

He surveyed the warehouse of case files, literally shelves and shelves of documents and bomb debris. In the department's impound lot, Gary's burned car served as a ghostly reminder that *someone* needed to pay. But police work was like marriage: pure drudgery peppered with moments of sheer inspiration and necessary secrets. What Gamber *couldn't* disclose—what might have pacified Heather during those accusatory phone calls—was his tireless behind-the-scenes investigation. He still had to juggle ancillary cases, take his on-call rotation, deal with suicides and unattended deaths, and contend with the daily interruptions of coworkers. He tried humor, placed a toy guillotine on his piles of paperwork, and watched the poor puppet dressed in stripes and shackles sputter his innocence before the blade sliced off his head.

But his bosses reprimanded even that, mistaking gallows humor for insincerity. The truth was Gamber needed the release. The grisly details of Gary's bombing permeated his life, destroyed his personal relationships and led to chronic insomnia. His annual review all but labeled him an asshole, a non–team player who broke convention. Gamber considered the remarks an unavoidable downside of his job. He dispensed with family life, believing that every major challenge required sacrifice. Little did he realize that police work would shatter loved ones, and leave a trail of human debris.

What he so badly *wanted* to tell Heather, but could not, was that he relied on certain investigative tools, like FinCEN (Financial Crimes Enforcement Network), managed by the Department of the Treasury, to gather information he was prohibited from disclosing or disseminating to *anyone* including a prosecutorial agency. Merely subpoenaing

Gary's bank records only ensured that no one could manipulate the figures, but as Gamber knew, wealthy people funneled money through other hidden sources. He sifted through voluminous records, searching for inconsistencies, large withdrawals, or deposits that stood out. Gamber needed more than circumstantial evidence—embittered lovers or ex-wives or failed business ventures—to build a case. He narrowed his list of suspects to those who might have benefitted from Gary's death. The information he gathered from FinCEN helped him develop a victim profile, a lifestyle that inspired killing.

He couldn't know yet which suspects were more significant than others. But he hoped that by following the money he would find a motive. And at least in the beginning, every transaction, investment, and debt that involved Gary might have been sufficient cause to kill him.

CHAPTER FIVE:
DIGGING DEEPER

High-profile cases demand special patience when deciphering truth from fiction. Witnesses, eager to help, offered leads that Gamber felt compelled to follow, if not to eliminate, then to investigate. But not every tip merited precious resources; he had no interest in chasing ghosts. The first of several anonymous letters addressed to "SHERIFF'S DEPARTMENT" arrived on November 21, 1996. The handwritten block print warned that investigative reporter Don Bolles's *real* bomber lived in a trailer park in Flowing Wells, a suburb of Tucson. Best known for his journalism on organized crime, Bolles was murdered in 1976 when a remote-controlled car bomb exploded in the parking lot of the Clarendon Hotel. Although the anonymous letter insisted that the lone mechanic-suspect was actually a Mafia hit man who had blown up a nightclub near the seedy Miracle Mile, three people had been convicted of Bolles's murder and now served life sentences. The only similarity between Bolles's bombing and Triano's killing was the hint that both crimes might have been mob inspired.

But a cursory investigation revealed that the lone mechanic identified in the letter was actually an eighty-four-year-old World War II veteran who had served in a tank squadron. In civilian life he worked in concrete. The letter included a recent photo; the man, with purported ties to mobster Joe Bonanno, wore coveralls and muddy boots, a cigarette between his lips. He balanced with a cane, the veins in his hands knotted ropes. His face like carved stone stared blankly at the lens, and Gamber concluded the mechanic was as likely to have detonated the bomb that killed Triano as he was to have participated in a marathon.

Most victims had some connection to their assailants. But the detective fielded numerous anonymous tips as random and useless, as if he had thumbed through the Yellow Pages himself and chosen exotic names to target. Psychics, too, called in and insisted they had "seen" Triano's killer on the grassy knolls that bordered the country club.

In late January 1997, FBI field agents offered Gamber leads as well; one reported he had received information from a reliable confidential informant that Gary's murderer was actually a member of the Hells Angels Motorcycle Club and an active participant in the Aryan Brotherhood, a white supremacist prison gang. According to the source, the Hells Angel bragged about bombing a Cadillac in Tucson and solicited the informant to share in the proceeds from that crime. According to the source, he and the bomber planned to rendezvous in Switzerland, where the funds were secured in a Swiss bank account.

Gamber cradled the phone to his ear, listened patiently to the speaker and took a long pull from his coffee cup. *A Hells Angel now?* Notwithstanding that a car bomb seemed far too sophisticated a method for a motorcycle gang to orchestrate, the detective could not fathom a motive, and no information that Triano ever had business connections with the Hells Angels had ever come to light. *Pam* had alleged that Gary might have been involved with drugs, but the Hells Angels did not traffic in cocaine. Gamber quickly dismissed the "lead" after he learned that the member had been released from prison two months *after* Gary's death.

But the FBI persisted the following week with yet another possible tip from an unidentified informant who had purportedly purchased four explosives for an individual in California named "Tony C." They planned to detonate a bomb in Tucson. The source elaborated about galvanized pipes, threaded end caps, and a blue Los Angeles Dodgers bag equipped with remote control devices. Gamber propped his feet on his desk and opened the latest *Tucson Citizen,* dated January 21, 1997. The headline article detailed the bomb components the ATF had recovered in Triano's case but omitted mention of a key piece of evidence, a shred of blue fabric containing the logo "Echo Bay" that crime scene technicians had retrieved from the rubble. It was a detail law enforcement deliberately kept from the media; only the real killer would know the type of bag used to conceal the bomb.

As it turned out, the FBI's proposed lead was a convicted felon with a history of false reporting, and although he had some relationship to "Tony C.," the alleged bomb maker was completing a ten-year prison sentence at the time of Gary's murder.

Gamber preferred concrete leads and returned to the money.

Bank reporting laws required that institutions disclose deposits in excess of $10,000 in cash transaction reports (CTRs). For those individuals who sought to circumvent the CTRs by depositing *less than* $10,000, the banks generated suspicious activity reports (SARs) and provided lengthy narratives. The IRS, in turn, used this information to monitor potential tax evaders and people who might have hidden assets, like Gary. While Gamber pored over SARs, he had insight into Gary's financial practices. Bank tellers found Gary "charming." He maintained several accounts with different banks and conducted nearly all of his transactions in cash. His money plummeted in 1994.

The beginning of the end for Pam and Gary's marriage had everything to do with the Arizona Indian Gaming

Association (AIGA), a 501(c)6 nonprofit organization established on November 21, 1994, by Arizona tribal leaders. The association was committed to advancing the lives of Indian peoples—economically, socially, and politically— so Indian tribes in Arizona could achieve their goal of self-reliance, supported by tribal gaming enterprises on Arizona Indian lands. AIGA served as a clearinghouse and educational, legislative, and public policy resource for tribes, policy makers, and the public on Indian gaming issues and tribal community development. Under new legislation, Gary could no longer exclusively keep his casino profits or lawfully control the gaming facilities; he had to defer to the Indian tribes,* who could now take control of their own operations and claim the money Gary earned.

Anticipating the looming legislative changes, Gary filed for Chapter 11 bankruptcy protection in January 1993 with an estimated $26 million in real debts, including a $10 million liability to the Tohono O'odham Nation. The Indian tribe sued Gary over the Papago Bingo gambling profits. But more than the lawsuit, Gamber fixated on information he received from a private investigator. The son of one of Gary's deceased partners threatened to kill Gary over the lost revenue from the gambling parlors. The man, identified only as "Cohn," stalked Gary, leaving him threatening messages on his home phone and mailing him empty bullet shell casings.

Curiously, Pam Phillips never mentioned Cohn to Gamber in her three lengthy interviews.

---

* Triano and partners Louis Cohn and Richard Hickey raised a $1.2 million loan for the tribe to build its first bingo hall in 1983. Triano and his partners created a management arm to run Papago Bingo in exchange for 40 percent of the profits. But tribal leaders wanted more for themselves and less for Triano and his crew of non-Indians. The dispute only escalated in the early 1990s with the addition of slot machines.

As a result of the Tohono O'odham lawsuit, Gary's annual income plummeted from a reported $1.5 million in 1992 to a mere $107,000 in 1993, the year Pam Phillips filed for divorce. In earlier depositions, Gary insisted that his business fluctuated: if one deal failed, he embarked on another, exhilarated by the "chunks of money" that flowed periodically into his bank accounts. But much like a gambler, Gary thrived on the highs and lows and the thrill of possibility. His financial practices made him an instant target. As Gamber's suspect list became almost unmanageable, he looked for common denominators; Pam's name continued to surface.

In addition to Papago Bingo, the detective investigated Gary's stock interest in another gaming venture, Bingo Enterprises. Operating as Milagro Inc., Gary owned a 65 percent interest in Barona Bingo, a casino in California. *Pam* owned 10 percent of the company, thanks to her father's substantial investment of $285,000. But before the business had a chance to thrive, four of its members, excluding Gary, were arrested for misdemeanor slot machine violations. Gary dissolved the company shortly thereafter, with no available assets for distribution, and when Pam's father demanded an accounting, Gary provided none. Meanwhile, Gary's accountant faced felony charges for forging checks in the amount of $400,000. Gary made a phone call to the Pima County Attorney's Office and the charges were conveniently dismissed.

Gary wasn't always rewarded by those he helped. Pam accused Gary of hiding assets following his bankruptcy, an allegation that, on its face, sounded reasonable for a disgruntled spouse cheated of spousal and child support. But for a detective investigating a murder, it provided motive. Two major creditors, First Interstate Bank (which loaned Gary $415,000) and Insurance Company of North America (which claimed it had a $92,312 judgment against him) filed lawsuits against

Gary, accusing him of shuffling assets "like a deck of cards." Without explanation, Gary surrendered his interest in Potrero, the 4,400-acre property in San Diego, to his brother-in-law. Gary shared a home on Airway Boulevard with his longtime business partner, Richard Hickey; Gary put the home in Hickey's name. The Lincoln Town Car Gary "borrowed" just weeks before his murder was also registered to Hickey. Gary's former residence on Skyline Drive was owned by brothers who engaged in insurance fraud and served several years in prison. The FBI scrutinized Gary closely in the weeks before his murder, theorizing whether *Gary* had anything to do with the fraudulent activity.

All the while, Gary's daughter Heather called sometimes two or three times a day, her tone accusatory and critical. *You're not doing enough. You're wasting time. The real killer is out there.* Dissatisfied with the progress, Heather made frequent appearances at the sheriff's department, and the detective's heart hammered inside his chest each time he spotted her long blond hair and attractive profile in the lobby. She looked older than her years, as if her father's inexplicable and violent end had caused her such stress, that she could no longer *be* young. Although Gamber had little experience with the kind of grief crime victims suffered, when he passed the door in his department labeled "Parents of Murdered Children," a lump formed in his throat.

It was a fallacy that he or any homicide detective could ever bring a victim's family "closure." Grief brought numbness and fueled a victim's loved ones' desperate need to feel part of an investigation, to feel anything but dead inside. Even the most ordinary things, like driving to work, required effort. He'd heard stories of mothers so lost in thought that they couldn't remember the route. Heather's profound sadness propelled Gamber to action. He worked feverishly into the night, ignoring his own family, battling migraines, surrounded by mountains of paperwork he was certain held clues, if only he could find them.

As the days stretched into weeks and spring approached, Heather lamented that she felt like the only person in the world still interested in her father's case.

"I can't see his face anymore," she whispered once.

Parents of murdered children had reported similar memory distortions. Psychologists dismissed the phenomenon as the mind's coping mechanism for trauma. Blurred or indistinguishable features supposedly helped the remaining family member "move on," but Gamber had never known a parent to move on after the brutal death of a child. He heard about the recurring nightmares, the parents who "found" their missing boy or girl in a blizzard or deep woods, but could never see their child's face. Instead, the hazy figure teased them like a mirage. The parents woke confused, frustrated, and never sure they had actually dreamed *their* child. Without certainty, they still had hope. Even though Gamber had doubts about ever solving Gary's bombing, he assured Heather emphatically that he would.

He started with sixty-eight boxes containing key players in Gary's history. The contents spanned a decade, from the 1960s through the 1970s, when Gary once dabbled in a business near the Tucson airport. Ordinarily, documents that old would be of little value; but in this case, where the suspect list went on for pages, any names that formed a pattern—that revealed a realistic victim profile—could take the case in an entirely new direction. He skimmed the names, jotted notes next to each, and soon found a disturbing common denominator. Gary's friends were all villains hidden in plain sight. All were either dead or missing.

He reviewed the list:

- Skip Creagor had family money, died mysteriously in an airplane crash, possibly flying narcotics in from South America.

- An ex–Pima County Sheriff's Department captain who went to prison for smuggling in aircraft.
- Samuel Manning* entered the witness protection program.
- Gus Huchean was a professional informant for the federal government and knew secrets about Gary.
- Gary's father was rumored to own a "chop shop" for stolen cars.
- Gary used to conduct business with a law firm by the name of Russo, Cox, Dickerson and Carter. Cox and Carter were dead; Dickerson left the firm.
- An ex-con contracted with Gary at the Desert Diamond Casino and lost his job. He had the technical knowledge to manufacture a bomb.
- The people who purchased Gary's Skyline Country Club property were now under indictment for fraud by the FBI; the key witness, a chiropractor, had gone missing.†
- A CPA who allegedly stole money from Gary had disappeared.

He stopped reading. Gary, adored father, spiritual poet, kind philanthropist, and jovial friend, had a distinctly darker side—a side that made it infinitely more plausible that he had something in common with Pam.

Over the next several weeks, each road, no matter how twisted or long, led back to Pam. But Detective Gamber didn't have enough to charge her with anything but a personality flaw. Pam relished money, had married and divorced for money, and, according to at least one witness, occasionally threatened friends with bodily harm if they allied

---

* Pseudonym.
† The FBI later determined that Gary Triano had never come up in their fraud investigation.

themselves too closely with Gary. *But was she a bomb maker?* Gamber reviewed the details of his interviews with Pam, mentally flagging inconsistencies, circling dates in bold red. Gary's birthday was actually November 6, not November 1; and yet, whoever had killed Gary wanted his death to coincide with the macabre Day of the Dead celebrations. Friday, the day of the bombing, was *not* part of Gary's typical golf schedule. According to Westin La Paloma employees, Gary usually golfed on the weekends. Despite Gary's delinquent club membership dues, the staff allowed him to play.

Who would have known about that arrangement? Someone inside? Someone monitoring his tee times? Would Pam have known Gary's golf schedule? Not likely. Pam hadn't lived in Tucson since 1994, and she rarely allowed her children to visit Gary. A number of witnesses disclosed to the detective that the club had received anonymous calls inquiring about Gary's tee times. His friend and partner, Ruben Lopez, arranged the golf session. He planned to lunch with Gary beforehand but then forgot about his date. Had Lopez insisted that Gary golf that Friday? Witnesses expressed relief that Lopez was not also in the car with Gary. *Should he have been?*

Gamber's first interview with Pam occurred on November 6, Gary's actual birthday. She had expressed no emotion over the phone, her cold, flat tone reminiscent of shock or tired anger from years of bitterness. Pam insisted in that first interview that she had a terrific job working for Heinz Interstate selling houses and lots on a golf course, and yet, no records corroborated her employment.

She insisted that she spoke with the FBI shortly after her divorce about possible death threats Gary had received related to his business affairs. But the FBI had no record of ever having a conversation with a Pamela Phillips. Pam express mailed her October life insurance premium on November 5; the company received the payment on November

6 and credited her account. Pam insisted she was unaware of the "problem" until *after* Gary's murder. She told friends that she had no life insurance policy ostensibly because "it was none of their business." Curiously, Pam never mentioned that *she* had ever received any threats as a result of Gary's business ventures.

In Gamber's third interview with Pam in Aspen on December 13, 1996, Pam mentioned her prenuptial agreement for the first time. She had $2 million prior to her marriage to Gary. Her net worth in 1995—allegedly $3 million—was secured in the Potrero property. She sold several items of Gary's prior to his murder because she didn't like his stuff; it was either store it or dump it. *But did that make her a killer?* No. It made her, as Robin had so plainly described, *cold.*

With new tips coming in daily to the sheriff's department, Gamber resigned himself to the fact that it would take weeks if not months to unravel the case. Ninety-nine percent of the leads would likely yield nothing valuable, but Gamber could hardly ignore any. Heather's voice in his head pounded like footsteps. *Pick up the pace, faster, faster.* It was never enough for Gary's daughter.

He didn't blame her. This was his job: human emotion, restless sleep, fractured personal relationships and pressure so intense he could hear his own heart beat. He preferred silence and dark, empty spaces. He declined invitations to decompress with colleagues after hours because there really was no such thing. Like most homicide detectives he could never shut off the images that swirled in his head; he lived as if shell-shocked. Suspects drifted in and out of his conscience like so many ghosts. Anger simmered at the surface. The shrill of a phone startled him awake. He had no time for idle chitchat, for his wife, for his dog, for anyone or anything unrelated to The Case.

And as time ticked by, pressure mounted from his bosses, his sergeant, Heather, his family, even himself. Soon no one *but* another detective could possibly offer him relief. His life had sharp edges, deep grooves, and steep cliffs. His mind raced. He didn't sleep like other people, love like other people, even speak like other people. What he did for a living was not a calling; it was a sickness. And Gary's case was a living organism that breathed under his skin.

CHAPTER SIX:
THE DEVIL IN THE DETAILS

The detective reviewed suspect after suspect, stopping briefly again on Richard Hickey, Gary's business partner. *Pam* knew about the relationship, knew Gary shared a home with Hickey, an arrangement the detective suspected Gary contrived to hide—and protect—his assets from his ex-wife and the bankruptcy court. She mentioned death threats from Mexican investors. There was some truth to Pam's revelation. Gary *had* secured a $2.5 million loan on a piece of property Hickey owned and he had personally guaranteed the loan. It was a pattern Gary practiced with investors, offering land as collateral. But Hickey filed for bankruptcy and lost the land. The Mexican investors sued Gary for fraud and threatened him with bodily harm if he defaulted on the $2 million judgment.

The detective circled Hickey's name several times in ink and formed a question mark. As far as Gamber could tell, Hickey had suffered no repercussions from the failed Mexico deal. But the connection intrigued the detective enough for him to begin focusing on Gary's other foreign investments, particularly the casino he built in China in the province of Hainan, a large island off the coast of Vietnam, in the Gulf of Tonkin where the locals enjoyed legalized prostitution and wore bright tropical shirts, in stark contrast to the plainer attire worn on the Communist mainland. The island, according to an associate of Gary's, resembled an "Asian Hawaii" and the governor hoped the gambling would boost tourism. Encouraged by his results in China, Gary made plans to build similar casinos in Saint Lucia, near Martinique, and possibly in Baja, Mexico.

"Gary was the money end," one former business associate, Walt Collins revealed to Gamber. "For the China deal, he secured two groups of investors; the first, headed by Michael Tsang, ultimately pulled out. One of the partners was diagnosed with cancer. The second group, headed by Gary Fears, didn't end so well. Fears financed a couple of trips, invested $600,000 into the Bank of China. But then Fears learned that some of the state gaming commissions where he had casinos in the United States considered his China venture a violation of his license. He pulled out and sued Gary for his out-of-pocket expenses. Gary countersued. If he had won that litigation, he would have stood to collect $10 million in lost revenue. Fears settled for $300,000. Gary died a few days later, effectively making his countersuit moot.

Gamber didn't believe in coincidences. If Fears had wanted to eliminate his problem, why resort to a bomb? Why not exact something more subtle, like a single shot to the back of the head, or poison in a cocktail?

"Did Gary have other ventures?"

"He considered opening up a floating casino in the Middle East along the Gulf of Aqaba. There's no shortage of tourists there. Gary considered himself somewhat of a pioneer." Collins laughed.

" 'Floating?' "

"A land-based casino might get blown up by the religious fanatics . . . The land is sacred, you know . . . Saint Lucia was another deal, like Jordan. There were always deals, no shortage of deals. His attorney John Fierramonte financed Gary's trip to the island."

Why would Fierramonte invest in a floating casino?
Gamber wondered.

"He had the mistaken impression that [they] were solid
investments. He put up $30,000 in consulting fees and ad-
vertising and had a vision of developing a five-star resort.
He had an idea to open a dude ranch, thought the German
tourists disembarking from the ocean liners might get a kick
out of horseback riding on the island. But nothing ever
materialized, just more invested money and nothing tan-
gible."

And Fierrramonte never got paid.

"How did Gary survive on a day-to-day basis?" Gamber
inquired.

"Commissions, percentages of deals brokered . . .
Fierramonte's loans." Collins lowered his voice. "The attorney was eventually [censured] for something fraud related,
but not before he loaned Gary $10,000 towards his back
child support."

Why would a lawyer step in like that? Gamber wondered. The attorneys *he* knew were hardly altruistic. He ran
the figures in his head: $30,000 for a failed casino, $10,000
for child support, other "loans" . . . and how many partners
could one person have?

Collins told Gamber about still other people with a potential motive for the crime. According to Collins, another
of Gary's associates filed for bankruptcy and hid assets
from the federal bankruptcy court. Collins suspected that
Gary knew about the debtor's fraud and feared that his
colleague knew Gary knew. According to Collins, this associate worried that Gary, if subpoenaed, might testify
against him and might expose him to potential criminal
charges.

Witness elimination could certainly inspire murder.

"Gary was definitely spooked. He parted his hair differently and carried a gun."

"What happened?"

Collins suggested that the associate offered Gary financial incentive for his silence. "He promised Gary $16,000."

"Not much compensation for a coconspirator," the detective voiced the thought aloud.

Perhaps Kevin Oberg agreed and took matters into his own hands? After all, he did own a construction company and often used dynamite to blast buildings.

Sergeant Keith St. John researched blasting permits in Pima County, the criteria to obtain one, the restrictions involved, the penalties and sanctions for noncompliance. More specifically, he looked into the activities of Cienega Property Development, of which Oberg was a principal officer. According to the mining inspector's office, regulatory policy concerning blasting operations (outside mines) was left to the discretion of local government; the fire marshal's office, like the Bureau of Alcohol, Tobacco, Firearms and Explosives, focused on explosives storage and handling, not permits. Pima County Regional Flood Control District concentrated on blasting operations of land development companies that threatened the integrity of water and sewer lines. St. John stumbled upon a little known subdivision known as the Summit; it was developed by a company named Swan Ina Properties; Kevin Oberg was its principal officer. There were no permits on file. But then St. John learned there were no serious punitive sanctions for noncompliance, either.

"So we have a lot of nothing." Gamber shrugged at his partner's latest revelation.

"Nothing conclusive."

"No blasting operations near Westin La Paloma resort in November 1996?"

"None that have surfaced."

"We need to dig deeper."

While the detectives focused on the human debris, the Bureau of Alcohol, Tobacco, Firearms and Explosives processed the bomb scene and turned their investigation to the technical aspects of the case. And though the two factions debriefed one another each morning, the sheer quantity of information overwhelmed even the most efficient of investigators. Short on manpower, the ATF commissioned select employees from bureaus all over the country to work in the Tucson office for three months. Their specific task was to catalog evidence, input documents into computer databases, and manage the enormous paper flow. The ATF office buzzed like a newsroom. Stacks of evidence littered the desks. Computers hummed. Employees worked robotically in their open cubicles, occasionally compelled to look over the walls.

But it was the bomb itself that offered the first real clue. Various fragments—wood chips, metal shavings, nylon threads, the end cap of the bomb, and the battery source—underwent forensic testing. Agents with the ATF concluded fairly early on in the investigation that the bomb was "a little more sophisticated" than most, a fact that only widened the pool of potential suspects. Although the Internet in 1996 was still in its infancy, bomb-making instructions were readily available. A person could easily order books and link with underground providers. But the agents made a startling discovery: the pipe bomb used to kill Gary was unusually long—seventeen inches—and stuffed with Red Dot, a smokeless gunpowder most often used to reload shotgun shells. Most pipe bombs, as Special Agent Anthony May would later explain to a jury, "were built with stock six-inch-long pipes purchased off hardware store shelves."

Gary's bomber took care to order a longer pipe, specifically cut to size and rethreaded.

"The killer used a pipe with a six-volt lantern battery, commonly used by bombers in the 1970s and 1980s before they realized double AA batteries would suffice," May said. His discovery allowed the agents to pinpoint the bomber's age. They developed a profile—the bomber would likely have been someone with knowledge of model planes or boats. The painstaking task of analyzing the fragments under a microscope using forceps, tweezers, and probes belonged to ATF special agent Bradley Cooper. He emptied the pieces, battery fragments, pipe nipples, end caps, and bits of red carpet into ceramic bowls in his lab in Walnut Creek. Over the next several months he discovered the Red Dot powder used was manufactured by Alliant Powder, also known as Hercules powder, commonly found in ammunition.

"The red dye was proprietary," the agent explained. "So it could easily be identified as gunpowder."

Agents replicated the bomb in a chemist lab by using components recovered at the crime scene. Fragments of wood, a radio crystal, toggle and slide switches, a battery holder, a circuit board, and other items led investigators to conclude the bomb was mounted to two-by-fours and a peg board. And although the bomber attempted to mask his identity by scratching off the battery label so that investigators could not trace it, the radio crystal confirmed that the bomb had been remotely detonated and that the bomber had to have stood just a few feet from Gary's car when it exploded.

The search for the person's identity began with a small piece of nylon recovered from the scene. The thread matched a diamond-shaped design on shreds of fabric found on particular duffel bags sold at Wal-Mart stores. Investigators quickly dispersed and traveled to hardware stores, Wal-Marts, and Radio Shacks throughout the country; inexplicably they overlooked Colorado, California, and Florida, all places detectives would later learn the elusive bomber had lived.

CHAPTER SEVEN:
THE ROMANCE

November 1995: *Two Years Earlier*

According to Joy, Pam glowed one morning in the meadow, the fine lines on her forehead smoothed with relief. Her blond hair swept back in a clip, she wore a cowl-neck sweater and a pair of cream slacks tucked into a pair of fur-lined snow boots. She chatted more freely than she had in the past. She talked about a man she'd met, Ron Young.

"She seemed content for the first time in years," Joy recalled. "Not happy, exactly, but hopeful."

Joy invited Ron Young for Thanksgiving dinner. Gray clouds filled the November afternoon sky. Joy's home smelled of spiced pumpkin and cinnamon. Classical music filtered through the speakers. Her sunken living room flickered with gold candles. Pam and her new friend arrived.

"He wasn't what I expected," Joy said. "Pam had always gone for striking good looks, impeccable hair, and a charming smile. There was something vacant about Ron Young, something unsettling. He was unusually tall, almost a distortion. But I smiled anyway and shook his hand."

As Joy led the couple into the living room and hung up their coats on hangers in the closet, she overheard their hushed whispers. Joy recalled Ron seemed to be instructing her friend "as if she was his student." Joy thought Ron was phony. "The first clue was that he kept telling us he owned businesses in the Bahamas and Italy. He talked about all he was and all he had. When people start telling you all they have and all they are, they're usually the people who don't have, aren't, and never have been."

But Joy kept her opinions to herself.

The whole meeting with Ron Young was entirely shocking and thoroughly distasteful.

"There was something absent about him, an emptiness to his gaze that told me his thoughts were elsewhere. He seemed so . . . cold."

Joy had impeccable social grace, and here was this man seated next to her best friend who scooped handfuls of leftover Halloween chocolates from the candy dish in their living room and stuffed them into his pockets. But that wasn't the worst of it. With the aroma of turkey still in the air the next morning, Joy's husband, Hugh, poked his head into the kitchen and instructed the couple's cook to prepare a stew with the leftover turkey bones.

"That's impossible sir." The girl blinked at him with large saucer eyes and wiped her hands on her apron. "The carcass is gone."

"Gone? You mean thrown away?"

The chef shook her head. "No, sir, your guest last night took it with him."

Neither Hugh nor Joy could fathom *how* Ron Young had walked out of their home with turkey remains—much less why—but Hugh was quick to demand that Ron return the bones. The afternoon had a grayish tinge to it, like a veil over the sky. Pam never apologized to Joy for Ron's behavior. She dismissed it, saying Ron was just frugal. He showed up alone at the Bancrofts' house and returned the turkey skeleton. It had been picked clean.

* * *

Ron noticed Pam a year earlier just as the first frost iced the Aspen sidewalks. He shared the same duplex as Pam on Snowbunny Lane. His sparsely furnished apartment had the stark, spotless feel of a medical examiner's office. After several preliminary inquiries he learned that he had an "incredibly striking" neighbor who socialized with some equally gorgeous and rich girlfriends. His tone was almost reverent when he spoke of Pam.

"I wasn't even in her league," Ron conceded later, but his date had "flaked out" on him for the evening and he spotted Pam at a popular chic martini bar at the base of Ajax Mountain, looking as polished as fine crystal. A light snow fell outside. A fire crackled in a corner and lit up Pam's hair like gold cotton candy. She wore all white, and her high-heeled boots glittered with a single studded diamond in the toe. She had company: a handsome older gentleman with chiseled good looks and jet-black hair that looked glued on. Ron slid awkwardly onto the stool beside Pam and his weight caused the cushion to exhale. He smoothed his navy slacks, draped his coat over his lap, wiped a bead of condensation from his brow, and without invitation interjected himself into the conversation with an uproarious laugh.

Startled at the intrusion, Pam pinned him with cool blue eyes that resembled glass.

"I'm a completely transparent person," she would later volunteer.

Ron invited her to ride the Silver Queen Gondola to the summit of Ajax Mountain with its steep glades and bump runs. At nearly twelve thousand feet, they had a dazzling view of the town below, with its opulent boutiques, paved streets, and globes of yellow light. Highland Bowl, Richmond Ridge, Buttermilk, and Snowmass glistened around them. Aspen's annual ski racing marathon was well under way. Hundreds of big-mountain enthusiasts whizzed past them at speeds reaching seventy miles per hour. As they rode the gondola to the summit, skimming the Everglades, Pam leaned close to Ron and confided, "I moved here for the quiet."

Her life, as Ron would soon learn, was anything but quiet. He observed Pam's "piles" of invitations to social events and dinner parties. She was considered an "A-lister" who really didn't exist outside the world she created. She made a point of pairing with a man whom others would approve, an *interesting* man, a man who had *money*, enough to charter luxury cruise ships for her friends at $30,000 a week, to book flights at a glance to lunch in Greece, or jet to Palm Beach for the afternoon.

"I couldn't possibly compete with that. My business* had come to a screeching halt in 1989, and I was sort of on permanent pause," Ron said. His attraction to Pam was akin to a crush, like Pam was the cool girl at school and Ron just wanted to hang around her.

But the two still shared dialogue and insecurities. Perhaps she felt a kindred spirit in Ron, a fellow impostor who craved the illusion of wealth. She loosened around Ron, peeled off her refined robes and wore her old self. And as their friendship blossomed, Pam spoke openly about her marriage to Gary, how he had abused her and invested her millions in "real estate scams."

One evening at dinner, Pam stabbed her fork into her potato for emphasis. She said Gary had left her "destitute," refusing to pay her child support or spousal maintenance. "I just don't know how he expects me to *live*," she pleaded. She *knew* how to make money, she insisted; she just had trouble with the "technical aspects." Her technology-based astrology company, Star Babies, languished as a result.

---

* Ron would later describe his "business" to another prison inmate as "flying drugs from the Bahamas to Aspen."

Ron patiently listened, sipped several glasses of wine, leaned back in the elegant chair, and offered to help. He had expertise with computers and Web-based businesses. He could be her "manager."

Three weeks later, Ron joined Pam for a late lunch at an Italian eatery. The place smelled of boiled pasta, spices, and beer. A warm fire blazed in the corner. Chunky candles served as centerpieces. They faced the street. Snow blew around them. Pam stiffened each time a car pulled into the parking lot.

"Gary has the kids this weekend," She said flatly. "I just worry so much [that] he'll kidnap them." She sat with her back to the entrance and ordered a salad. She drizzled vinaigrette over the dark leaves and grimaced at the couple next to them. They ogled each other with naked adoration as their pizza grew cold. Pam described her marriage to Gary as being like a "disease"; when she divorced him, her system "flooded with a strange relief."

She sensed his presence like an amputated limb: "It's like I can *feel* him even when I know he's not there," she said. Then, as if on cue, Gary entered the restaurant and slid quietly into a booth behind Pam. He ordered a glass of ice water. Pam's face registered her alarm as she dropped her fork; it clattered on her plate. With shaking hands, she pulled the napkin from her lap and slowly placed it on the table. Ron later recalled her stricken expression: he said it was like the bottom had just dropped out of her life and she was free-falling.

CHAPTER EIGHT:
KILLING TWO BIRDS WITH ONE STONE

Following Gary's impromptu appearance at the restaurant, Ron saw Gary only one other time, two weeks later, while walking in town with Pam's children, Lois and Trevor. Gary *was* a presence, appearing without warning or fanfare, curiously opposite from what Pam had conveyed. "Gary hated Aspen," Pam insisted. "He never really fit in; he needed to be 'Mr. Big,' loud, larger than life; locals never really cared *who* he said he was." Ron could understand why Pam found him unsettling. But the truth was, even Ron saw the affection between Gary and his children. And the love disturbed him. He couldn't fathom how a man who clearly adored his kids could be so abusive toward their *mother*.

But Pam insisted Gary "terrified" her: "He's threatened to kill me," she said between mouthfuls of grilled salmon at a quaint bistro in town. Her hands trembled. It was November 1995, and chilly even inside the restaurant. Ron secretly recorded their conversation. Meanwhile, he shared very little about himself; instead he listened, absorbed, and slowly cannibalized Pam's life.

"I feel like I'm being closed down all over. This is breaking me. It's costing me so much money to live here. Still have no child support, and meanwhile Gary's taken a three-week vacation to Europe. I'll probably have to pull the kids out of private school."

She spoke about Potrero, how she still could not sell the property. She blamed Gary. He had borrowed $270,000 from his business partner, Gus, and rather than pay him back, he agreed to give Gus 10 percent interest in Potrero. But Gary never recorded the money from Gus. Gus had 10 percent of nothing.

"There was no *transaction*. It was a sham," Pam whispered across the table. She swallowed and said, "My mind doesn't work so well. I think I'm fucked-up. I'm usually stressed out, worried about cash flow. Need to leave my money invested, can't be draining it."

Ron countered, "But you don't *make* any income. Don't be unrealistic and think you have enough capital to live off stocks. The market could go flat in a year."

"If I sold my property, I'd take a huge hit," Pam agreed.

"What do you mean by 'a huge hit'?"

"The estate has no garage or apartment addition to inflate its property value. I'd have to sell it at a loss." Invariably her conversations focused on money, how she could expand and improve her surroundings, build upon her finances, unload her assets. All the while, Pam earned nothing. But she spoke as if she did and had a remarkable ability to manipulate the truth to suit her own purposes. Ron encouraged the mindless Ping-Pong. He listened to her banter and occasionally he smiled; the expression came awkwardly, forced, as if he were smiling from inside a mask.

In the early stages of their relationship, Ron helped Pam leverage Star Babies, though he claimed later to detectives that he actually knew nothing about computers. Some people, he reasoned, were "closers or cleaners. I was a fixer."

But Pam infuriated him. She needed a "committee" decision, twelve of her closest friends' approval, before she accepted Ron's advice unconditionally. He counseled her time and time again about her finances, offered her "sound" suggestions, and by January 1996 even went as far as proposing solutions to her mounting cash-flow problem. "First, don't panic," he wrote to her in an e-mail.

> There is adequate time to repair this cash problem . . . The following are areas where solutions may lie: lower expenses . . . get on a budget and certain expenses like lawyer bills should be evaluated closely to determine when you really need to pay them. If you change a few lawyers for instance you can string out the old ones on an agreed upon payment schedule. Basically you may not have the freedom to pay everyone right on time.

He reminded her that her available cash in December was $137,977, in January it had dwindled to a mere $70,899. By May, he predicted, she would have a "frightening" $5,355 remaining. But when, two weeks later, Pam still failed to address her "problem," much less properly acknowledge his advice, Ron grew agitated and advised that conversing with her about "certain issues" was becoming "increasingly awkward":

> I have been glad to help you with your financial and legal difficulties. But I am getting less glad as you depart from my carefully thought out plans and strategies . . . this is a source of me getting discouraged and depressed like carefully building things only to have them erode by the ones you build them for. One recent example is your "Gary problem." As you explained to me he is the most intelligent man you have ever met and he has declared that he is going to ruin you. You have told me he has cheated you, outmaneuvered you legally and financially . . . he

is constantly behind in child support, has harassed you over the phone, gone into your house,
into your bedroom . . . I've been endeavoring
for the past four months to get this 800 pound
monster out of your life as best as possible under the law. I have spent really a lot of hours
discussing this with you, reading over and over
again the court order and mediation agreement,
composing many faxes to Gary, sending them
on my phone bill designing a phone system to
be used by you, to avoid Gary being able to call
them, all with the purpose of winning a battle
with him. It was quite distressing to me I guess
I shouldn't care but I do that you are back making legal decisions on your own after all the work
I have put into this. It is not an ego problem
but I just hate to lose anything I'm involved in
and I hate waste.

Pam placated Ron, insisting their relationship was "so
much more" than that of a teacher and pupil. She thanked
him intimately for his efforts but cautioned that, despite their
divorces and their single status, their sexual affair should remain discreet "for the children's sake." But secrecy did not
necessarily translate into exclusivity. Pam enjoyed multiple partners. Ron accepted her weakness, and while he
may not have been her only lover, he vowed to be her most
memorable.

Pam prepared a complimentary "birth chart interpretation" for Ron. The cover page read: "The inner you may not
shine through and others are in for some surprises when they
get to know you at a more than superficial level . . . [B]eware
of the real person inside the costume."* She compartmental-

---

* Birth chart interpretation for Ron Young, May 7, 1942, Star
   Babies, Inc.

ized Ron; his utility had limits. He helped her with her business affairs. He sympathized with her about Gary. That's all he was to her: an ear. And she had already tired of him.

But Ron had not tired of Pam. He convinced her that Web design and computer issues had a "monstrous learning curve" and she could waste months trying to do "cheap crap." Their affair continued "off and on socially . . . she was never exclusive with anybody," Ron said, and added that he wasn't rich enough for her, though she never questioned his fickle financial resources. Sometimes he carried wads of cash; at other times he was dead broke and used her money. She never offered to pay Ron for his services, either, although he estimated his value to be worth $10,000. But each time he broached the subject, she complained that Gary paid her "peanuts" and that lawyers were "screwing her over" on trademarks, copyrights, and patents related to her business.

"I knew a lot about that," Ron said. "That's all I handled for years. Plus, I [was] good with lawyers." In a recorded conversation he schooled Pam about attorneys, warned that they were "notorious for fucking off and blaming their screw-ups on the client." He advised her that it was "a good idea to put things in writing." He drafted letters to Pam's lawyers, pretending to be *her* and listing "bullet points" for them to follow. Pam complained that she had wasted hours trying to communicate with her lawyers, who only "yawned and scribbled notes on sticky pads." She complained they gave her nothing but "lip service."

"I figured I saved her $1,000 to $2,000 in legal fees. Her friends thought I was too vicious, but I knew exactly what I was doing."

Pam wasn't as appreciative as Ron would have liked. And the fact that Pam never offered to pay Ron for his services "pissed [me] off."

He invited Pam to lunch and slipped her an invoice for $3,500.

Pam was incredulous. "What the hell is this?"

"You've never mentioned reimbursing me, so . . . ," he said, miffed that Pam had never offered to pay him for his services.

She leveled her strange flat eyes at him. "Is this about the guy you saw me with the other night?"

"We're not engaged; you can have as many affairs as you like," Ron lied. In truth Pam's promiscuity bothered him. He wanted her to be exclusive, to understand that she *needed* him. Ron reminded Pam of all of the grunt work he'd performed for the company, for her, for free. Pam's face flushed. She folded the invoice carefully and shoved it across the table.

"I'm sorry if I misled you," she began, but her voice held no emotion. In the next breath she offered Ron a deal, 5 percent in her company, Star Babies.

"How about a *majority* interest."

Five days later, Pam's son, Trevor, delivered an envelope to him containing a thousand dollars in cash. No explanation accompanied the bills, but Ron understood her implicit message. She found Ron's request for payment insulting; future arrangements would be handled differently.

Star Babies became more conversation and intrigue than business venture, though Pam earned an estimated $200 or $300 a week predicting newborns' futures. Gary originally purchased the mail order astrology company during their marriage but, according to Pam, frustrated her efforts to develop the business for profit. She "dabbled" with the generic software program, personalizing the astrological charts with her own interpretations. She thought parents might find it useful to know that their children, born Scorpios, like Gary, might have a secretive nature despite their outward shimmer. Or Aries children, like Pam, would likely be preoccupied with social acceptance, appropriate behavior, and good etiquette. Parents of Leos were warned that *their* children might possess an "active imagination and powerful fantasies . . . [T]hey might never feel secure no matter how much money they possessed and tended to be attracted to people who [were] not quite what they professed to be."

Prospective parents, interested in their babies' futures, eagerly paid Pam $50 for tales of prosperity and promise. Pam considered herself a sort of modern-day soothsayer. Her passion for astrology led her to embark on a number of self-improvement retreats.

"She considered herself a flawed human being," Ron remarked. And though Pam complained regularly to Ron that she barely survived in her $3,500-a-month duplex with a nanny and nanny's quarters, she traveled frequently to South America and various tropical islands to meditate and continue her "Yagya work," a Hindu astrology that involved a tradition of sacrifices around firepits. She was experiencing a "very bad astrological period" and required cleansing.

Ron offered his help. He proposed solutions to her perpetual-cash flow problem but grew increasingly irritated by her ingratitude.

"My friends think I should handle my own affairs," she told him flatly.

"I'm wondering why I submit myself to this head-bashing," he responded in a scathing e-mail, "when it is all for [naught]. You don't listen. You don't take advice . . . [F]or my sanity I don't think it wise for me to stay involved in your financial life. I feel like a classified ad salesman . . . trying to get you to commit to something *you* want. You can't ask someone to devote the time and energy to your life that I have and not trust them to do anything."

"I just can't *be* with him, you know?" Pam confided to her latest nanny. "He's not my type."

"What type is that?" the woman asked as she folded Pam's lace panties into a suitcase.

"Rich."

Pam smoothed things over. She invited Ron to an intimate dinner, complete with candles, soft music, and expensive wine. Wind roared around them. The fireplace crackled. Pam wore a low-cut blouse that exposed her substantial cleavage. She tucked her legs beneath her, careful not to pierce the cushions with her stiletto heels. Pam tapped her wineglass with her perfectly manicured nails and the sound amplified in the stillness. Ron leaned forward, his elbows on his knees; he downed his third glass of wine and his heart raced with irritation. Dinner lasted three hours and still no check.

"Did you get my fax?" He'd billed her for 25 percent of his time, at $12.50 an hour, "a maid's wages."

Pam uncurled her legs, smiled, and smoothed his long hair with her fingers. She led him wordlessly to her bedroom, passed her sleeping children and the nanny's dark room. At dawn, Ron rolled over and whispered in her ear, "Am I ever going to get *paid*?"*

"Do you really *need* it?" Pam groused. "The bank isn't even open. Besides, I don't have my checkbook."

Later that morning, Ron sent Pam fourteen faxes. One contained a spreadsheet and referenced Gary's financial affidavit. With expenses staying the same and almost no revenue, Ron warned, "you will hit the wall in May or June." He suggested she sell Star Babies. "I know you will ignore my advice again but I feel obligated to give it. I am completely confused as to why you are back trying to handle all your matters yourself?"

On March 21, 1996, Pima County judge Margaret Maxwell delivered a devastating blow to Pam. In a damning minute entry, she found Pam's conduct toward Gary "contemptuous" and "petty"; worse, she characterized *Pam* as *Gary's* tormentor. The divorce proceedings, according to the judge, had left *Gary* penniless, unlawfully deprived of his children, drifting between friends' homes and borrowing

---

* Reconstructed conversation from correspondence between the pair.

cars. And yet, Gary continued to play golf. He purchased lavish gifts for his girlfriends; his latest an unemployed twenty-something, drove around Tucson in a shiny Pontiac Grand Am. Gary's niece, Melissa, who insisted "she had done a few things for Gary's business," owned a black Corvette.

"He's mocking me," Pam confided to Ron one night over drinks. She suspected Gary had hidden assets, money that lawfully belonged to *her*. She wouldn't be in "this situation," she insisted, if Gary would just cooperate. But she knew he had placed his company, GLT Corporation,* in his friend James L. Matison's name† and used Matison's credit cards. She knew he played games.

"What are you going to do about it?" Ron asked.

"What *can* I do about it? He's won." She threw up her hands in mock surrender. She looked panicked: no more exclusive memberships, no more meetings with the Trumps, no more Aspen.

"Maybe I can help you . . . kill two birds with one stone."

---

* GLT Corporation performed consulting work for Victor Fears Trust.

† Matison's own father had mysteriously disappeared in 1991, leaving behind nearly $17 million in judgments against him.

CHAPTER NINE:
THE NOTES THEY LEFT BEHIND

April 5, 1996

Before Pam had a chance to seriously entertain Ron's proposal, reality clobbered her over the head. She discovered large sums of money had disappeared from her bank accounts. Livid, she reported Ron to the Aspen Police Department. Detective James Crowley took the call from Pam's lawyer, John Case, who explained somewhat apologetically Ron's relationship to Pam. Ron served as her contract employee and handled a few business affairs for Pam. No romantic entanglements. None whatsoever, he assured.

And while Case downplayed Ron and Pam's connection, Pam drafted a scathing sticky note to her paramour:

> You have no idea how betrayed and angry I am.
> After we just had a conversation about integrity . . .
> If I have to proceed to prosecute you I will.

But when Crowley attempted to follow up with Pam, she avoided his calls, claimed she was "too busy" to interview with him further and suggested that he just "drop it altogether" even though she was one of three victims Ron had allegedly defrauded for $300,000 each. Pam refused to produce her financial records: "she didn't have time," and after all "it was her own accounting error," Crowley noted. She apologized for "bothering" him. Curious at Pam's sudden disinterest in recovering her money, Crowley attempted to connect with the alleged perpetrator of the fraud, Ron Young. But when he arrived at Ron's Snowbunny Lane address, he found an abandoned vehicle parked in the driveway and several large trash bags containing business documents, bank account information, and private contact numbers piled like compost in his front yard.

"He teased us," Crowley said. "Who *does* that?"

Crowley had enough probable cause to obtain a search warrant of Ron's duplex. A neighbor supplied him with the key. Once inside, Crowley found a stark, sparsely furnished space with alphabetized cans of food on the pantry shelves. The room reeked of antiseptic. A monitor illuminated the shadows and cast the room in a hazy blue glow. The detective seized the computer.

April 15, 1996

Pam agreed to meet Ron for dinner at the exclusive Caribou Club. She had hopes of recouping her money. With no name on the heavy mahogany and brass door, the place boasted "quiet old world, well bred, like vintage Bordeaux." Pam dressed comfortably in jeans, a silk blouse, and a belt with a silver buckle. They entered the wood-paneled foyer, strode past the nineteenth-century paintings of western landscapes and views of Capitol and Pyramid Peaks, and settled in the cavelike, dimly lit Wine Room.

Antler chandeliers suspended from the ceiling bathed the linen in soft gold. Hundreds of vintage bottles of wine protruded from wooden sleeves tucked into the ceiling, alcoves, and arches. The ripe-tomato-colored walls shimmered with glass. Pam's face was elongated in the reflection. She

and Ron slid into the intricately carved chairs at a table set
for six. Pam fluffed the oversize white dinner napkin and
trailed her manicured nails along the elegant heavy cutlery.
She ordered whiskey-glazed filet of beef with farm fresh
vegetables. Ron ordered a rack of lamb with exotic herbs
and a bottle of Martin Ray. They spoke in hushed tones,
sipped wine, leaned earnestly across the table. And when
the bill came, Ron paid with his American Express credit
card. He signed his name Phillip Desmond.*

What transpired that night would become the subject of
conjecture and heated debate in Ron Young's ensuing trial.
But one thing was certain: the couple shared more than
dinner. According to the prosecution, the two conspired to
commit murder over crème brulée. They plotted how and
when without much thought to why, and they memorialized the anticipated "event" with receipts, recordings, and
handwritten lists that included, among other things, a
sawed-off shotgun and a tube of toothpaste.

"And I can assure you," the prosecution argued, "Ron
had no interest in brushing his teeth."

Before dawn on April 15, 1996, Pam left Ron a cryptic message on his Snowbunny Lane answering machine: "I love
you and want to go ahead with the thing we talked about."
But Ron would never get the message. And police detectives
would never hear it until years later, in 2005, after forensic
computer analysts discovered a folder titled "All before
D-Day." Ron left abruptly after his dinner like a gust of
wind. His computer still hummed on his desk. He planned
a cross-country trip, looking forward to traveling with his
son, Brady, and catching up on his lost time. He hoped to
reconnect with his daughter, Kelly, as well as his ex-wife,

---

* The real Mr. Desmond never met Ron Young and never
    authorized him to have an American Express credit card in
    his name.

Linda, with whom he still shared confidences. The contact would have to last him a while; soon it would no longer be safe for him to officially exist.

He smiled as he drove through California, Texas, and parts of Florida. In Lincoln, Nebraska, he paid for groceries with a black American Express card in someone else's name, though he carried $1,700 cash in his pocket, courtesy of Pam. He had already wired several thousand dollars of Pam's money to his bank account in Florida. He hadn't *wanted* to forge Pam's name on the checks—not really— but it had been so *easy*. He couldn't help himself. His world consisted of "givers and takers." It would have been foolish not to exploit a person's weakness. She'd get over it. After all, they were *friends*. Still, if he proceeded as he planned, he needed to change his name as a precaution, alternating between real and fictitious people: Phillip Desmond, Doug Franklin, and Richard Perez. The idea of reinventing himself excited him. He had downloaded a pamphlet off the Internet: *How to Get Lost—and Stay That Way!*

Have you ever felt like running way? Yes.

Are you running from something or someone? Yes.

Do you wish you could just drop off the earth? Absolutely.

Ron was like a child again immersed in his world of play. He lived in the present, as if he had no future, no past, and no anchor roped around his neck in the deep end of the ocean. The future, rife with worry, fear, and guesswork, was all a lie and the past a mere distraction, a label, a way to categorize events as failures, mistakes, and lessons. The present was the only *real* thing in his life.

Before he left, he sipped coffee from a paper cup and indulged in his fantasy life, the one he lived overseas in his mind, the one he composed to his mother and younger brother, the one that made him swell with importance. On paper he could be anyone he wanted, travel anywhere he imagined. He didn't need a passport, an identity, or even money. This morning he wrote from Berlin and saved his thoughts in a computer file titled "Great Britain, Scandinavia and East Germany." He expressed relief that he had "a few moments to expound . . . on the previous weeks of [his] life."

"You can't imagine how busy I've been being a good traveler, keeping up on current events, writing impressions in my diary, writing letters to this fantastic English girl I met in Dublin." Orange neon blinked through the vinyl blinds. A car honked. A door slammed in the room next door.

> Most British are against European unification because they fear loss of their remaining independent power and their national identity . . . [Y]ou're probably interested in British views on the cold war in Berlin. Let me say first that my judgments are based only on the citizens I have talked with . . . [M]ost English don't want to risk a war in Berlin. They favor giving West Berlin to the East Germans . . . I was in a pub recently and two British students were discussing communism . . .

He tapped away on the keyboard elaborating for several pages about Germany, communism, and his extraordinary travels. Since Glasgow, he wrote, he'd been in "Edinburgh, Scotland, Newcastle, England, caught a ferry to Bergen, Norway, and onto Oslo, into Sweden, and wound [his] way down to Copenhagen." He took another pull on his coffee. "Describing each country in any detail," he observed, would be "hopeless." His mom would do well to consult *National Geographic* or *Holiday*. Ron revealed that he found the Irish "refreshing," the Scottish "humorous," and the Swedes "terribly dull." Copenhagen, however, had "beautiful women. I couldn't stand it. So I left."

After composing page after page of his travels to exotic locales, the words took on a life of their own, unfettered by the author's knowledge that the reader was likely aware of the facts—that Ron had *not* recently traveled to Europe, or engaged Communist leaders in heated political debate, or sailed with gorgeous women on private yachts. In truth, Ron never left his duplex on Snowbunny Lane. But he was good at embellishing. He peppered his tales with "bad experiences," hoping to bolster his own credibility and convince his mom that he really did lead the "crazy life" he described.

"One midnight in Copenhagen four million insects smashed into my eyes and I collided with a Porsche." Ron insisted he wound up in the hospital as a result but had only $3 in his pockets. He didn't want to be regarded as "a deadbeat" so he devised "an escape plan." He located his clothing in a closet, wriggled his bandaged arms into his sleeves, and slipped past hospital guards, through the double doors, and onto the lawn. But as so often happens to expert liars, Ron forgot an important detail: Danish hospitals offered free medical care. But it hardly mattered; he had no expectations. On paper, Ron could imagine anything, be anyone he wanted, even an exotic cruelty.

April 25, 1996

And while Ron invented fantastic adventures, Pam cut into his reality:

> Did you send the money you owe me or part of it?
> I'm getting calls from a Detective Crowley . . .
> I think the apparent connection between us is
> best kept at a minimum. I don't want to appear
> as too much of a helper though you know I am.
> I want to arm you with all the information you

need to really problem solve . . . I'm feeling
pretty helpless and not real healthy. I think I've
been through such an emotional drain on so
many levels. Everybody and everything feels
like quicksand lately. Aspen may never feel like
home again to you but there are lots of fantastic
places to be if you have the freedom and resources to go. Please call. I love you and count
on you . . .

　　　　　　　　　　　　　　　　　　—Pamela.

　A few hours later, when Pam had still heard nothing
from Ron, she wrote:

No call, no contact. Is your computer still there?
I didn't talk to the detective. I guess I should in
the morning. My trust wants to stay steadfast
but how do I know you will do what you say?
You always have yet the checks [you wrote] blow
me away. Maybe I don't really know you as you
always accused me of and you're just playing
on my insecurities. I can march right into the
bank and get my money back . . . [T]he others
can't. I need to hear from you. . . . Hope you're
stable in your head?

　　　　　　　　　　　　　　　　　　—Pamela

May 1996

Secretly, Ron fumed when he read Pam's e-mails. *He* was
the helper. *He* was the one who had been helping all along.
I'm the guy. I'm the one. And he proved it to her. Ron flew
his son, Brady, back to Aspen and purchased a single
round-trip airline ticket for Pam to fly to Denver and saved
the receipt from John Hollinger's American Express card

in a special folder he stored on his computer. Ron joined Pam by car at the luxurious Loews Georgio Hotel in Denver. He planned to discuss "their event" over a light lunch. He gathered a list of resources from Pam of contacts to explore in Denver: the addresses of a local Circuit City, a nearby Federal Express office, and a gun shop, and the phone number to an obscure gunsmith who owned a shop in Superior, Colorado.

Ron sampled a biscotti appetizer in the hotel's Tuscany Restaurant. Powdered sugar lingered on his lips. Pam browsed the extensive wine menu. A harpist strummed lightly in the background, her flowing jeweled gown and white porcelain-like face evoked illusions of heaven. The marble fireplace in the entrance crackled invitingly. Floral displays bloomed on the elegant tables. The room was tastefully accented with antiques and fine art.

As Ron picked at his fresh cucumber salad drizzled with exotic oils, Pam tore into a loaf of bread and stabbed the soft center with a square of butter. In hushed tones, they reviewed the details of their business transaction, a discussion that prosecutors later asserted involved conspiracy to commit murder, a $2 million life insurance policy, and Ron's proportionate share. He could not receive a lump-sum payment without attracting "loads of attention," he cautioned, then went silent as the waitress poured more wine. Ron devised a formula, a way to keep Pam "safe and sound" while she funneled him nominal cash increments every two weeks. He could be patient: better to "be cautious" than hasty.

"Just don't mix my stuff up with yours," he warned. "I'll need earnest money."

Pam bit into a cream pastry and arched a brow at him.

"A good-faith advance." He shrugged, nonplussed by her hypnotic gaze and perfect alabaster skin. She looked . . . appropriate, not happy, normal, like everyone else.

"Haven't you already stolen that?" Irritation dented her expression.

"Twenty-five thousand should do it," Ron replied, deflecting the barb. He knew she would produce the money; it was like baiting a piranha with a slab of steak. They were one and the same, motivated by need, not conscience.

"So, how is this going to work?" Pam asked, dabbing her lips with the cloth napkin and glancing around the restaurant.

Ron detailed how Pam should execute future money "drops" at a FedEx office in Basalt, Colorado, a tiny snow-packed village nearly forty-five minutes from Aspen. The town boasted two grocery stores and a handful of quaint eateries. She could be discreet, turn the twice monthly trips into "outings" for her nanny and children, promise to buy them each "something nice" for tagging along.

"Avoid *staffed* offices with real people who can put real faces to real packages," Ron warned. "There are five drop boxes in Basalt, two to three different trucks with different drivers who pick up at each box. Use a different box each time."

Ron droned on about air bills, three pieces of paper handwritten and preprinted with information, his address in Pompano, Florida, and his account number.

"Send the packages as 'Richard Perez' *to* 'Richard Perez,'" he instructed.

"The same person."

"Different zip codes."

'Who's Richard Perez?" Pam frowned.

"A former client." Ron said dismissively.

"Won't he—"

"He's dead." He crunched a cucumber.

"How much do I send?" Pam didn't flinch. This was business.

"Small amounts, less than $2,000 each time."

The prosecution theorized that with the payment plan established, the couple focused on the "event" and the method of execution. The two drove in silence to Superior, Colorado, an old coal-mining and farming community in Boulder County. Purple flowers speared the rolling hills. Dilapidated homes crumbled on their foundations. Even in early May, frost crusted the roads. There were no signs, no guide-posts, only a dirt trench marked the path to Joseph Nord's gun shop.

"How does this guy make a living if no one can find him?" Pam complained as their car lurched over grooves and rocks in the road. The sun dipped over the Rockies. Nothing for miles. They were truly in the middle of no-where. Pam lit a cigarette, rolled down the window, and flicked the ash into the dirt.

"What's the plan?" Pam asked.

"The *plan*," Ron stuttered, rubbed his temples with the thumb and index finger of one hand, "is to buy a gun."

But, the prosecutor speculated, Pam could not know then that Ron had no intention of ever *firing* the weapon.

CHAPTER TEN:
IDENTITY CRISIS

"You won't get much sympathy today if you try to blame someone else for your mistakes, Leo"
—Ron Young's horoscope, April 12, 1996

Murder requires meticulous planning. Ron had never been to Tucson, Arizona, and he wasn't about to visit unprepared. A simple map of the area would not suffice. Ron needed to physically experience the desert terrain, the sizzling heat. He had to navigate the roads, monitor the tee times at the Westin La Paloma golf resort. He needed to observe his target, note patterns of behavior and preferred contacts. But he certainly wasn't going to *fly* into Tucson: too conspicuous, not to mention costly. The distance between Tucson and Phoenix was exactly one hundred miles. On May 29, 1996, Ron purchased a cheaper airline ticket to Phoenix, paid cash for a rental car, and produced a Texas driver's license bearing the name Michael Woodcock. Ron, aka Woodcock, returned the rental two days later; the odometer confirmed he had driven 522 miles. On May 30, 1996, the Phoenix department of motor vehicles reported an Avis license plate stolen. Detective Crowley later recovered it from inside Ron's abandoned Plymouth Voyager. He speculated that Ron must have put the stolen license plate on his rental van to avoid detection.

In Tucson, Ron cruised near the Westin La Paloma golf

resort and scoped out possible reconnaissance locations. After a short visit, his "cursory overview," he traveled to California to see his parents in Yorba Linda; he thought it might be his last opportunity before he "officially" disappeared. He made plans to return to Tucson in July, amid oven temperatures. The Residence Inn where he eventually reserved a room for eighteen days remained largely vacant in the summer. Dust devils swirled in the streets. Monsoons darkened the sky each night before dusk. Torrential rain spit against the windows. The hotel, situated one mile from Gary Triano's residence and a few blocks from Woodland, Pam's former home, provided excellent surveillance opportunities. Each day Ron paid cash for his room, never uttering a word to the concierge, who described his guest, "Phillip Desmond," as "mysterious and strange." Ron was in complete control. He didn't worry about cash flow or objective. According to prosecutors, he had Pam's assurance the "event" would progress as planned. He had her money, all $25,000. And he had multiple credit cards belonging to various business associates he could use in a pinch.

From his hotel room, Ron composed another letter to his mom entitled "Europe, Hitchhiking from Seattle to Minnesota": Hi out there! I'm sitting in the "Y" in Duluth, Minnesota, thinking over the last 2,000 miles . . . I can't get over the number of small towns I've gone through, probably millions. One term can describe all of them: they're dead. Their deadness differs in degree and kind." He interrupted his prose with an important "HISTORICAL POINT": "Nellie Curtice, the proud, respectable leader of hundreds of prostitutes . . . End of historical point." His letter read like a tourist brochure as he highlighted the various cities and towns he'd recently traveled to in his mind: "For the sportsman, Seattle is the most ideal . . ."; "musically, northern California, part of Oregon, Idaho, Montana and North

Dakota enjoy nothing more than to listen to Gene Autry"; "Montana is second to none in hunting, fishing, primitive area and beauty"; and so on. He ended with his impressions of the Blackfoot Indians: "They receive permanent relief . . . they do absolutely no work . . . the money disappears as fast as they can drink. They live for today, only.

For the next eighteen days he collected information, license plates, names, addresses, and places of employment for Gary's contacts. Ron recorded everything on little notepads: Gary never locked his car (check); Gary played golf regularly in the late afternoon (check). Ron stalked his prey at the movies, conducted surveillance of his home on Airway Boulevard. He watched Gary's girlfriends, too, taking note of their fancy cars, their rich lifestyles that they could not possibly afford on their waitress salaries. Later, Ron would insist to his captors that Pam asked him to investigate Gary's hidden assets. The control, the power, that he experienced was intoxicating. He invoked anxiety in others. Fear had a vibration. He felt it reverberate off him like a current. Just knowing that his presence was causing Gary's heart to flutter thrilled him. Ron could be anything he wanted, do anything he wanted. He could take his time.

"Remember," the prosecutor said. "He had no warrant yet for his arrest, no one looking for him, no reason to disappear . . . [H]e gained the confidence he needed to later walk through that parking lot unawares and place a bomb in Gary's car. He wanted to be in control. Information is control. He decided when to walk away, if he walked away, and when to pull that switch." The prosecutor spoke haltingly, almost in a whisper, as he imagined Ron's thought process on the day of the murder. He reenacted the scenario for jurors.

"I'm Ron Young," he said walking deliberately around the courtroom. "I'm wearing a polo shirt, a pair of shorts, a golf hat. I'm walking through the parking lot. I know there are no cameras. I know there is nothing conspicuous about a man carrying a bag. I open up Gary's car door because I know it's unlocked. I know he's playing golf. I flip something on inside the bag I leave on the passenger seat. I walk away. That's it. I look around because I know I can bail out anytime. But I don't. I don't want to. I know the safety devices. I know I can drop the bag on the seat and it won't explode. The safety is a switch. It's a toggle, a drop-down. I know how to be careful. I am in complete control."

"It was curious," Pam's former nanny, Samantha Stubbs, reported later to police. "For someone so concerned about money, Pam was fairly dismissive when I informed her about a recent $5,000 wire transfer to a Ron Young. She claimed it was compensation for his services. But Pam, to my knowledge, had never paid Ron anything before. And I never really understood what Ron was meant to have done for her."

Ron's role in Pam's life was a puzzle to most who knew Pam. By all accounts, Ron was an unemployed drifter with no apparent income and an undefined history. He *said* he had several failed business ventures overseas and that he sought investors in Aspen, but no one the detective interviewed during his investigation could ever confirm Ron's past. Pam's nannies offered theories about him, but none could explain why Pam had not yet cut him loose.

Samantha reported an odd sensation in Ron's presence, a feeling that made her skin crawl, as if each time Ron spoke, his speech sounded scripted. She reported that Ron stalked Pam, appearing unannounced as Pam prepared for dates with other men. He left her threatening and insulting messages on her answering machine. He convinced her she needed technological and financial help with her business affairs and offered her free advice concerning Star Babies and her Potrero property.

"She disliked hurting people," Samantha remarked. "Pam once hired a couple to care for her children after I quit. I learned that Pam's new hired help had dumped the children's puppies in the desert to die because they grew tired of cleaning up after them. Pam was *kind* to them, said she *understood* why they had killed the puppies. She said she might need their help in the future. She might need more house trolls. Pam didn't like conflict, and she certainly didn't want people to think badly of her. I could see her doing that with Ron . . . [I]f he did blackmail her, as she claimed, she would have tolerated it for years, hoping he would just . . . die or disappear. She might have even rationalized it as payback for the work he did for her. I could see Ron calling her up after Gary's death and collecting. And if she started to pay him and didn't contact the police, she'd already be in trouble."

It was an interesting theory, blackmail. The detective's phone vibrated in his pocket a few times but he didn't answer it.

"You did her books?" he pressed.

"I tried, but mostly I just organized her papers."

"Hypothetically speaking, if $25,000 suddenly disappeared from her bank account in March of 1996, would you have noticed?"

"I might have. I didn't know *all* of her finances. But there were times when she had big expenses looming and she'd stress and . . ."

"Would Pam have had that kind of money to give?"

"She had sold her home in Tucson. When I worked for her, she had approximately $30,000 of those proceeds remaining. And she always had her friend Joy."

"Would $25,000 have been a red flag to you?"

"Not necessarily. She had big business deals, investments . . ."

"But she had no income, right?"

"Right." Samantha frowned. She looked pale and harried. "She worried constantly that her money was running out. Once, when she was supposedly down to her last $60,000, she announced it was time to find a husband."

"When was that?"

"February sometime."

"Nineteen ninety-six?"

"Yeah."

Meanwhile, in August 1996, Detective Crowley issued a warrant for Ron Young's arrest with respect to the other two fraud victims. And Pam's neighbor on Snowbunny Lane, Susan Spaulding, noticed Pam's little blond daughter, Lois, no more than six years old, crying in the woods. The child claimed to have been locked out of her residence. Susan investigated, but her subsequent knocks on Pam's door met with silence. She later learned that the child and her eight-year-old brother, Trevor, were being cared for by a male nanny, a choice Susan found to be "inappropriate" and "a little dangerous" for a girl. Susan invited Lois to her daughter's birthday party and eventually to participate in Susan's religious-based learning and play group called the Pioneer Club. The child appeared daily, quietly absorbing the lessons "like a little ghost. We hardly knew she was there."

Once, Susan planned a hike with her family and Lois joined them. "Are you sure your mother won't mind?" Susan inquired, but Lois wrinkled her nose at Susan and stared at her blankly as if the question were absurd. "My mother doesn't care what I do," she said.

Lois lagged behind on the wooded trail. The afternoon chill made her hands shake. She sat on the dirt, her legs folded beneath her, the rubber on her shoes worn. Susan waited patiently while Lois pulled her jacket tight around her, and watched the child toss rocks over the cliff's edge. Lois blurted out that she was "angry." Her father, Gary, she explained, "had held a gun to her mother's head" and threatened to kidnap her and her brother and take them away from Pam. Susan did not know whether Lois had actually witnessed the violence she described or was parroting her mother's complaints, but she made a mental note to confront Pam about it. But by the time she actually connected with Pam sometime in late November, it was apparently too late. Lois greeted Susan at the front door to her home and announced calmly, "My dad got blown up."

Susan reflected on the girl's chilling delivery and remarked to police, "I always thought it a little odd that Pam kept a ceramic pot on the mantel that read "Ex-husband's Ashes."

CHAPTER ELEVEN:
THE BIG REVEAL

In October 1996, an officer with the Yorba Linda, California, Police Department received a citizen's complaint about
a Plymouth Voyager parked askew in an upscale residen-
tial neighborhood one block from a "Neighborhood Crime
Watch" post. The doors were locked. No sign of a break-in.
The license plate identified the vehicle as a rental reported
stolen out of Aspen, Colorado. The officer impounded the
van in his police department's lot and contacted the Pitkin
County Sheriff's Department.

Detective Crowley, believing he may have acquired a
lead in his fraud investigation, flew to California a week
later to search the van. He recovered, among other items, an
Arizona license plate belonging to a 1996 Cadillac DeVille
registered to an Avis Rent A Car in Phoenix. Crowley
thought the discovery odd but insignificant. More compelling were TRW credit reports in the name of Phillip Desmond, Desmond's American Express credit card, and a
notepad containing scribbled names of seemingly random
people: Gary, James Matison, Melissa T., Taylor, and Don
Redman. Logic dictated they were possible creditors, business associates of Ron's—perhaps people Ron had defrauded. The detective impounded a Ramada Inn hotel

receipt dated July 1996, hoping it might provide information on Ron Young's whereabouts.

There was nothing extraordinarily revealing until Crowley uncovered a modified shotgun tucked inside a plush velvet case. Scattered on either side were empty hollow-point bullet shells, a Taser, and an air pistol. Crowley frowned: white collar criminals were not typically violent. A con artist's only weapon, in Crowley's experience, was his brain. So, *what was his suspect doing with a shotgun, and why would he leave it exposed in plain sight?* A cool breeze blew through the van, fluttering the papers around him. Crowley's legs tingled, a signal that he had been crouching too long in one position. His mind raced.

The man saved everything, even bullet shell casings belonging to another gun. Ron was either extremely arrogant or extremely stupid. Or, option three, a combination of both. Crowley had experienced the game before with fraud suspects, scam masters, the "Catch me if you can" bait that often accompanied cagey, sophisticated criminals. News headlines reported daily about "crooked promoters," people who scammed the stock exchange to lure naïve investors. And with such nominal penalties, was it any wonder con men continued to thrive and prey on the innocent? Financial institutions were mere watering holes for psychopaths. Typically, the resources available to law enforcement proved useless in tracking and detecting the professional con man who thrived underground, completely autonomous, undetected. Any leads garnered were generally "after-the-fact," like popcorn kernels strewn in a dense forest on a path toward a gingerbread house inhabited by a wicked witch that never materialized.

With his misdeeds completely exposed in the van, Crowley instinctively knew that Ron was long gone from Yorba Linda. His suspect had likely relocated to a faraway city in another state and started anew. No doubt Ron manipulated innocent "helpers": respectable folk, perhaps even family members, completely duped by his easy banter and perceived "charm." In Crowley's experience the true "professional criminals" had no moral compass, no "right way" to commit a wrong. They studied methodology, adopted suitable personalities, mimicked the dress and style of success, always acutely aware of details and subtle nuances in conversation.

But the shotgun raised Ron to a different caliber of evil.

"Only reason to have a sawed-off piece," his colleague remarked, "is to conceal it, to deliver a blast close-range as powerful as twelve-millimeter pistols."

The modified weapon, seized in another state three weeks before Gary's murder, would ultimately disappear, never to be produced for Ron's later trial. The missing gun would become a source of contention between prosecutor and defense counsel, an "irrelevant piece of evidence of highly prejudicial value."

Crowley impounded a Pima County Superior Court minute entry dissolving the marriage of Pamela Phillips and Gary Triano; a map of the Tucson area; receipts for a FedEx office in Basalt, Colorado and a restaurant in the Loews Giorgio Hotel in Denver. The paperwork confirmed Ron's brief and random travels but, in Crowley's opinion, little else compelling. Con men typically lived lavishly and spent other people's money freely. But something else caught Crowley's attention: a Hallmark card entitled "Reflections." The glossy front depicted an ocean scene; inside, a handwritten promise from "Pam" of "visions coming into focus. Dare to dream for in dreams lie the foundation for happiness." The name "Pam" jogged Crowley's memory. Could she be his initial fraud victim? Had he just caught Pam's lawyer in a lie? *No romantic entanglements, none whatsoever,* the attorney had assured him. But even if John Case had lied to the detective, Crowley considered there were always neutral reasons for omissions. And while the lie was curious, it was not extraordinary. He filed the Hallmark card.

Crowley stumbled upon communications between Ron and a man he identified as his lawyer.

"I'm not his lawyer," George Rombach quickly clarified when they met. "I am a certified public accountant with a law degree from Irvine. But I can understand the confusion and why people might *think* I was an attorney . . . I have five published legal decisions and I argued before the United States Supreme Court in Washington, D.C., once."

Detective Crowley suppressed the urge to laugh. "Well, I'll be darned," he said instead. "That's . . . good. Well, Mr. Young holds you in high regard."

"We're old sailing buddies. I helped him obtain a small business loan for his company, Orangematic, a commercial orange juice machine maker. He's like America suburbia, that guy." Rombach chuckled and shook his head.

"Is that so?"

"My education," Rombach continued, as if the detective had posed the question, "is what you might call second-chair . . . I have a handicap. I'm dyslexic and my parents were told I was so mentally deficient I should have been institutionalized. All the alphabet soup after my name is partly overreacting, refusing to accept the decree of being dumb."

"Okay," the detective said, and then returned to the reason for his visit. "Any idea what the connection to Yorba Linda might be?"

"Ron's mother lives there."

In the detective's experience it wasn't unusual for a suspected criminal to seek the comfort of his mother. He had heard of an investigation involving a member of the Bloods, a gangster known on the streets as "Block Monster"; alone, away from his peers, the boy still curled up in his mother's bed at the age of twelve and sucked his thumb. In fraud investigations, so-called soft crimes, the perpetrator oftentimes cannot identify with the acts he commits. The denial is so great, in fact, that the criminals sometimes go out of their way to be "honest," to conceal nothing, because concealment implies guilt. Twice now the detective had discovered a virtual treasure trove of evidence. Ron had left his home untouched, his computer on and available, with all files accessible. Now the van stuffed with documents and weapons seemed almost as if . . . Ron were baiting him.

Intrigued, Crowley began to investigate the discs recovered from Ron's computer. One, a document entitled, "All before D-Day," piqued his interest.

The detective approached Rombach again: "We found several e-mails between you and Ron."

"He asked for my help in recovering his shotgun, said it was specialized for hunting. Strangely, he didn't seem that upset about not getting it back." George had no explanation for why his name appeared on a fax Ron sent to the Avis Rent A Car. But he *did* think it strange that "Esquire" appeared after his name.

Homicide investigations are 90 percent luck and 10 percent tenacity. Crowley had never heard of Detective Gamber in October 1996. He assumed that the paperwork he recovered from Ron Young's van had some relevance to Ron's fraud investigation. But on November 1, 1996, he watched the evening news: a bombing had occurred in Tucson involving Gary Triano. Recognition skittered across his brain. He knew that last name, had seen it before. He sat transfixed on his couch. Ron's van flashed in his mind's eye: the map of Tucson, the divorce papers, Pam's love notes. *Dare to dream . . . Visions coming into focus.*

Crowley reinterviewed Ron's fake lawyer.

"When did you last see Ron?" he asked George Rombach.

"Just three days ago, November 2, 1996."

Most detectives have keen intuition, and while Crowley didn't have proof yet that Rombach had lied to him, he had much more: a *feeling*. And when he reviewed the many folders stored on Ron's computer, he found one titled

"Manager/Owner, Avis Rentals, Aspen, Colorado." The letter, dated October 26, 1996, contained a detailed "inventory" of items locked inside the van. Ron implored the rental company to appoint a "responsible representative" to store the contents until he could "safely retrieve them": sport coats, ties, dress shirts (both long- and short-sleeved), "hiking shoes, dress shoes, casual shoes, biking shoes, socks," and one "Bernardelli shotgun initials RKY." The list continued: several boxes of shells, a knife, one pellet pistol, electrical and mechanical devices, and several Briley choke tubes.

Computer forensic analysts would later confirm in 2005 that Ron actually *composed* the letter to the rental company on November 5, 1996, several days *after* "D-Day." He had apparently modified several of his files after April 26, 1996, and requested a memory upgrade sometime in August 1996. But detectives discovered something far more revealing: despite the "thousands and thousands and thousands of documents Ron saved," experts would find no activity whatsoever from October 26 through November 5.

"He was too busy," the prosecution marveled to the jury later. "The computer spoke to us, said to you: Ron Young has no alibi."

CHAPTER TWELVE:
HIDDEN IN PLAIN SIGHT

January 7, 1997

Pam deposited $2,035,000 into her checking account. Although versions varied concerning Pam's reaction to being a multimillionaire again, the most reliable source revealed that Pam tossed off her bedsheets after a restless sleep and padded to the kitchen to prepare a light breakfast. She ate quietly at the table as snow fell outside, and for the first time in many months she exhaled with confidence.

The clock on the wall ticked 6:00 a.m., three hours still before her bank opened. Pam dressed for the occasion in an oatmeal knit pullover, stylish black jeans, and a sapphire blue scarf. Long black boots hugged her calves. She tucked her blond highlighted hair into a wool cap and applied rouge to her cheeks and eyelids. This was the first day of her new life, and it promised to be incredible. As she drove to the bank, she felt light-headed and buzzed down her windows.

Frigid winter air smacked her cheeks. The road glittered in front of her, the ice catching the sunlight like crystal. The sharp pine scent tickled her nostrils. She felt like a newly released inmate. Pam slammed her car door shut, left the windows down and her keys in the ignition. She hugged her purse tight against her hip and entered the bank. She beamed at the dowdy middle-aged teller with the pinched face and rabbit stare. She could afford to be generous with her emotions now; her energy had changed. She had cleansed all negative thoughts from her pallet. She had been propelled into the stratosphere, where anything was possible. She handed the woman her life insurance proceeds.

Next, Pam opened several accounts at different banks and soon began what would become her bimonthly routine. As she paid for her groceries, she asked for an additional $300 cash back. She wrote checks to herself and collected the funds at that same institution. She wrote larger checks off her Morgan Stanley account, removing $17,000 in funds, depositing $15,000 into her Norwest account, and taking the balance as cash. She placed the money into envelopes and slipped them into a drawer, divided into sums of $2,000, $1,800, and $1,600. She thought of the women she had watched as a child shuffling multiple coupons, traveling to several grocery stores because some boasted better discounts. Food shopping consumed their afternoons. But by dusk they returned home satisfied, their pantries stocked with groceries. Pam complained that it sometimes took five withdrawals to make a single payment. *Safety first,* Ron's mantra echoed in her head. He had schooled her on the risks involved in cash conversion: "Banks have to report services of transactions, six thousand today, seven thousand tomorrow."

In order to appease Ron, she followed his instructions to pay him for services rendered. She mailed him cash installments, what he termed his "things," in sums of $1,600 ("16") or $1,400 ("14"), traveling to Basalt in blizzard conditions, using the prepaid air bills that identified the sender and receiver as Richard Perez with different zip codes. She sent him confirming e-mails with tracking numbers. He reminded her constantly to use code words when referring to money: they were "items," "things," and "information."

Ron required advance notice to collect his cash at the

Federal Express drop box; he had no driver's license and no vehicle. He needed sufficient time to hire a chauffeur, arrange a taxicab, and coordinate his various stops to the local 7-Eleven where he could purchase a money order so that he could deposit his check into his Bank of America account.

"It's quite a production," he explained to Pam. "I can't just deposit the funds into my account without converting them into money orders. If you don't tell me when you've made your drops, or you cancel a scheduled delivery, it costs *me* money. I have to hire a driver, fire a driver, and start the whole process all over again."

By September 1997, according to the prosecution, Pam had concealed cash conversions to Ron for a total of $68,000. Ron kept meticulous records of payments, a spreadsheet identifying the loan amortization schedule, $400,000 at a rate of 4 percent interest.

"That wasn't part of our agreement," Pam protested.

"But *you're* earning interest," he insisted. "It's not right that you should get interest on someone else's money."

"You're bringing this up *now*? You can't just change the rules of play mid-game. We never discussed interest in 1996."

"The number's 248 with interest," Ron said.

And while the two continued to bicker over money and their exhausting transfer schedule, Pam used a large portion of the life insurance proceeds to purchase her dream mansion in Meadowood, a "dark house with black painted walls" that needed "major renovations" but had its own ski lift. Situated just one mile north of her modest duplex on Snowbunny Lane, the house stood in sharp contrast, buttressed against the Elk Mountains and the Aspen Chapel. Massive wood doors marked the entrance like a wide mouth. Sharp stakes framed the windows. Iron railing wrapped around the second-floor balcony. Cold marble accented the bathrooms. A spiral staircase led upstairs. Crossbeams framed the ceiling. A stone chimney hugged the side of the house. The surrounding pines scratched the narrow windows. The home had sharp angles, slanted rooms, wide spaces, and too much echo. Brick pillars accented the circular driveway and twin garages. Pam had moved from a nondescript duplex to an overstated mansion, a "chic house that made a statement." She had arrived. If only she could remove the darkness.

She lit a cigarette and inhaled sharply.

"What did you have in mind?" a contractor asked, his hands on his hips.

"I'd like to gut the place. Start over."

Renovations dragged on, and by the spring of 1998, Pam's nights were fitful. The wind banged against the loose shingles on her roof. Gary loomed from the darkness in her dreams, alive again, his face twisting like a ghoul's Halloween mask. Familiar panic clogged her throat. The room swallowed her. She clawed at her sheets, feeling trapped, suffocated. She ran to the small window and pushed open the glass. Frigid air burned her lungs.

She called Ron the next morning, still breathless. "I'm totally losing it. Talking to you, getting hounded by you . . . I've snapped. I've been handling this . . . arrangement for a long time."

"Two years." Ron cleared his throat. He waited patiently for her to continue. His calling card beeped at him. He had used up two minutes.

"What you do with the rest of your money, whether it's drink yourself to death or buy clothes . . . ," she prattled on.

"I drink myself to death," he volunteered.

"I'm not a big girl. I am a totally messed-up girl," Pam said. She choked back a sob. "Where are you living now?"

"I'm not going to say."

"Why aren't you going to say?"

"Because my level of trust for you has shrunk to zero. I asked you if anything ever happened to me to watch out for my kids and you—"

"I can do that, of course I can do that, but it's all in stock," Pam said flatly.

"*Stock*?" Ron sputtered.

"I'm just a basket case. I'm throwing up. I've got to get myself together. I have diarrhea. I need to meditate. My friends say they don't know how I'm functioning."

"You've been talking to your friends?"

"Joy's been asking some pretty direct questions."

"How direct?"

"Pretty direct."

"What have you told her?"

"Nothing. I haven't told a soul anything. They just don't know how I'm functioning."

"Functioning? You've taken trips to Peru . . ."

"I might die there. It'd be a good place. Maybe I should eat a bunch of coca leaves."

The detective learned later that the "direct questions" Joy posed to Pam had everything to do with the thousands of dollars she had loaned her over the years. Pam might have let it slip that she used the funds to pay back Ron, though she was never specific about the services he rendered. As their friendship soured and Pam's money source disappeared, she romanced her house contractor.

"How else am I going to ever finish my roof?" she justified to Ron. But as with most of Pam's male relationships, the contractor had limited utility. He'd be gone once he sealed the drafts, "like breath blowing through [my] thoughts," she confessed.

"I'm never going to feel really safe in this town," Pam confided to Ron. "I mean, it's horrible. It costs me more money to try than you make. I'm haunted. I shake all the time."

Ron tried to help. He took great care to disguise his e-mails to Pam, using at least fifteen different addresses: weatherlee@freedom.net, sky10@mediaone.net, sailzone@ mutemail.com . . . all untraceable. Pam, by contrast, used only five, and all of them identifiable: Paminaspen@hot mail.com, Phillips@sopris.net, starbabies1@aol.com, baby stars@hushmail.com, and meadow781@yahoo.com (her address in Meadowood).

"You're not quite getting this code thing, are you?" Ron scolded Pam over the phone as he admonished her once again to exercise discretion.

He implemented elaborate computer software programs to preserve his two hundred floppy disks containing their recorded conversations. He organized Pam's voice mails into folders and created spreadsheets detailing payment schedules. He installed software that allowed him to communicate between computers from distant locations, all presumably to avoid detection. He stored faxes inside his computer, installed zip drives, purchased memory upgrades, and developed mirror images of his hard drives; in short, he obsessed over his deception.

"I've always been on your team, always tried to help you," he reminded Pam.

"If you really want to help me, you can skip the whole deal. Give me a call a year from now and we can check in with each other."

"Are you joking? I'm sure you don't want me to flip out."

"Just do me a favor: Let me know ahead of time before I get the knock on my door so I can check out."

"You promised me . . ."

"The promise I made to you is never talk to anybody about you. This is like a fucking nightmare."

"But it's totally safe. The nightmare is in your head."

CHAPTER THIRTEEN:
THE NIGHTMARE

Pam lay awake after midnight. She balanced the phone on her chest and called Ron's number. The dial tone buzzed in the dark. Her mind raced. The room spun. Her breath labored. She had no energy to replace the receiver. The phone beeped at her, loud and obnoxious, like a warning. She clicked to disconnect. The seconds ticked by on the clock on her nightstand. Pam picked up the phone again. She called Ron's number: still no answer. Pine needles scratched at her windows. *Where was he?* She shivered in her plush sheets. Blood satin bunched at her waist. She was alone, completely, utterly alone. She drifted into a restless sleep, clutching her cell phone, checking it, pointlessly, for any missed calls, watching the screen, hoping it would blink blue. Obsessively she hit "Send," connecting with Ron's voice mail over and over until finally he answered.

"I couldn't talk to you, couldn't get ahold of you. I freaked. Absolutely freaked. Freaked. Freaked. Freaked . . ."

"Okay, okay, stop," Ron interrupted.

". . . I mean, to where all of a sudden I became unable to move . . ."

They started yelling, speaking over each other unintelligibly. They reacted to stress by fighting with each other. Eventually, Ron calmed her with detailed discussions of money, debt consolidation, and cash-flow options. He suggested that she stop repairing her roof. Maybe it was foolish to start a business when she had no income. Potrero still had not sold. Maybe it never would.

"Make sure you do the right thing," he said patronizingly. "Make sure there's money for Pamela." But it wasn't Pam's money he worried about. It was *his*.

On a blustery afternoon, she piled Lois and Trevor into her Mini Cooper. Their nanny slid in beside them. Pam blasted the heat and drove in silence over washboard ice. She tightened her grip around the steering wheel. It would be foolish to have an accident *now*, after all that she'd been through, when she was so close. She counted the number of drops remaining: if she continued her twice-monthly ritual of cash withdrawals and trips to Basalt, she could be done with Ron as early as . . . What if she doubled the amounts, mailed him more than sums of $1,400, $1,600, and $1,800? Too risky. She glanced at her children in her rearview mirror and felt an overwhelming emptiness, as if time were running out, as if she were dead already and had somehow prolonged her fate without permission. She had done this for them, for their financial future. Her children belonged to her; they were her possessions and she was responsible for their well-being.

"They'll get over it," Ron had said. "Give them time. Kids are resilient."

Thirty minutes later Pam parked on the curb in Basalt and left the engine on. Her brain screamed, *Run!* But where would she go? Her children climbed out, held the nanny's hands, and crossed the street to the corner grocery store. Pam shuffled to the drop box inside the warehouse-like structure, stuffed the envelope from "Richard Perez" to "Richard Perez" inside the dark hole. Her heart hammered against her chest. Wet snow dampened her hair. She shivered. *How much longer was she going to have to do*

"The Happy Couple," Gary and Pam, on their wedding day. *(Photo courtesy David Bean)*

Pamela Phillips: "A Toast to the Future."
(Photo courtesy David Bean)

Gary Triano, demure on his
wedding day.
(Photo courtesy David Bean)

Gary and Pam.   *(Photo courtesy David Bean)*

Bomb debris of the '89 Lincoln Town Car.
(Photo courtesy Pima County Sheriff's Department)

Gary Triano's '89 Lincoln Town Car after the bombing.
(Photo courtesy Pima County Sheriff's Department)

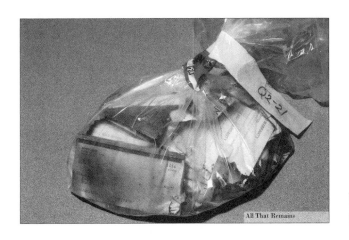

"All that remains."
(Photo courtesy Pima County Sheriff's Department)

Parking lot, Westin La Paloma, following the bombing.
(Photo courtesy Pima County Sheriff's Department)

Front view of the Town Car.
(Photo courtesy Pima County Sheriff's Department)

"Self portrait." *(Photo courtesy Pima County Sheriff's Department)*

Investigators at the bomb scene.
(Photo courtesy Pima County Sheriff's Department)

Inside view of Gary Triano's bombed car.
(Photo courtesy Pima County Sheriff's Department)

Gary Triano with his children, Brian and Heather.

(Photo courtesy David Bean)

Gary Triano playfully holding a knife near his new bride's throat.

(Photo courtesy David Bean)

this? Her children emerged a few minutes later with pastries. As they bit into the cream centers, they stared blankly at their mother. The nanny secured their scarves tighter around their necks. They stood on the white sidewalk. As snow fell lightly around them, they resembled figures in a snow globe, trapped in their cold, stark world.

By the end of October 1998, Pam had paid Ron an estimated $153,540 dollars, leaving a balance due of $246,460 *without* interest.

"I can't handle the stress." Pam sounded flustered over the phone. "I'm not able to go out. I feel handicapped. I'm not able to free my mind from being, like, totally underwater. Really nervous . . ."

"Well, you know . . . you need to . . ."

"You don't understand . . . you have to use your head to come up with a different way you know to do this. There must be . . . there must be . . ."

"Well, you certainly don't want to be writing checks; that's how the dumb people do it."

"Well, then come up with a smart way. Either I pay some bills or you know some kind of automatic something or [I] give you an interest in something."

"I think what's bothering you—and I'm not trying to be critical here; I just want to put this out—you're making the mechanics of this—"

"It's horrible. I can't even tell you."

"I think you've made it far more difficult than it has to be."

"I can't even tell you what it does to me. I mean, I can't even . . . I cannot even . . . I can't go there. I can't go there."

"It's undeserved stress."

"I can't get rid of it. I'm meditating. I'm totally a mess. I'm, you know, my dreams, my this, my that, it's all, like, it's . . . you know, I can't even run from it. I can't even run."

"Let me just say this . . . anybody, when they have layers and layers and layers of unresolved issues . . . they're going to . . ."

"Blow up."

But of course Ron produced no alternative plan, and Pam continued with the ritual cash withdrawals and deposits to the Federal Express drop box in Basalt. She felt like an experiment, certain that if she were ordered to deliver electric shocks to a stranger seated in another room out of sight, she'd continue to administer the jolts, no matter how loud and tortured the screams from the other room, because someone in authority told her to do it. She'd keep pressing that button until someone told her to stop, until Ron told her to stop, until the nightmare ended and the coast was "very very clear." But there was no stopping. And instinctively she sensed the coast would *never* be clear. They would function like strangers, each teetering on a thin tightrope, afraid the other might snip the end.

She fantasized endgame scenarios. *There had to be a way to stop this.* She imagined herself an old woman, sealed inside her Mini Cooper, heat blasting her withered face until she melted entirely. Ron's creepy power burned into her subconscious like a fever. She would never be free of him. Money connected them. *Sin* connected them. If she stopped answering his phone calls or responding to his e-mails—if she pretended for a week she had no obligation to him, didn't even know him—he would find her. He always did. She knew instinctively she was a marked woman. If she snapped, if she betrayed him—even if he only thought she did—he would kill her.

That's what happens when you bargain with the devil.

Meanwhile, large trenches snaked through Pam's living room. Construction debris formed piles in the kitchen. Surrounded by paint chips, dust, and leaking faucets, she admired her gorgeous wooden deck. Her house had enormous curb appeal. Her friends marveled at the allure, the carefully placed stone pavers, fountains, and topiary. She hoped soon the inside renovations would reflect the outside. But even Pam knew a perfect eggshell could conceal a rotten yolk.

She needed to end her relationship with Ron.

She left him a message on his answering machine: "You know, Mr. *Friend*, I'm getting tired of this charade. I can't make ends meet. I have two little charges that demand everything but can't *have* everything."

"Welcome to parenthood," Ron condescended. But Pam barely heard him. She ranted on about the exorbitant cost of private-school tuition for Lois and Trevor, taxes, health insurance, life insurance, car insurance, home insurance, how her cost of living was so high it was painful, absolutely *crushing*. And then, almost as suddenly as the floodgates opened, she dammed them up again.

"How are you?" she asked brightly.

"Doing very poorly. I've been kicked to the curb." He pouted, because he knew Pam had only pretended to love him.

"You know I feel bad about that," she lied. "I should have been more forceful about us, but we're just *friends*."

"Well, *friend*, you spent my stuff . . . I'm not accusing you," Ron said icily.

"If I'm spending this much money, I must pay taxes, no?" she prattled on, seemingly oblivious to Ron's tone or the fact that she had dipped into his share of the proceeds without a thought to reimbursement. She distracted him by pretending to ask for his advice.

Ron took the bait and explained that he was not her contract employee: "I'm not working for you, so there's no 1099 [tax form]. Have you sent my principal yet?"

"I'm thinking we should just cool it for a while."

"What?" Ron dissolved into a coughing fit.

"It's just too much. I'm stressed all the time. The bank woman is starting to look at me funny."

"If I'm being fucked over by you . . . ," Ron wheezed.

"I have to go. Bye." Click.

Ron immediately called her back. His prepaid calling card reminded him that he had used twenty-two minutes.

"If there's anything that you've done to compromise our understanding, it might be a good time to talk about it. Just like the phone records, the hundreds and hundreds of calls from you and me to you . . . going back six months prior to the event. I suggest you fax me your records. Just fax them instead of implying I'm some sort of cheat. I'm really sick of the implication. It really makes me crazy when you question my integrity while you sit in your $2 million home that you have absolutely no business having."

Ron groused, and when he received no answer, he continued: "Whatever I know about you or you about me, that would stay quite confidential, no matter what . . . do you understand what I'm saying? 'Cause if I ever found out that you compromised me for your benefit, that would be really unfortunate [for] you, because, there's plenty of stuff that . . . you're, you know, a fried duck. Understand that I'd rather not be in that position."

"Well, *I'm* sure you'd rather not be in that position as well," Pam said quietly.

"I just hope there's not a silliness about somebody's trying to . . . you know, and I'm trying to help you on something that was, you know, nobody else in the world would probably do and especially somebody you can trust. And I think that deserves some consideration. Since you're living off the benefits."

"I'm willing to talk about it." She switched on a vacuum cleaner.

"But don't start talking, you know, adios for a year kind of stuff, okay? Just stop!" Ron shouted over the phone.

"I wanna get Potrero sold. If I could get Potrero sold I could—"

"Yeah, yeah, there's a million dollars in the bank. Well, so you get a million bucks for that in a couple years. So, what's gonna be different?" She shut off the appliance.

"I'll buy something nice for you. I'll donate something. There's gotta be another way to do this."

"Well . . ."

"There's got to be another way. It was supposed to be a short-term thing." She stood and walked over to one of her tall windows. She caught her reflection in the glass, eyes bleary with sleep, hair tousled, more brittle than usual. She had always appreciated her easy prettiness, good skin, well-formed features; but lately, deeper lines creased her eyes and mouth. Lack of sleep and too much stress gave her a greasy sheen. Somehow youth softened the hard edges of disappointment that gnawed at a person's life. *But it took so much energy to fix herself.*

I wanted security. I never wanted to worry again.

"Until the coast was very very clear . . . we just keep it extremely cautious, untraceable," Ron insisted.

"You know that's what you said. But this is like a fucking nightmare." She blew out a sigh.

"Okay, well, I got a nightmare, too, so we just need to deal with this. Just so you know . . . 248 is the number without any interest."

"You add this interest business. I get interest. You know, I mean, that's . . ."

"Not after the fact."

"Yes, after the fact. After the fact."

"I was honorable with you. I mean, I could have said no. Everything's in the kids' names. I could have done all kinds of things. I could have . . . I was straight with you."

Ron could barely contain his anger. "I lived up to my word and you have not had any problems. *I* haven't had any problems."

"Well, I'll tell you what . . . if you don't give me a break . . . ," Pam trailed off, her voice like ice.

"We should talk about it and figure out how to unwind whatever you did . . . ," He warned.

"I have not talked to anybody. I have not talked to a soul."

"And nobody's contacted you?"

"Nobody's contacted me."

"Okay." There was a pause.

"If I have to kill myself . . . I can't even move forward. It's like I can't get rid of . . . this constant . . . take my phone and just throw it. I want to change my number. I want to leave. I just can't. I don't have a dime. I mean, going to the bank . . . which is totally illegal."

"What do you mean, 'illegal?'" Ron sounded incredulous.

"It's illegal."

"What's illegal? Spending your money is illegal?" He chuckled.

"No." Pam lowered her voice to a fierce whisper. "I am paying money to somebody. I am not spending it. I'm getting money and I'm not declaring it. And you're getting money and . . . are you declaring it?" Pam had reason to worry: interest earned from her life insurance proceeds was taxable income. And if she construed Ron as her "non-employee" and paid him for services rendered from that interest, she was obligated to issue him a 1099. Even if Ron considered Pam's payments mere "gifts" in exchange for his favors and therefore did not have to declare the income, the money he received from Pam far exceeded the lawful annual limit of $13,000, thereby creating tax implications for Pam.

"No, you're completely confused." Ron was tempering his impatience, never sure whether Pam actually believed she had to pay taxes on money she spent or whether she just pretended to be dim.

"Am I?"

"Look, I want a little bit of it so I can get the surgery. I gave you my word. I gave you my word . . . when I get back some strength, we'll come up with a figure . . ."

"I don't have time for this."

"When you're sitting in a women's prison for murder . . ."

"Please . . . I have to fit this in a budget. I need to slide this by a money manager."

"No, when you're sitting in a women's prison for murder . . ."

"You know what? I don't have time to discuss this now."

"You're going to be in prison for murder."

"I'll be back at four."

CHAPTER FOURTEEN:
NEW PLANS

By late 1998, Gamber worked almost exclusively on Gary's unsolved homicide. He had come to know both his victim and his many potential killers. Because he could not know *which* information would prove to be vital, he collected minor details and intimate secrets; and while he could never really *know* his victim except through others' eyes and recollections, he would *know* his killer better than he knew his own wife. The dead, even long buried, bothered the margins of his conscience. He wished he had the luxury of some of his colleagues who "lived" in the crime scene, shut themselves in the quiet, in the middle of the floor, in darkness, and listened, trying to "hear" what had happened there. It wasn't as if Gamber could sit inside the shell of Gary's bombed-out car and *feel* his killer's presence, or sift through his ashes searching for metal shards that might offer the missing clue.

Some victims, so desperate for answers and guidance, seek the assistance of psychics. Gary's former girlfriend, even his mother, enlisted the services of Sylvia Browne, a renowned spiritual teacher and psychic whose predictions have led to national television notoriety.

"I don't know if you believe in that sort of thing," Gary's

girlfriend advised Gamber. "She told us Gary's murder would never be solved, but that his killer would surface in Florida. Strange, huh?"

"Yeah, strange." Gamber never judged his victims' choices, or whatever sources gave them comfort. Whether it was psychic reassurance or physician-prescribed medication—pills for sleep, anxiety, depression—Gamber could only offer his own version of hope, his promise that the case *would* be solved; he just wasn't certain when.

Meanwhile, Pam's body erupted in hives. Chunks of hair fell out in her brush. Some mornings she lay curled in the sheets in a cocoon of darkness, listening to the bustle of activity around her, her mind racing. She needed the arrangement to end. She needed a solution.

"Why do I feel there's something wrong?" Ron badgered her a few hours later.

"I haven't done anything to compromise anything," she answered him wearily. She held up a hand mirror and pretended to smile, then frowned, then smiled again. She didn't recognize the woman in the mirror, the strange rubbery complexion.

Ron's words sliced through her: "We made a deal. I told you I'd protect you to the death and I'm willing to do that unless I'm being fucked over."

"I haven't compromised anything," Pam repeated, barely listening. She was like a small animal caught in a hunter's trap: the more she twisted, the tighter her binds, the more she yelped, the thicker the darkness. Desperation gnawed at her bloody wounds until, two years later, she fought again for her release.

Gary's case was "closed," she announced, but provided no proof.

"Let's not get cocky." Ron bolted the chains in place again and shot her an e-mail:

a. First, there's no such thing.
b. A case like this would never be closed. It would be placed in the active files.
c. Coincidentally this remarkable news happens just about the same time you float the concept of blackmail by me.
d. The same time you mention record keeping . . .
e. You do realize don't you that anyone with access to your office, where you said you leave your computer, can read all of your e-mails while you're gone, including mine . . .
f. I better not hear that word in your vocabulary. The word that starts with "black."
g. I'd better not hear it.
h. That pisses me off. That really pisses me off. I'd better not hear that word.
i. I'd better not hear it.
j. By the way you seemed surprised when I mentioned "interest."
k. You shouldn't be earning interest on someone else's $. It was mine when it was earned. I'm only asking for my fair share. You got 1.6 million tax free. I want my four.

Pam called Ron the next day as if she had never made any grand announcement, as if there really was no "end" planned. "I'm thinking we should take a break."

"A break?"

"I have to start making money." She launched into grand plans for renovations.

"You could jack up the value of your home, put in a garage, a maid's apartment . . ."

"Maybe put in a second-story structure, even if it's faux, up on the top of this one-story structure. And then do a two-story garage . . . I just have to start making some money."

She was breathless. "I mean, I had to license my car. Between homeowner's dues and taxes, it's unfucking believable. I just borrowed money on a credit line."

"You've been writing to me in crayon," Ron said flatly.

"This is draining me," Pam said.

"You still have a Dean Witter account with like six hundred grand in there . . ."

"Not really. That account was drained for the house. I figure I have roughly enough to live on for one year."

Pitkin County Assessor's Office records confirmed Pam purchased the house at 781 Meadowood Drive for $1,050,000.

"Don't even think about—"

"I haven't talked to anyone if that's what you're worried about. I will kill myself first."

By July 2000, Pam and Ron had resorted to pen names. "Dear Ann Frank's Diary," Ron wrote to Pam, signing his name as Doug Franklin. Meanwhile, Ron's repeated requests for his share of the money, his so-called information reached urgent tones as he berated Pam for inexplicably altering the order of the scheduled payments.

"You did the 14 instead of the 16. Did the 16 happen? Do the 14 in the next few weeks. The 14 is overdue. Please confirm 14 was done and when."

Pam always assured him: "Mail going out today. #812791370350. SB [Star Babies] taking a little longer." She remained steadfast that Star Babies would "someday" produce steady income. Ron warned her about privacy; he cautioned her to use security measures when deleting e-mails. He encouraged her to install spyware and adware and destroy e-mails "even from the 'trash.'" He made lists for her, drafting pages of comprehensive step-by-step instructions on how to remove compromising correspondence from her computer.

But she rejected his advice: "A friend of mine told me the only way to remove e-mails from the hard drive is to break it in two."

Ron grew anxious again when his expected Saturday delivery did not arrive. He called Pam's cell phone. She answered on the fifth ring.

"I'm just hanging out in the aisle with the birthday candles." She sounded irritated.

"Are you alone?"

"Yeah, except for all of Wal-Mart." And he could hear the loudspeaker advertising fresh rolls of bread.

"Well, do you want to find a pay phone?"

"Yeah. God, I'm just running on such a tight schedule. I have to have the kids back by 4:00. People are coming over for cake."

"How much did you send this time?"

"Two."

"Any reason it wasn't a Saturday delivery?"

"It was." She said defensively.

"It doesn't say."

"Shit, I don't know. I mean I put it in there on time. I marked on there 'Saturday.'"

"Okay."

"You know, I mean, you know, I just can't even . . . I just don't even . . ."

"No reason not to trust this line we're on, is there?"

"I have no idea. I have no idea. I mean, I really have no idea."

"You know our original understanding was that whatever I knew about you or you about me, that would stay confidential no matter what, right?"

Silence.

"Any reason to believe that I should be concerned that you have not lived up to that promise?"

"No." She sighed.

"'Cause I know you've thrown around the concept of blackmail in your interviews with the police."

"Why are you so paranoid?" she spat.

"Several reasons: your urgency to have stuff faxed to you. Why do you need to know ahead of time when I'm going to call? I explained to you two or three times a fax is the easiest way for both of us to be in a lot of trouble. Every phone call we've had for the last two weeks you've demanded a fax memorializing the call."

"I still want a fax."

"Why do I feel like something's wrong?"

"I don't want to do it anymore."

"What does *that* mean?"

"I don't know. I don't know. I'm standing here in the middle of Wal-Mart and you know I just . . . don't want to do it anymore."

"The way we had it working was just fine."

"I'm sure it is just fine."

"ATMs three or four times a week."

"I'm going nuts. I don't want to live like this anymore." Tension crackled between them. Pam shook in the aisle surrounded by Mylar balloons, bloodred roses, and candles that fizzled and sparked. Her heart raced and she exhaled slowly. "Hey, there's no problem. I'm just . . . maxed."

"You seem anxious."

"I'm aggravated. Would you just leave me alone?" She choked back a sob.

"I hardly ever talk to you," Ron lied.

"I want you to leave me alone," she whispered fiercely. "You've stolen my *life*."

"I'm bothering you"—a statement not a question.

"Right now you are. I've got to go. I've got kids waiting . . ."

"You bothered *me*—" He was like a fencer circling his opponent.

"For Lois's birthday."

"—for some help so you could get rich," he finished, plunging his rapier into her heart.

"Will you leave me alone? Good-bye."

A year later, in April 2001, Pam turned forty and announced her plans to travel to New York City to celebrate. "The pace should get me up for great work and money year astrologically. Sent today 812791470257." And while Pam was exhilarated, Ron revealed he had skin cancer and needed an advance of "400 extra of his stuff," to pay for his anticipated surgeries: "not finished with the butchers yet."

Days later, when the money still had not arrived, Pam assured him, "I'm doing my best . . . [I]t's really ugly and scary."

She believed her home had become a refuge for bats. Guano seeped through her leaky roof. And as hard as she tried, she could not get rid of the overwhelming stench of rot. Wind whistled through the cracks. She tried to seal the holes. The bats roosted. They filled empty passageways. Still no money arrived. Doubt plagued Ron's conscience. He depended on Pam's communications, needed regular assurances that she planned to fulfill her obligation. He looked forward to her icy voice mails, her stainless-steel edge. He lived like a drifter, occupying borrowed spaces, hiding in dark hotel rooms, gauzy rentals in dismal parts of town. He waited for the reprieve, the cash. Sometimes it took weeks for Pam's response. Meanwhile, Ron prowled his tiny prison and agitated at the blank screen. He willed her confirming e-mail to appear with the tracking numbers. He was *sick*, literally rotting from the inside: How could she be so cruel as to make him wait?

He wrote to his mom:

> I know you're wondering about my eating and sleeping habits. Most of the time breakfast is had at a café serving only pastry and coffee. The pastries, especially in Denmark, are like nothing

you can find at home. For lunch, I purchase
bananas, peaches, plums or other fruits and de-
vour them with tomatoes and a half pound of
cheese. Dinner is liable to be anything, as long
as it's inexpensive. I'm eating hoards of bread
because it fills like nothing else and is cheap
and good. It's never the sliced sponge they sell
in the states.

Pam complained she had resorted to "bottom fishing,"
the real estate market had crumbled, and she was left
with mere million-dollar homes to sell. She'd had to borrow money "just to meet her expenses," which she kept at
a minimum until the stock market recovered. Potrero
still hadn't sold. And her home needed more renovation.
Her roof leaked. Part of her overhang rotted and col-
lapsed. Ron delayed his cancer treatments. He needed his
stuff.

"*Where* is it?" he demanded, his fingers pounding on
the keyboard.

"Houston, there's a problem," Pam wrote, pretending to
be "Anne Frank." "I need to raise money to meet my mortgage and only emergency cash outlays. My account is
overdrawn and my credit limit is maxed. Thinking about
meeting with a financial planner to help me restructure or
raise money in less expensive manner. I need ideas." She
added that her regular installments to Ron might be delayed, and the thought of sending him his "14" and "16"
were making her "numb."

Ron panicked: "What are you *talking* about? Four days?
Did you send it another way without asking me? We are
talking about my property not yours. When I want my
property and how I ask for it to be done should be respected
by you. Especially when I'm on a delayed cancer irradiation
program . . . [F]or the foreseeable future let's just keep
things simple at 18 at a time, a lousy snail's pace. You're

blessed to have a house, a new car and most importantly full health insurance. I must be mad to take risks, tempt fate, stall cancer procedures. If this crap gets into my lymph or blood a major shitstorm will erupt."

Pam delayed payment again and then wrote: "Life's too short. You should let it go."

Let it go? Let what *go?* Then it hit him: Pam wanted him dead, needed him dead. It would be easier that way. He would no longer be her obligation; she would be free, truly free. No more secrets, no more hidden identities. If Pam delayed payment, his cancer would spread.

"I made a huge mistake. I live like a fucking immigrant while you live in the most expensive place in America, travel, ski passes. You don't bother to work for the last eight years. Really helps my attitude when playing Russian Roulette with cancer. Guess why. Someone else has MY fucking property."

And while Ron fumed and waited for his money, he arranged to travel to Mexico to have his surgeries; detection was less risky there. Still no word from Pam. Days morphed into two weeks, and just as he began to think she had double-crossed him, he received her breezy explanation,

"Sorry for the delay, I was on a cruise."

In many ways Ron lived undercover with heightened awareness. He dressed unassumingly in jeans or shorts, a baseball cap, sunglasses, and sometimes a beard or stubble. He was somewhat restricted in his disguise choices, careful to blend with the crowd. Cash limited his options. He stashed thousands of crisp bills in his freezer along with a second firearm. *Just in case.* Without a credit card, air travel was not an option. He could not rent a car, own a cell phone, or purchase Internet service. He traveled by taxi, used prepaid phone cards, and assumed several identities. He could never date or connect with another human being.

"It was a little like being a serial killer," he mused in his journal. "The only safe company is your own."

* * *

Later, when Pam didn't hear anything from Ron, she wrote: "We are aligned. And I am not effective for so many reasons. I am very fragile and transparent."

Still she failed to send the money.

"Haven't heard a word from you which is really nice. Please get this BS straight and get this 4 done and behind us. Please remember what I'm referring to: MY STUFF." He signed the e-mail as "Maureen," a vague reference to Norman Bates's dead mother.

Pam responded a few days later: "I'm doing what I can to salvage my situation . . . [T]he truth of the matter is two children that need to be supported, a house of cards, my roof is falling down and the house needs a remodel. SB needs attention because it could pull me right out of my problems. I have great connections. Sent 400 today. This is not your stuff. It is all woven together in one big existence of family future and past."

Ron again reminded Pam about being diligent and the importance of "e-mail security."

"Not good at typing," she replied. "Would rather call."

"Don't want a 'long' call. Bye."

But the next day Ron relented. He *did* call: "What's up, Captain?"

"I can't keep bouncing between banks. The manager is suspicious. Even Morgan Stanley is asking questions about my business venture: I'm draining $30,000 a month from their account."

"Look we can stress or we can solve problems."

"I'm ready to go marry someone I don't love just to solve the fucking problem," Pam spat. "My life is just shit. I have to run around with the kids, projects, back and forth; I'm doing everything and it's too much. I've got furniture lying in the middle of my house."

"Maybe you should put Star Babies aside for now," Ron counseled.

He began to discuss spyware and adware so that they could communicate better in codes.

"I have a maid who has to vacuum." Pam hung up.

Ron's growing distrust of Pam compelled him to connect with her almost daily, either by e-mail or phone. He paced like an inmate in a dark cell, waiting for his dose of human contact. Pam confirmed his existence; she validated his purpose. Even their spats comforted him. Without her he faced nothing but blank space. Theirs was a true partnership, more intimate than any marriage, bonded together by need, the survival instinct . . . and fear. No one could ever know their dark secret.

But by early November 2001 an article surfaced in Arizona's *Tucson Weekly* that threatened to expose them. According to "Requiem for a Heavyweight," Pam remained a "loose end," "not completely excluded as a suspect"; it described her "boyfriend" Ron as "a bad guy" a "slippery" villain "wanted on weapons and fraud charges in Aspen." Ron found the description of him "provincial." *He was hardly an amateur.*

Pam came across as a "ruthless" woman "who would not hesitate to rip a person's heart out for a commission." The article mentioned her failure to submit to a polygraph . . . *as if that detail offered any insight into her state of mind,* Ron reasoned. He knew the press salivated over these tidbits, hoping they might lead to real meat. *Don't panic. That's what they want.*

But when Pam found unflattering articles in the *Aspen Times* as well, she could barely contain her hysteria. Using the code name "Spider," she wrote Ron: "I'm ready to commit myself, but I don't want to offend the Catholic Church and in turn offend everyone else. Is that awful or what?"

"They're totally fabricated, the articles," Ron replied.

"I'm just shaking."

"I've never even heard of the publication. Was it a little magazine or something?" Ron pretended, almost enjoying her stress.

"A pretty big *free* newspaper."

"Tear it up. Just flush it in the toilet, it's upsetting you."

"Of course it's upsetting me!!" she wrote.

"Other than the guy going into details about . . . Well, you've been portrayed badly before and my name has shown up twice in two previous articles. The only *new* thing he wrote in there is that apparently you're a vicious businesswoman."

"Yeah."

"Ripping commissions out of people's throats."

"Unbelievable."

"Are you really *that* bad?"

Pam didn't respond immediately.

"I'll do some research on this, find out the circulation of this thing. The article didn't get picked up by anybody else, so that's good."

"Yeah."

"The journalist said you were . . . someone they considered at first, which is natural. I found it quite interesting about the beneficiaries to the thing, you know, the policy and your kids. They clearly got it wrong, said your *kids* were the beneficiaries and that's why they lost interest in you."

"Well, they are the beneficiaries . . . I'm their trustee until they reach majority." she clarified, then added, "I'm still on the list."

"No, the article was black-and-white. You *were* on the list and then you were eliminated. Towards the end the goofball representing the sheriff's office, whoever it is, wanted to remind the reporter that of course even though nobody's working on the thing these things never do get closed. 'And you know we always keep an eye out for people and stuff like this' and general PR bullshit. The article stressed that you didn't have any direct benefit, your kids did. It lists about four thousand of Gary's enemies."

"This town is really small."

"What happened to your boyfriend?"

Pam deflected his question and quickly returned to the subject of money. "I have so many obligations. I'm going to have to borrow money against the equity in the house because my roof is collapsing. That's going to cost me about $100,000 to replace."

"You have to redo the whole thing?"

"Yeah. The guys that worked on it before used an ice pick to break the ice and snow and perforated the metal lining. The outside is literally seeping through my house. The facades, the overhangs, are actually rotted. The wood is falling off."

"You're becoming exposed."

The pair exchanged communications for several days without mentioning the dreaded newspaper articles. But Ron almost preferred the subject to Pam's other obsession: cash flow. He resorted to phone calls, finding it tedious and unproductive to e-mail. At least with the phone he received instant responses. And they could dispense with the code names.

By February 2002, Ron was calling almost daily, partly to infuriate Pam but mostly to remind her he still breathed, still waited for his payments. Rain spit against his apartment window as he dialed her number. He watched his reflection in the glass smear.

"We shouldn't talk on the phone," Pam whispered.

"I've purchased phone cards," Ron stuttered.

"I'm just really stressed . . . you have no idea—"

"Hey, I've sacrificed too," Ron cut her off. "I'm pretty aware of your losses and gains. I'm happy for you, *Grandma*, but you've spent my stuff."

"I borrowed $500,000. My home is valued at $3 million. I need to know what I'm going to be taxed on and what's going to be considered a gift."

"A *gift*? What are you *talking* about? Have you sent my principal?" Ron exploded, not eager to have yet another conversation about taxes and money management.

"I'm not sending you more money until I know you're going to honor our agreement. I want to move on. I want something definitive, capping at four. I don't want some nebulous number."

"Nebulous . . ."

"That's right. You hit me with interest . . ."

"Can I finish a sentence? I need an advance to get to Mexico."

Silence.

"Maybe I'll agree to four," he relented. "I did something for you that no one else would do. I could literally dig up some evidence and you'll spend the rest of your time in a women's prison for murder."

"I have nightmares every night over lack of income," Pam began. "I have to start making some money." Her voice cracked with desperation. She spoke of panic attacks, paralysis, delusions. Some nights she sat on her bed, arms curled around her knees, and smoked until dawn. When she did sleep, nightmares swirled in her head. She shuffled barefoot through shrapnel and bomb debris in a broken, abandoned building. The windows had jagged glass like teeth. Doors banged shut behind her, others swung open into wide, white nothingness. Exit signs flashed bloody neon down the dark hall, and as she approached, the pungent odor of burnt flesh choked her.

She saw her daughter's face. She wanted answers, needed closure. *How did her daddy die?*

"She can't find out," Ron advised Pam.

"Well, of course she can't find out," Pam spit. "But she's curious. She's going to find the articles . . ."

"She'll get over it," Ron said evenly.

"What if she doesn't?"

CHAPTER FIFTEEN:
STARTING OVER

Pam reconnected with her stepdaughter, Heather, who was attending college in New York. She treated Heather to a luxurious lunch in lower Manhattan and pleaded with her to return to Aspen. She needed her help to run Star Babies.

"After all, it was your *father's* company," Pam beamed over a crusted salmon salad.

"What were you thinking?" Ron fumed when he heard of Pam's new "houseguest."

"I was *thinking* it would be smart to keep my enemies close," she responded coolly.

Pam's house bustled with people, nannies, bookkeepers, boyfriends, and children. Each of the teenagers had her own computer. Lois and Trevor "drifted in and out of the house" unannounced, walked alone to school through the meadow, and had little if any supervision. Pam commissioned a girlfriend of Heather's who lived in the neighborhood to periodically check in on the children. More often than not, Lois and Trevor spent the night with the woman. Pam preferred to travel, to pretend that her life was normal, that she had money, that she was free.

"She was a spiritual person," Heather's friend remarked, "very into self-improvement and cleansing the body of toxic energies. She traveled to Europe for the weekend, Chicago for the week, spent three thousand dollars on popcorn for the movies, and always she'd call on the final day and ask to extend." The friend didn't necessarily balk.

"She gave me free reign of this gorgeous house and always promised compensation. To a single mom, the carrot of an extra $200 in my pocket was attractive . . . only Pam rarely paid me anything. Instead she offered me nice dinners. There were few groceries in the home, and I replenished the pantry and refrigerator. She always promised to reimburse my expenses, but that was just the way she was . . . always writing checks to people, promising to reimburse, asking them to just fill in the appropriate amounts. She trusted people: so generous . . .

"She always spoke about money, how much she needed, how much things cost, how important it was for women to have financial stability. She teased Heather often about the importance of marriage, instructed her to 'go after what she wants,' to make a list of eligible bachelors and have specific criteria." The friend paused. "Gary [had been] on Pam's [own] list of eligible wealthy men."

Heather never suspected her stepmother of involvement in her father's murder; Pam was so kind to her, took her in, gave her a gorgeous home to roam, a business to manage. Heather developed hives from food allergies and Pam took her to cleansing spas in California. She taught Heather about the virtues of juicing and eating organic foods. She provided Heather with naturopathic supplements.

"Sounds great," Ron said sarcastically. "Except that my brain just clicked in the middle of the night and I remembered Heather is vigorously pursuing her father's killer."

"Well, I'm definitely going to have to clean everything up," Pam assured him.

"In case it's escaped your notice," Ron fumed, "there *are* news articles on the Internet that name us."

*   *   *

While Ron agitated over the increasing threat of exposure, Detective Gamber continued to pursue leads in Gary's homicide, nonplussed by the fact that the case was already five years old. The passage of time often fueled investigations and offered fresh perspectives. Witnesses formed new alliances, divorced, severed partnerships, or unwittingly leaked information. Gamber explored new angles on old leads and returned again and again to people he had originally "cleared." Gary's ex-girlfriend Robin Gardner resurfaced in 2001 in splashy litigation against her former fiancé, real estate agent and mortgage broker John Kenneth Orms. But more than Orms's flamboyant personality—he peddled his services on television and radio—or his position as founder of Platinum Luxury Real Estate and Platinum Mortgage and Financial Services, Inc., Gamber was interested in his real estate business relationship with Gary.

Orms had a reputation as "fast and loose": he expedited mortgages by offering "drive-by" appraisals and papers a spouse could sign later. He had acquired New Frontier from Gary and, in 2000, sued the Westin La Paloma golf resort for failing to activate the company's corporate membership; he alleged in his claim that the bombing must have been "too embarassing" for the country club.* That same year, Orms also sued Robin Gardner for failing to return her diamond engagement ring. Court papers confirmed domestic disputes in their relationship and money bribes: Orms purportedly offered Robin $500 in cash and promised "more where that came from" if she would agree to have dinner with him.

But Gamber was more interested in Robin's revenge: in a stunning court victory, she sued Orms—and recovered $919,000—for slander and infliction of emotional distress. What unnerved Gamber was Robin's unfailing "coopera-

---

* The lawsuit was later dismissed with prejudice.

tive spirit" in Gary's homicide investigation. She was like a rash that mysteriously appeared and disappeared without explanation or treatment. And yet, Gamber had no evidence that implicated either Robin or Orms in Gary's murder. Instead, he had instinct, a nagging sensation that Gary knew his killer, that his bombing was no random act.

Still, less obvious targets emerged, "people who lurked in the shadows of Gary's high-rolling deals," individuals his colleague, Sergeant Michael O'Connor, called "hardworking people low-rent" like "a little old lady, who [gave Gary] her life's savings, $1,000, $2,000, $3,000" and got the feeling Gary ripped her off. Plenty of those scorned people demanded Gamber's attention: "What if one of them ha[d] a former Navy SEAL doing some handiwork or errands for them and all they heard [was] the complaining about Triano? What if they said one day, 'want me to take care of that for you?'" Sergeant O'Connor suggested.

"I'm having serious cash-flow problems again," Pam announced the next time Ron called. "The guy at Merrill Lynch keeps pointing out how much cash is leaving my accounts."

"Well, when you have no income . . ." Ron tried unsuccessfully to temper his sarcasm.

"Yeah, I know. There's just got to be some other, you know." She started her rant again and the words filled Ron's head like white noise.

"Look, I'm the one that's being victimized here with this method. There's two sides to this thing," Ron retorted.

"Well, I don't even, you know, I mean, that's not even . . . I mean, I'd rather just send you a note. I mean, I just can't go through this drill. The lady at the bank keeps giving me weird looks."

"Why you don't open another account is just silly. You need to fix far more than me. You need to fix your cash situation. By the way, did you accidentally or on purpose splash any perfume on the last thing you mailed? It was literally soaked in it."

"I don't think so," she waffled, sounding unconvincing.

"Something you just . . ."

"Nope."

"I thought maybe you did something just to be—"

"No."

"—cute. It must have been a coke addict, then, who poured it on there as the thing circulated through."

Silence crackled over the line.

"I can't handle this drill. My assets are so bad right now; I mean, for a while—"

"Well, your *assets*—" Ron interrupted.

"I can't handle it. I mean, I—"

"Stop," Ron shushed her. "You never let me finish my sentence. You get paralyzed . . . I need you to do one thing for me . . . and then you can fly off to South America to make yourself feel better."

"I'm not going to South America."

"Just do yourself a favor—do us all a favor. It'll take two minutes to get a blood test or whatever they do. Make sure it's not your menopause thing kicking in . . . [M]aybe they can prescribe something that will snap you back to normal."

"I'm just so stressed . . . ," Pam seethed.

"Can you go to a doctor?" Ron interrupted, sounding impatient.

"No . . . ," Pam replied.

"Maybe I can do something to ease the pressure off you."

"*Maybe* what you could do is total up your—"

"I don't need to total anything up. It's fucking half. Half . . . [I]f anybody should be stressed and pissed and crazy, it's me. I try to hold it together."

"Well, I have to. I don't know how else to cover my ass."

"Maybe you're out of balance. At least get fixed and maybe that will help you feel better."

"Well, anyway . . ."

"Every time I mention menopause, you change the subject." He heard a crackling sound as if Pam were eating potato chips.

"Maybe it would help clear me up for a year," she said thoughtfully.

"Why? What happens in a year?"

"I don't know. At least it could stop the drill."

"Pam . . ."

"I'm constantly hearing police sirens in my head."

"Pam . . ."

"Maybe you're right. Maybe it's just my hormones."

Was Pam instinctively sensing Detective Gamber closing in on her? He never tired of the chase, certain that the piles of paper in the evidence warehouse hid a blood trail. And while financial documents were less sexy than gore, they were sometimes far more revealing. Money, as any seasoned homicide detective understands, is never about money; it masks deeper psychological wounds. Distracted people lack self-control and are more likely to spend recklessly. Malls at Christmas are a prime example: bright colors, exotic scents, and soft music prompt even those on a budget to overindulge. A murderer, complacent with the passage of time, might come out of hiding. Stress, sleep deprivation, alcohol—all contribute to carelessness. Gamber looked for slipups, impulse purchases, cash-flow problems, even "cooling-off periods" during which lump sums remained untouched in bank accounts. Financial "freedom" always comes at a price. And Detective Gamber patiently waited for his killer's mad desire to become inflamed.

CHAPTER SIXTEEN:
OVEREXPOSURE

Pam alternated between sleeping and weeping. She didn't smile. She hardly ate. She smoked packs of cigarettes a day, pacing her office like a caged animal. Clumps of hair came out in her brush.

She confessed to Ron that she was "feeling weird things." She elaborated: "It's hard: hundreds of e-mails a day, and then all of a sudden nothing. Thirty a day and now nothing. One or two. I can't reach you. No signal. I'm freaking out. Sporadic e-mails, five-day delay."

Ron noted the quiver in her voice and interjected, "Did you send my stuff?"

"Something's up with the planets. They're not aligned now. It'll last for a while. I mean . . . I get really suicidal, totally suicidal. You know, it's like I just want . . . to get everything cleared up and move on somehow and . . . I can't handle the monthly drill. I can't handle it. I just can't . . . believe this happened. I'm telling you, I just start shaking. I mean, I'm, like, crazy. I wake up in the middle of the night and I'm, like, in a sweat. I mean, I'm not even . . . can't talk to anybody and all I can think of is the next drill, you know?"

"Did you see the doctor yet?"

"This is stress, it's not fucking menopause."

"How much is your first mortgage?"

"A million and fifty thousand."

"How much is the house worth?"

"Three million."

"That's fantastic. You're one of the lucky ones who still has equity in her home. You could borrow quite a bit . . ."

"Maybe I'll just sell it." She wasn't listening to him.

"You could do that too . . . ," he said, trying to be helpful.

"And move."

"You could do that, cut all connections, break away, get some walking-around money . . ."

"Maybe I'll just commit suicide." She hung up the phone.

You could do that too, Ron thought.

And when his regularly scheduled installment of $1,400 dollars failed to arrive from Basalt on time as planned, Ron sent Pam a reminder:

> Hello. Following is part of just one of a dozen of terrible articles that should be interesting reading for anyone knowing any of the parties involved. Notice your name pops up several times in the article . . . what a surprise. A copy of the article, four long and grisly pages will go out to people who should know about certain parties involved. I think it's only fair considering how one of the parties continues to fuck certain people. Each day beginning Tuesday morning one person in the valley will receive the full article until information* is received.

Pam sent him the money.

---

* Robert Sample, the state's forensic accountant, later testified at Ron's trial that "information" was a code name for "money."

* * *

Secretly each hoped the other would expire on his or her own *naturally* and end the mutual obligation, but year after year each lingered, like an old married couple, hating each other for what their lives had become and already living their worst fear: prison. Pam viewed Ron's cancer as an omen; it seemed fitting to Pam that he suffered from melanoma, a deep skin sickness that permeated his core. His death would free her. She could breathe again, still her trembling hands, shut off the dark voices in her head, the constant demands for money.

"I'm worried about your new 'houseguest,'" Ron said in a later phone call. "In the articles they list me as a 'bad guy.' She might know me. Make sure she doesn't know me," he warned.

"Heather knows nothing. She has her own computer," Pam insisted.

"They won't find me. They can't contact my friends. I made a conscious decision that there's nothing to be gained by talking to the police. I can't deal with the Aspen problem without attracting suspicion. I would *still* face humiliation if I'm put in the slammer overnight. I would shoot myself first. I'm not going to embarrass my kids. I never made the local papers. I have to stay low-key. It's bad enough that my son has to lie for me."

Dear Mom,
You can't imagine all there is to being a good traveler. Ireland isn't all rock fences and grass as I expected. It resembles a saucer, mountainous on its edges and fairly flat in the middle. In Limerick I looked up an acquaintance I'd met on the Atlantic crossing which resulted in an enjoyable stay. Home-cooked meals, a bed and the most unforgettable hospitality . . . [O]nward to Glasgow, Scotland."

By the spring of 2002, Ron, disguised as "Sailzone@
mutemail.com," wrote an e-mail to Paminaspen@aol.com:
"Got a note, looked like it was printed by a little kid. You
have my concern meter up to full red alert." Pam, writing
as "T.S.," warned him about a "really bad article": "They
say they know where you are. *I* am the sitting duck." It took
Pam weeks to scan the article and send it to Ron.

"Just remember," he warned her, "you came to *me* out of
your mind, going crazy, seeing bats in the night, and most
of it seemed to be related to going cash broke."

Pam responded the next morning: "828524517005. Ya-
hoo! Tomorrow."

By summer, Ron exploded with frustration:

Dear Anne Frank's Diary: I asked you if you got
[the] money. You told me the stars were not lined up
so you put off the transfer. Did you happen to notice
that the rest of the world including banks and their
billions of fund transfers just went along fine through
this bad star period? You told me the bad star shit
was over *last* Saturday.

Pam promised to send the money. It was delayed again.
She stalled on purpose, hoping for a plan. She'd had a
nightmare, Ron towering over her in a cloud of blue flame,
his voice gravelly and cold. Each time she ran, the roads
disappeared, dropped away, or circled back to the closed
door she would never walk through again. Her life was
gone, erased.

"Okay, Frank," Ron seethed. "You must relish jerking my
chain. If I don't know the information* it costs me money.
No urgency to answer my e-mail of *nine* days ago."

Silence.

---

* "Information" meant "amount."

You don't e-mail or call to say you missed the
event, or perhaps apologize or tell me when you
will do it. You never ever do this. You just wait
around for me to go crazy. Makes no sense to
me and I can't imagine you enjoy my reactions.
Getting me angry and crazy at getting fucked
around doesn't seem to be the smartest thing to
do. Can you think of *any* positive reasons to
screw around with me to continuously miss your
obligations? Maybe I'm missing something here
but I cannot for the life of me understand why
you do this to me and why you subject yourself
to the unpleasantness. It is particularly shitty of
you to be doing this when you know I'm not
well, a fact I will not forget. Maybe you can put
your thinking cap on and see if you can understand why I would be upset? Each time I have
to unschedule it costs me money.

"Why are you so *mean* to me?" Pam could feel his
negative, furious energy channeling through the e-mails.
"You have no idea what I'm going through over here, the
stress, the uncertainty . . ."

In truth, Ron knew exactly what Pam was experiencing
because he, too, lived with heightened awareness, waiting
perpetually for something to happen. He stored his belongings in a small suitcase, wore his laptop as an accessory,
and carried a pistol in his waistband. He borrowed identities, used his son's and daughter's names to promote a fake
consulting business. He had no driver's license, no job, no
home, and no human contact. He lived suspended. His
world existed in a one-mile radius bordered by 7-Elevens. At
times he felt like a windup toy, programmed to travel
from his apartment to the Federal Express box to the
7-Eleven to the bank. Like Pam, he worried about money,
about his "stuff."

"You have an unbecoming habit of whining about everything," he scolded. "Retrain yourself to count your blessings. What a horrible hassle it is to raise your kids. What a horrible burden it is that you've had to do it alone. What a martyr you are for doing it. You don't work [and] have a nice home and a life insurance policy blessing you out of nowhere. The Potrero partnership for some strange reason is drawn up as a trust with no provisions to dilute partners out who don't pay their share of the carrying costs (like you). You still own 20 percent of the property, totally amazing. Once again, Pamela comes out smelling like a rose."

"Please don't slam me. I have done the best I can. Why are you always so *mean*?"

"Help me to understand something, 'Anne Frank.' You claim you are broke, credit cards gone bad, credit lines maxed. What on earth are you *talking* about? Joy gave you a half-million-dollar interest-free loan. What do you mean you 'chose' to refuse acceptance of a 2nd mortgage because ten days ago there were astrology problems?"

Later, Ron/Sailzone@mutemail.com soothed, "Level out your head, start using Prozac again to calm yourself. You can't go on being so freaky. How's the 'houseguest'?"

"Lois is searching for information on her dad again," Pam replied.

"Delete bookmarked history setting. She will know you are filtering her information and will be pissed. Have her ask you directly for information about her father."

"Call me tomorrow."

"Okay, Frank, tomorrow it is, assuming I'm not bedridden, which means I'll be unable to carry on a conversation. If I don't have the information it costs me money, long-distance phone calls, scheduling with another person and so on. I am confounded as to why you never do this on time?"

"You act as if I'm doing something on purpose to torture you."

CHAPTER SEVENTEEN:
SKIPPING CHRISTMAS

In November 2002, just after Thanksgiving, when Pam still had not sent Ron's money, Ron wrote to "Anne Frank": "Working on a bulletproof way of getting this thing finished so neither of us has to handle anymore. Send 18 each time on time, please don't make this a magic horror show again."

"I've decided to skip the month of December," Pam wrote.

"Dear Pamela," Ron replied, resorting to her formal name, like a parent scolding his insolent child, "please forward my information." Two weeks later, Ron again demanded his money, referring to her by code name, "Anne Frank." "I tell you what to do with my stuff. You don't tell me. 18 on the 12th, 25 on the 26th. If you find this inconvenient we can do it all at once and get it over with. Your choice. Either way, please no BS, you can save yourself 'trauma' by opening up another account in an Aspen institution."

"Your e-mail leveled me. Let's total this up and do what I have wanted to get done for a long time."

"Send me a ten word e-mail. That shouldn't be too much trouble. Tell me you sent it."

"I'm not saying I can do it but I need to try. Remember,

I have two kids to support with no father. I need to *talk*: no more e-mails."

"E-mail me back, 'I WILL DO DECEMBER.' Five words. Until I get this, no phone call. There is only one person on this planet who saved your bacon and you now choose to hassle with him? This is not only immoral and unconscionable but also stupid. Sometimes people who are being screwed react in a negative way. You can definitely bank on that, my dear."

On the evening of December 10, 2002, just two weeks after Ron's warning, the two exchanged e-mails.

Pam wrote, "I'm ready to snap. I am having so many problems and I keep asking for a simple call . . . money money money demand demand demand. I'm getting sued for $584,372 . . . I am trying to raise two teenagers with no hope or savings for the future. You were the one who claimed to be looking out for my best interest, would never have me do anything illegal or uncomfortable, would always be there for me. You have problems. I am there, Kelly, I am there, etc., etc. I am asking for a fucking phone call."

Ron seethed at Pam's slip of the tongue; she had never before called him by any identifiable name. The faux pas was unforgivable. He had stressed discretion, the need for secrecy. Now it was "out there"—his middle name, "Kelly." If anyone ever found their e-mail exchanges, their relationship would be revealed. *Was that what she intended? To screw him? To throw him under the bus?*

Ron tempered his sarcasm: "Hello. You want a call or do you want me back helping you for free? Tell me the December payment is fine. I've sent you ten messages since your November 27th pronouncement. Even before you dropped this silly bomb on me I asked you to e-mail me the web marketing software you are using for your company. You said it was 'Mom' but I couldn't find it listed anywhere. You act like it's an important secret I might steal?"

Ron received no messages from Pam over the next two

days. As he paced his tiny space, he felt the blood drain from his face. *Now you've done it. Bravo! You've pissed off your lifeline. What are you going to do now?* his internal monologue thundered in his head. *Do something!*

He needed to make her care. The next morning he fired off a threatening e-mail: "Well, it seems you have decided to shoot yourself in the foot again. Since you are going down this path, others will go down theirs. In the next day or so a handful of people in Aspen will receive a twice-weekly bulletin on your past and a steady stream of published articles that I'm sure will make great party favors in the rash of Christmas parties. The articles include such great snippets as 'Pam will rip your heart out for a commission.' Boy, can I relate to that. Or how about this gem, 'Pam remains a loose end. She is not completely excluded as a suspect.' "

Two days later, on December 12, 2002, Pam, using her code name again, wrote, "I will be sending something today."

But by December 26, 2002, Ron had still received nothing.

"Please tell me you have done today what I asked."

Pam responded by insisting on an accounting. She needed to know how much money she'd sent him over the years. She was "getting tired of the charade," the constant "hounding." She needed "a break," especially if she had "overpaid" him. Ron could barely contain his rage. *An* accounting?

"Welcome to the Walgreens Phonecard Plus network. Please enter your card number now," the prepaid phone voice droned.

"Hello? Hello?" Ron heard a toilet flush.

"I'm in the bathroom. I'll use my cell phone," Pam whispered.

"I just want to make a few notes on this. What I'm going to send you is obviously as I mentioned before, very sensitive, and I want to make sure we have an agreement that you treat it carefully. It's kind of in code and when you get it . . . I'll just stay on it. Are you alone or . . ."

"Sort of." She ran the faucet to dull the sound of conversation and caught her reflection in the mirror. Her skin looked ashen, her gaze glassy like a corpse's. Startled, she flicked off the lights and stood in the darkness. *What's happened to me?* Familiar panic clogged her throat. *I can't do this. I can't do this.* She started to shake.

"Well, who else is with you in the bathroom?" Water roared in the background.

"Oh, okay. I thought you meant . . ." She slid onto the toilet.

"I'd prefer if you just got in a quiet place when you have time and copy down what you need to copy in your code and throw this away. Even though this is sort of in code . . ."

"Okay, so I'm sitting in the bathroom."

"Just listen. You don't have to talk much. I just wanted to have a meeting of the minds, get back on the level of privacy. I've set up my apartment so that if somebody broke in and rifled through all my stuff, no matter who they were, there's nothing that shows me having any contact with you since I left Aspen. You should function under the same rule, because, you know, you never know, somebody might accidentally do something or some nosy boyfriend that's accessed your office or bedroom . . . or wherever, you know. Those things that you said you were keeping, which sink us, let's put it that way—it's just not me or you, it's both of us. And there would be some awkward explaining to do. So if you for any reason need to keep dates or numbers or anything else, obviously just transpose it into codes someplace else and get rid of those things. I'll make this real quick. They're sort of . . ."

"You can call me in my office," she whispered.

"I can finish this . . . real quick. The other thing is that those things generally unless you're a . . ."

"Can you fax right now?"

"Yeah."

"I'm going to go stand over it, okay?" Pam shut off the water. She cradled the phone to her ear and listened for movement outside the door.

"Okay."

"I'm going to hang up now," she said.

"I'll call you back. I'll call you right back."

She cracked open the bathroom door and peered into the empty hallway. Sun streamed through the skylights like dirty patches of heat. She felt like a thief in her own home. The phone in her office shrilled. With shaking hands she picked up the receiver.

"Are you still standing there?" Ron asked.

"Yeah." Her voice shook. She glanced over her shoulder. *Where were her children?*

"How's the weather?" Her heart raced as her fax machine beeped: ready.

"Beautiful. Gorgeous." Ron waited a few minutes. "Did it go through?"

"How many pages is this?"

"Two. If you just want to grab them and walk outside the building, I'll tell you what the . . . it's real simple, unless you're in a hurry. I could talk to you another time."

"That might be a good idea." Pam hung up the phone. She spotted her daughter in the street.

Ron called back two minutes later with the prepaid card. Pam stood at the window with fax in hand and listened to him describe his coded number system for payments generated and received. He recounted in laborious detail his spreadsheet of monies paid and months received throughout the years, but all Pam heard was the balance remaining. It never occurred to her to challenge his numbers or his accounting methods.

"Did you ever give me credit for that one that got lost?" she interjected.

"Yeah, that's in that first 25. The dots are the same as a comma. So 25.0 is really $25,000 and 2.0 is $2,000. I tried to make it not look like numbers, but they are." He spoke too slowly, deliberately, as if she were a child with hearing issues.

"So what you're saying is I'm only halfway there?"

"Yeah, a little over."

"Shit."

"Well, you know, the thing is, it makes sense when you look at the, you know, the last two years, really. It slowed down and . . ."

"Well, we need to come up with an alternate plan here. I know you're working on that."

"Yeah."

"'Cause that's frightening. I could end up with no money."

CHAPTER EIGHTEEN:
BAD ENERGY

By May 2004, Ron had not yet devised an alternative plan for recouping his share of the profits. He had bigger problems. His continuing cancer treatments necessarily risked exposure. He would have to provide his name to any area hospital. He would unwittingly generate a paper trail. If he survived the radiation, he might not survive his imminent capture. Illness required a deviation from the plan.

He struggled with how to tell Pam:

> I have three melanoma skin growths, one on calf, chest, back, doctor is going bonkers. If goes beyond 'Clark Level II or III' it will be in my bloodstream and it's all over. The procedure is the pits; it's going to cost $7000 overnight hospital, 4-5 thousand and one baseball sized tumor located on the outer wall of the intestine, full blown operation has to be done in hospital with surgeons, nurses, drugs. They want me to start chemo and I won't do that. They think it's related to non-Hodgkin's problems. I was quoted $42,000 without health insurance, because I can't afford to show up in the national database and expose myself I have

arranged to get all the above done in Mexico.
This includes two to three days in the hospital.
I'm getting to drive over the border. A friend
has agreed to fly me down in his private plane
to Guadalajara. The cost will only be $12,000
plus travel. Canada is out of the question: even
if I could acquire an expensive phony ID none
of what I have would allow emergency treatment. I need to do this yesterday. Melanoma
will simply kill me. I need 13 of my stuff. You
are not the suffering victim in this deal. You
have the stuff and I don't. I need you. You have
something of mine that I need to save my life. I
won't be doing chemo. I'll just use my version
of chemo, a Glock 9mm.

Nine days later Pam finally responded to Ron's devastating news: "I am mortified. I know I can't do this from
the bank without flags. I don't know how to handle this."

Then, after she had a moment to calm down, she wrote,
"I need to know that interest is not being calculated into
this. You can imagine my attorneys' bills as well as the
$500,000 note that's coming due."

"Since my life is at stake and the doctor says I have to
quit stalling and get immediate surgery, split up the payments into two installments—$5500 today and $3500
tomorrow."

A week later, Pam, writing as Anne Frank, counseled
Ron about "Poison Ivy," hoping he could decipher the sub-
stance of her e-mail despite the misleading title.

"It was meant to be a diversion," she explained later.
"So no one knows what we're really discussing."

I hope you can honor your commitment as
originally made for both our sakes. You want
an end to this as do I. I have had major losses,

expenses, you can't unilaterally change something to your benefit. This has been an ongoing
thing for a long time. I want the end.

She attached a "Self Care/First Aid instruction for Poison
Ivy" to the e-mail for added authenticity. Several more
e-mails followed with the same Poison Ivy instructions.

Ron was incredulous.

"Are you actually suggesting that my cancer was something I planned for my benefit?"

Pam shared her nightmares with Ron. She saw him as a
spider, his spindly legs and large torso caught in sticky silk.
Fat black flies gathered on his head and, in an ironic twist
of fate, sucked the life out of him.

"You embody the disease," she interpreted. "Your own
energy is eating you alive . . . I have a guy who works with
energy over the phone: he can clear up your negative spells.
He doesn't even have to know your history, name, or details. He is also effective in clearing out past karma."

But Ron wasn't interested in karmic help. He wanted
his money.

"Did you send what I asked for?" he fired back.

"Did you read what I wrote?" she pleaded.

"Yeah, yeah, I'm a spider."

"A *cancer*," she clarified.

No money arrived. Ron hired his taxi driver anyway, no
longer able to stand the quiet. He clutched his laptop to his
chest, felt his gun press into his waist, and focused on the
familiar blocks he traveled twice a month. The same neon
sign flashed at him with its missing letter; the same woman
with the blue sneakers and pink blouse smoked on the corner,
waiting for a different ending. He watched people hustling
along in their busy lives, balancing coffee in one hand, a
cell in the other, big bags slung across their chests, not at all
present, distracted by lists they'd created, things they had

to accomplish by nightfall or suffer overwhelming self-disappointment.

Routine restored order to Ron's life: his weekly appointments with the chiropractor, regular visits to the dentist—all reminded him he was still human. Starved for conversation, he engaged the taxi driver in inane banter about the Miami heat and regaled him with details about his latest invented personality. He pretended for a moment that he didn't inhabit a roach-infested apartment in the city's poorest section, didn't migrate between 7-Eleven stores, hoping to convert his cash to money orders or rent a hotel room at the Beach Comber when his paranoia and boredom replaced reason. He had created an insular world for his own protection, spun a web so thick he poisoned every human contact. He had no choice. He lived a kind of paralysis. Still, he felt no remorse, no tug of regret for the world he had created.

"Where to this time?" the driver interrupted his thoughts.

Ron stared at the blinking 7-Eleven sign and shook his head. "Just take me home."

The next day Pam wrote, without apology or explanation for the delayed funds, "We have energetic clean up to do—pronto, as soon as you are safe and strong." He had lost her to her world of healing. Her e-mails floated in white space as if she had drifted away already, and for the first time in his life he felt vulnerable.

"Did you send the stuff?" he managed, though he already knew the answer.

"You need to make an appointment with the energy healer—you have lots to clear and heal."

But of course Ron never would take Pam's advice. He already *had* a cure for his ailments: money. His plan had seemed so simple at first, so organized and precise. If only Pam had followed the rules. Ron could not have imagined so many years later that he would still be living undercover, still waiting for his share, still reliant on Pam. Part of him considered that she enjoyed the control. Maybe they both did. Neither could move, breathe, or live without the other's knowledge or counsel. Unwittingly, they had each become both warden and prisoner, each serving his own life sentence.

PART II

CHAPTER NINETEEN:
THE KILLER'S IN THE BOX

By the spring of 2005, Detective James Gamber had pieces of a jigsaw puzzle and subtle inconsistencies that bothered the margins of his conscience, investigative leads that dead-ended; and yet, instinctively he knew his victim's killer was hiding in plain sight. Boxes were stacked against his cubicle like a makeshift wall. Papers fluttered in the fan's breeze. Facts swirled in the detective's head: bomb, money, players. The movable parts had led to distraction and indecision. Somehow he had missed his target. He needed to backtrack. Prey, initially startled by footsteps in the woods, always returns to the meadow, when the animal feels safe, alone. Exposed in the stillness, the hunter picks up its scent again.

The detective returned to his widow, a socialite who knew the music but not the dance, clean by most accounts, but cold. Pam had no criminal history. She thrived in Aspen on Gary's life insurance proceeds. Closed up and closed in, her statements to Gamber just days following the bombing seemed rehearsed and controlled. The detective had initially attributed Pam's brittle veneer to shock. But now he wondered if it hadn't been something else: fear? But what did Pam hide? She had reported her employee for fraud and then refused to cooperate in Detective Crowley's

investigation. She had lied about her romantic entanglement
with Ron. And yet, the contents of Ron's van revealed that
the two had shared an intimate relationship, dreams and
visions of a future together. But both were divorced and
single. Why insist on discretion? Ron, according to Pam's
nannies, knew Pam was involved with other men. They
said that Ron stalked her, left her threatening messages on
her home answering machine, and appeared unannounced
and uninvited on her dates. Why hadn't Pam reported
him? Why had she kept these details from even her closest
girlfriend, Joy Bancroft?

The godmother of Pam's children, the woman who had
assumed responsibility for Pam's life insurance premium—
the one person in Pam's life who would have done anything to help—knew nothing about an intimate relationship
between Pam and Ron and, after the spring of 1996, never
heard Pam mention Ron's name again. Not even when Pam's
money disappeared from her bank account. Did Pam
worry that her disclosure might invite scrutiny and risk her
one financial rope? But what did Pam fear Joy might dis-
cover, and why would she care if her girlfriend knew the
truth about her sexual relationship?

Pam's *nannies* knew about Ron—knew he helped her
with her business affairs, knew sometimes he stayed the
night, knew Pam paid him for his services. They knew
because Pam dismissed them as subservient and insignificant. She entrusted them with her children, her home, her
personal and financial affairs; they blended into the fabric
of her life, threaded the quilt together, and quietly watched
as the edges unraveled.

Pam, by all accounts, dated only wealthy men, *useful*
men, men who could finance her lifestyle. Love never fac-
tored into the equation. She didn't *need* affection; she
needed money. Gamber stretched, reached for his empty
coffee mug. He glanced at his watch: it was nearly midnight. He had been at this for hours, poring through his

notes, drawn to Pam's case like it was an addiction. She had benefited from Gary's death. She was the *only* one whose lifestyle improved. She had motive. He knew that. He knew it after his first interview with Pam in November 1996. But he hadn't put the pieces together yet: the lies, the deliberate alibi, the masterful distractions.

He padded to the snack room, shoved a dollar bill into a vending machine, and retrieved his bag of M &M's. Pam, the single struggling mother of two young children, living alone in Aspen, removed from the grisly murder, blamed everyone but herself for her "situation." She delegated her affairs to other people: Joy handled her life insurance premiums, Ron supervised her business and financial affairs, nannies assumed responsibility for her children, various rich men entered as lead roles and exited as extras after she drained their resources. The bomb itself had left federal agents steeped in fragments, wasting precious time hunting down Radio Shacks and hobby stores for elusive receipts connecting Ron—or Pam—to the purchase . . . receipts they never found.

Gary, too, posed a distraction, offering a trail of potential suspects that needed to be eliminated. His killer had law enforcement chasing their tails. *That's what he wants.* The detective had spent years mired in leads that led nowhere, ignoring the one person who blinded him the most: Pam. But sometimes the most obvious suspects are rejected *because* they're too simple. Their *cover* is their simplicity. He thought of serial killers: some of the most famous— Dennis Rader, Gary Ridgeway—had families, respectable careers, children. They thrived in the community and masked their darkness in the ordinary. They deflected scrutiny because of how they conducted their lives. Gamber had pushed Pam to the background, fearful that his first instinct might foreclose other possible killers. But he realized now that her very lifestyle might have provided the perfect alibi.

Beautiful-looking people like Pam thrived on appearances and perceptions; they conducted their lives like a shell game. Pam, consistent with that theory, would have suppressed or buried any *feelings*. Her whole life was illusion and *de*lusion. She would never have loved *anyone* unless he gave her something she needed. And what she needed, as far as Gamber could tell, was money, and she had already allegedly stolen Ron's share. Yet, she sent him love notes; she would not have pursued a "bottom-feeder" unless he had something she needed. Ron's van contained a map of Tucson, Pam's dissolution papers, and a sawed-off shotgun—*circumstantial evidence that raised more questions than answers.*

Gamber shoveled the chocolate candies into his mouth and chewed thoughtfully. He caught his reflection in the vending machine glass: he looked ghostly pale, dragged down, and acutely alone. *What are you still doing here?* Nine years had passed without closure. Occasionally he had received a tip and pursued it, but mostly he combed through the files again, propelled by raw instinct. Nothing placed Ron at the Westin La Paloma golf resort on November 1, 1996. According to agents from the ATF, the bomb that killed Gary was detonated just a few feet away from the car. The killer *had* to have been present, had to have known *how* to release the switch that ignited the bomb.

Ron had all but disappeared. And what Gamber knew of Ron was what Ron chose to reveal. The van flashed in the detective's mind and he thought he heard Ron's cackle. Ron believed he was in complete control. He had left behind a treasure trove of evidence, and the detective *still* had nothing. Ron was playing him—playing all of them.

Gamber needed to find him. The detective crumpled the M&M's bag and tossed it in the trash. Ron may have gone underground, but even a mole needed air. The detective had the perfect blood meal to coax him out of hiding: national exposure. *America's Most Wanted* had just featured the ATF's infiltration of the Hells Angels motorcycle gang.* Three members accused of beheading a female groupie had escaped police detection. John Walsh, the show's host, flashed the killers' head shots and implored the American public to "bring them to justice." *Someone* had seen Ron Young in the past nine years. *Someone* would help the detective catch him.

Gamber dialed his longtime friend, Special Agent Jay Dobyns of the ATF, the lead undercover operative in the Hells Angels case.

"I need your connections," he said.

Their paths had crossed early in their law enforcement careers when Dobyns, fresh from the academy, caught a bullet in his chest during an ATF raid. Gamber, a rookie sheriff's deputy and first responder, accompanied Dobyns to the hospital. Thereafter they formed a close friendship, shared a similar "dark horse" reputation, and thought nothing of calling in a favor.

A flurry of activity followed as the producers of the show arranged to air the case in less than fifteen hours. Special Agent Tom Mangan with the ATF contacted Gamber for a case synopsis and relevant photographs. Gamber confirmed with Detective Crowley that Ron still had an outstanding Colorado felony fraud warrant and secured a known driver's license photograph of his suspect from the Texas Department of Public Safety. On February 1, 2005, producers of the show traveled to Aspen to conduct interviews. Among those selected were former victims defrauded by Ron. They also contacted Heather, who informed Pam of the show. Per Gamber's instructions, Heather emphasized to her stepmother that police were focusing on Ron.

Prior to the show airing, Sergeant Keith St. John placed

---

*   The story is featured in *Running with the Devil: The True Story of the ATF's Infiltration of the Hells Angels* by Kerrie Droban.

a call to Pam's cell phone. He left a message and requested that she return his call. She never did. Anticipating that the *America's Most Wanted* broadcast might spark dialogue between Pam and Ron, Gamber requested that the Tucson office of the Federal Bureau of Investigation place traces on Pam's four telephone numbers in Aspen. He hoped the records might reveal Ron's location, solidifying their suspected relationship and any connection the two had to Gary's murder.

Then Gamber boarded a flight to Bethesda, Maryland, to be at the studios when the show aired on November 19, 2005.

Pam processed Heather's warning by meditating. She had devoted the past year to the study of Vedic astrology, an ancient Indian philosophy that attempted to dispel the darkness of illusion and underscore the purpose of the soul's present and the consequences of karma. In its purest form, the Vedas forecast human behavior and projected events. Pam subscribed to the old Indian proverb, "If you want to get rid of a snake, get rid of it when it is really small." She took the warning literally when she had minor surgery on her face to remove a cyst. The procedure left a faint scar that trailed down her cheek. She detested imperfection. Her face was a pretty mask, her beauty raw power. She couldn't afford to lose her only asset.

In the winter of 2005, Pam arranged healing sessions with an Indian priest, Pandu Dubay. She traveled to temples in India, hoping to scrape off the mark through prayer and Yagyas. She paid healers $1,200 a day to remove the scar. But in the harsh morning sun her skin still looked discolored.

"It isn't working," she complained to her friend as she rubbed her cheek raw. She found it symbolic, like a scarlett letter.

"There's no guarantee. It's a process," her friend pointed out.

Pam had no patience for *process*. She paid another $81,000 to Pandu Dubay to heal her.

"It'll fade in time," her friend assured her. "You could cover it up with foundation. No one will ever see it."

Pam studied her reflection in the bathroom mirror. *I have lots of scars nobody sees.* She applied magenta lipstick, cream foundation. When she smiled, her skin cracked like chipped paint. She looked . . . damaged.

Pam's home, too, remained in disrepair. Three remodels later, scaffolding and debris still cluttered the foundation. Elevated ceilings left the rooms airy and empty. The wind howled against the skylights. Pam shuffled through the halls, acutely aware she filled too much space. Her ski lift rusted. And the gondola outside swung violently in the snowdrifts.

If she could just fix her cash-flow problem, sell Potrero, find a man . . .

But the past year had proven futile. She had flown often to Chicago to be with "her Tom," a man she hoped would rescue her from financial ruin. And indeed, he invested $1.7 million in her home renovations. Secretly, Pam shopped for engagement rings at Meridian Jewelers in Aspen, though Tom had yet to propose. She warned the employees who recognized her to pretend she was never there.

"He probably would have married her," an acquaintance of Pam's disclosed. "Except that Tom's family detested Pam." She accused them of drugging her fiancé with prescription medications, of having her followed by a private investigator, and, in the end, of reducing "her Tom" to a state of dementia. Pam visited him in the hospital. He drooled at her, frighteningly pale, the skin on his hands nearly translucent, the veins beneath looking like thick blue ropes. When Tom no longer recognized Pam, their engagement fizzled and Pam soothed her loss with alcohol.

She listened as Detective Keith St. John's voice filtered through her living room. She closed her eyes and prayed.

When the producers of *America's Most Wanted* attempted to contact Ron's children—his daughter, Kelly, and his son, Brady—for information, Ron's ex-wife, Linda, had had enough. She threatened to "tell Kelly ALL things about her daddy" if he did not come clean. Ron begged her not to, whining that he had "been trying to deal with his personal shitty problem" for years without impacting his children. He had remained "off the radar screen," never informing his parents where he lived, never providing a telephone number, using a "completely untraceable" e-mail address. He lamented that he had already "compromised his security" by disclosing his warrant to Brady in 1998.

He disconnected the 800 number he had given to his children so they could reach him without knowing his location. He hadn't wanted to involve his ex-wife in his ruse, but without her cooperation he might never have a relationship with his children. Still, he was careful to disclose only his fraud warrant to Linda. The less she knew of his other activities, the more protected his children would be and the safer it would be for him.

"I will not call them anymore," he promised Linda over the telephone. "Please destroy anything you have at your office, home, purse, or computer with my address, FedEx account number, or anything else about me. Forget me. Erase me. I don't exist. I'm not sure I ever did."

He told her his whole charade had made him sick for years and it "haunted him" that Brady knew the truth. Still, he insisted "I will not go to jail." Nonetheless, he liked to be prepared. He drafted a will of sorts for Brady "just in case" his plans changed dramatically or he was suddenly "run over by a truck" or "struck by a comet." He warned Brady to keep the document "very private (like burn it when you no longer need it) or staple it to your forehead."

He instructed Brady to take his cash, "whatever I have [stashed] in the reefer . . . in the freezer [and my] two bank accounts." He enclosed unsigned checks for Brady's use and offered a crash course on forgery techniques. Ron included scribbled signatures he'd replicated of Brady's with a note: "Obviously these are not yours but the bank keeps cashing them. I started signing this way out of laziness." He produced several different signatures and disclosed that he had recently opened an account and forged his daughter's "real" signature. "Do you see how easy this is?" He scribbled his duplication.

Ron explained there might be "worst-case scenarios," like a car wreck or choking from a slab of ribs or a hospital visit, that left him incapacitated. Note, he wrote: "If I am conscious I will be feigning amnesia, especially when it comes to my exact name, SS# and birthdate. If you decide to visit, tell them you are a friend, or my maid or my acupuncturist." Then, as an afterthought, he wrote, "If I'm dead, no problem." He left nothing to chance; his children needed him.

"What to do," he wrote in boldface in the document, and provided a list of options. Choice number one: "Call your mom . . . she works in a law firm that services mostly dead people." Two: "Call the morgue." Three: "Ask for a cremation, maybe they'll give you a discount if you allow them to use a pitchfork." His possessions might pose a problem. He counseled Brady to "leave the apartment forever and never look back." He cautioned that there was "nothing to gain from talking to the landlord," but if he did, Ron had instructions for Brady to avoid any "hassles." He provided another list: "a. If I'm dead don't tell him, he may ask for rent; b. if he asks where I am, tell him I'm in the Virgin Islands on a sailboat; c. I'm probably being overly cautious."

But loose ends played on Ron's nerves. With regard to Kelly, he clarified what he believed to be "the central issue in case the cops question her." Ron wrote in a side note the looming question: "Did you know there was a warrant out of Colorado for your dad? The answer has to be no." He covered all grounds, offering his children suggestions on what to do if the authorities asked them, "Why was the car in your name?" "Why did you cash checks after your dad died, or was incapacitated?" The best answer: "I don't know." Ron closed with a kind of apology:

> I'm making this expansive because I want to make sure you know the tools you have if you get hassled. You are completely clean on this, and the bank is stuck—not my intention, by the way, just want to cover all bases if I become incapacitated.

Satisfied that he had taken care of his children's needs, Ron left his hotel lobby at exactly 10:00 in the morning for his regularly scheduled chiropractor appointment. He tapped on the window of his rented taxicab and slid into the cushioned seat. He held his briefcase containing his computer on his lap. The cool butt of his .38 pressed into his side. He wore khaki Bermuda shorts and a loud Hawaiian shirt.

When he arrived at the office, the receptionist greeted him by name, smiled politely, and offered him coffee. Light jazz filtered through the speakers. An ordinary day, a routine he appreciated. Pain reminded him he was still human. And though Ron's bill was delinquent, his chiropractor continued to schedule his appointments. Ron made excuses: delayed insurance, relocation, lost mail, expired credit card. He marveled at his doctor's foolishness—any savvy businessman would have canceled further visits— but Ron's chiropractor persisted in making weekly adjustments not only to Ron's back but to Ron's self-described "difficult circumstances."

Ordinarily Ron looked forward to his appointment, but

this day he sensed a disturbance in the air: his chiropractor appeared more anxious than usual, glancing regularly at his watch, distracted by the sound of the door opening and the little chime sounding. After his session ended Ron tucked his computer under his arm, nodded good-bye to the receptionist and walked outside into bright sunlight.

But before he could put on his mirrored glasses, loud voices barked around him. A wide hand shoved him to the pavement. Sharp pain ripped into his knee. Someone with a name tag that read "Abby Tiger" wrestled his arms behind his back. Badges flashed at him. Cameras winked from the bushes. He heard the click of automatic weapons near his temple. Panic clogged his throat. And as he lay still on the pavement, he felt the butt of his gun crease his belly. He had always prepared for his unlikely capture, carried his secrets on his person, used fake identities, cash. He had been so careful. *Where had he messed up?*

Only later would Ron learn that his own chiropractor had betrayed him, notifying the authorities of his next appointment and ensuring Ron's arrest.

CHAPTER TWENTY:
THE CAPTURE

*"This is a tricky period in which it becomes
necessary to focus on reality."*
—Ron Young's horoscope

**November 21, 2005
Broward County Sheriff's Office,
Fort Lauderdale, Florida**

Ron towered over his captors, special agents from the Bureau of Alcohol, Tobacco, Firearms and Explosives, as he was processed through booking in the Broward County jail. Special Agent Hugh O'Connor, still dressed in his black raid T-shirt and bulletproof vest, emptied Ron's pockets of petty cash and loose coins.

He glanced up at his giant fugitive. "No ID?"

"No," Ron stuttered, and smiled weakly. "I never could get one."

"How about a Social Security number?" The agent tossed the money into a property envelope. It didn't matter what answer Ron gave him: the result was the same. Ron was like a machine powering down, his battery juice depleting slowly.

"I don't know."

"You don't know the number, or you don't have one?" O'Connor motioned for Ron to sit. The room was small, intimate, and smelled of antiseptic. O'Connor sat across from him, produced a pad of paper, and smiled kindly, hoping to disarm him. Ron relaxed, chuckled unexpectedly, and condescended to O'Connor,

"I'm . . . a . . . a c-consultant."

"Of course." The agent nodded, mindful not to alienate his subject. He appealed to Ron's sense of outrage at being handcuffed and "assaulted" like a common criminal, an "overreaction" to his "simple situation."

Ron cleared his throat. "I'm dying."

"It's a little warm in here," O'Connor agreed. He motioned for his partner, Special Agent Richard Coes, to bring them each a bottle of water. Ron looked a little startled, apparently unused to respectful treatment.

"You go by the name 'Kelly,' right?" O'Connor asked. Coes returned, handed him a cold bottle of water. "That's your daughter's name, isn't it? Looks like you changed your date of birth."

"I couldn't get a driver's license."

"You used your son's name on business cards?" O'Connor added, moving to adjust Ron's handcuffs.

"This won't hurt, will it? I have unusually big wrists. The ankle shackles are okay . . . my feet are so big, I couldn't get them off anyway." He winked at the agent.

Coes glanced at his partner and raised his eyebrows. "You *do* understand you've been arrested, right?" he asked.

"Yeah, for a warrant out of Aspen, for a forgery from 1996, I think. Bizarre, huh?" Ron shook his head and picked at a thread on his shirt.

"Bizarre," O'Connor said.

"It was a relatively minor deal to be put in this federal . . . place, but—"

"Right," O'Connor cut him off. "You ever had your rights read to you before?"

"I've watched enough TV," Ron laughed.

"They usually get it wrong on TV," O'Connor said, and read the warnings verbatim.

A dam broke and a virtual flood of information rushed forth as Ron fixated on his warrant and his reasons for fleeing. "I was not very fluctual [sic] with cash, got screwed on an international deal," he hastened to explain. He had a problem with the Aspen district attorney and the police department: they were vigilant with criminals—*which he was not,* he assured O'Connor, and would not be treated so commonly. He embellished his lie and added that "a guy from the ATF," apparently impressed with Ron's cooperative spirit, negotiated a deal with Ron's lawyer, a "prearranged white-collar" thing that would allow him to fly "undetected on a Learjet into Aspen" and avoid having to be "booked, photographed, or fingerprinted." In short, he could surrender "without all the humiliation." He couldn't believe the district attorney had rejected the idea, told him in so many words to "shove it." Ron shook his head, insisting that he became a fugitive "mainly for his kids." "I couldn't have my son see me get arrested . . . I couldn't do that. I've watched TV. I know what happens . . . bad decision, good decision, whatever, obviously not a completely normal decision."

O'Connor absorbed Ron's fantastically long-winded explanation without comment. He subscribed to the less-is-more theory of interrogation: psychological Ping-Pong that required short, pointed questions and rapid, blunt answers. Action, reaction. But Ron had just led the agent down a hall of funhouse mirrors, each image more distorted than the last.

"Let's start with preliminaries," O'Connor said, redirecting Ron's focus.

Ron listed his credits, boasting to the agents that he once attained the rank of Eagle Scout; Norman Schwarzkopf had "embroidered" his shotgun; he had owned three successful restaurants in the Bahamas, Jamaica, and Rome as well as businesses in Germany and Italy; and, in between, he worked as a yacht broker. He "raced boats all over the world," he insisted, before settling down to become "one of those bums." O'Connor quietly processed Ron's verbal vomit, mentally checking off the contradictions: Ron had no passport, no driver's license, no identity, and apparently no income for at least the last ten years. Before that, Ron drifted as a "ski bum" and held "odd jobs" in what he dismissed as a "renowned drug hub."

O'Connor pulled the rope and the noose tightened around Ron's neck. His suspect hardly needed prompts. He figured the "embroidered" reference was probably a slip—nerves—and that he meant to say "engraved." Still, he seriously doubted Schwarzkopf personalized Ron's shotgun. Ron rambled, filling the pauses with fantastic anecdotes, convinced of his own charm and wit. He regarded the whole interview/booking process thing as a necessary formality; he assured O'Connor that there would be no repercussions, he wouldn't press charges. He fully expected to be released soon and any "misunderstanding" would be rectified. Meanwhile, he expounded on the whole "drug smuggler" ordeal and insisted he wasn't one, even though his restaurants were "fairly high-profile" and he became an inadvertent target for U.S. Customs agents, a victim of the random sweeps under "Nixon and the whole Operation Intercept" thing.

"Anybody who owned his own plane was a suspect. It's comical going to Aspen . . . you know it's such a hub."

"The drugs, sure." At the risk of alienating his suspect, O'Connor played along, marveling at Ron's expansive and generous detail in areas that had absolutely no relevance to his case.

"Big guys."

"Sure. So, how did you get to Florida?" A large fan clicked above them, slicing bladed shadows on the ceiling.

"I needed to get back to the ocean," Ron laughed. "Aspen was full of Donald Trump types and I had a hard time putting deals together. I helped buy and sell some businesses, but it was all chump change."

Agent Coes, who had been quietly taking notes, asked

about the detour to California. Why had Ron parked his rental van down the street from his parents' home?

"I thought I'd be a nice guy."

O'Connor glanced at his watch. He and his partner had been in the boxing ring, circling their opponent for at least an hour, and neither had initiated any solid punch yet.

Coes swung: "Did you see yourself on *America's Most Wanted*?"

Ron smiled slightly as if the whole thing were incredible. His son had "texted" him about the show, mentioning that authorities considered Ron a "suspect in a bombing or some nonsense." He insisted to the agents that "everybody" he knew in Aspen "was just clear as a bell" that Colombians had been involved. They were, after all, a "pretty violent group" who seduced the "Aspen guys" into their cocaine business. Ron lowered his voice, tapped his index finger forcefully on the table, and whispered confidentially, "I know nothing about it whatsoever."

O'Connor sighed. "So I've got to ask you: What's with the gun?"

"My dad was a cop." Ron shrugged, as if that explained all, but he could not resist elaborating. "I know things about shotguns. I went to shows . . . I carried it around in a satchel . . . for protection . . . [S]omeone once pointed a gun at me."

O'Connor pretended to understand completely. "This is Florida: time to get a gun." The state had its "dangerous element." He put Ron at ease; told him he would have hauled around a shotgun, too; assured him it was perfectly natural to chop off the barrel: How *else* could he walk around and not telegraph to the whole world that he carried a concealed weapon?

"There're all kinds of weird people in Florida." Ron nodded, liking the rapport he had established. "Homeless people walking around, you know—*criminals*."

The thought of violence apparently triggered an unpleasant "flashback" for Ron, who now lived in a "cheap, crappy two-bedroom" apartment in a dirty part of town. He reminded the agents that he hadn't always lived in squalor. He'd been rich once, owned nightclubs and bakeries in the Bahamas.

"Let's stay on the gun," O'Connor said, reeling him back in.

"You know, I just got a hair up my butt one day . . . I wasn't, like, being threatened on a daily basis . . . all the rounds that have ever been shot . . . you know they're not hollow-points."

That detail was new. Had he meant to let it slip that he had actually fired the weapon?

"Yeah, in some industrial place . . . ," Ron said, recovering. He cleared his throat, leaned back in his chair, and suddenly shut down.

"So we're not going to find any dead bodies lying around, are we?" Coes tossed out, unsure what response he would receive.

"Well . . . I . . ." Ron grabbed his water bottle, took a sip, and wiped his mouth with the back of his hand. His eyes watered. The whir of the fan distracted him momentarily and he glanced at the ceiling. Despite the slight breeze, he looked wilted. O'Connor registered the cracks in Ron's calm veneer.

He played on Ron's vulnerability: "Tell me about the gun that was found in the van."

"The shotguns?" *There was more than one?*

"The sawed-off one in the velvet case." O'Connor braced for the invariably long explanation.

Ron smiled slightly, enjoying the spotlight. He elaborated about his days in Italy when he worked in the factory business. He hadn't known anything about shotguns at the time, but he arranged to meet with a distributor in Milan.

He underscored that he "always flew first-class" because he was just "too tall for coach," and once at the factory he had "wined and dined" his prospects in the "lake country."

O'Connor didn't interrupt. He just gave Ron a longer rope. He didn't think it important to point out to Ron that Milan was located nowhere near a lake. He scribbled the details, noted the inconsistencies, unsure what information had relevance, what kernel Ron might reveal about his character, his alibi, or his fantastic past.

Ron shook his head. "Unbelievable."

"Yes," O'Connor agreed.

"That's the way we did business. Heavy socializing, breaking bread, and all that kind of crap."

"Right."

"You were telling us about the gun," Coes prompted, his amusement mixed with fatigue.

Ron began again as if his tape had paused in the middle and someone had pressed "Play." "So I bought two barrel sets, with adjustable chokes, just all the fancy, needless toys, and then it came in this velvet beautiful case with my name stamped on the stock."

O'Connor put down his pen. Was the man playing him for a fool, or did Ron really believe his own tales?

Ron's eyes widened, his voice agitated, and he spoke quickly, words tumbling out of his mouth without stuttering.

"I had [a gunsmith] chop it down. You hate to do that, because it's from Italy, but . . . I told him to shorten it up. I didn't know the rules about sawed-off shotguns, which is stupid for a . . . what do you call it?"

"Breaking action," O'Connor said dryly.

"See, I knew you guys would know what I'm talking about," Ron chuckled. He sat forward, clasped his hands together, and said cheerfully, "Maybe you guys can help me out with this. Does the law say it has to be twenty-one or twenty-six inches? I can never remember."

Coes cleared his throat. Ron reminded him of an underdeveloped photograph: white hair, pale face, transluscent skin against white, white walls. His dark eyes, which stood out like two bullet holes, unsettled him.

"Eighteen inches" he supplied.

"But the overall length . . ."

"Is twenty-six."

"Anything less is illegal?"

"Right."

Somehow Ron had steered them off course again. Each question the agents posed skimmed the surface and left ripples of answers. Not one of their stones sank to the bottom. In the end, they had learned nothing about Ron except that he lived in a world he had created, a world he controlled, a world he believed.

"My story's remarkable," Ron said, as if echoing their thoughts. "Something to put in a novel. No one would ever believe it. It's so phenomenal, fantastic, this saga that I lived through . . . I mean, it's just ridiculous . . . I was moving to Rome . . . they had this villa for me, a driver, limousines. I had my kids enrolled in school . . ." Ron's voice droned on like white noise in the room, static the agents struggled to clear. He forgot about his "crappy" apartment, the shotgun he carried. He blamed *America's Most Wanted* for ruining his life.

"After you saw the broadcast, did you think they knew where you lived?"

Ron squinted at O'Connor. He leaned forward and lowered his voice. "My problem is I'm so tall."

O'Connor glanced at his partner. The thought had crossed their minds that Ron might not be well, that his profuse sweating and frequent bathroom breaks might not be a ploy.

"Have you had any medications today?"

"Just a couple Excedrin . . . I have ulcers and I get headaches. I'm supposed to take Lipitor for high blood pressure, but I haven't been taking it. I can't hold my pee very well." Ron started to shake.

O'Connor was like a lion that smelled blood on its prey. Weakness spelled opportunity.

"We're almost done here," he said. "What can you tell me about the contents of the van? What are you doing with Pam's divorce paperwork?"

Silence hung in the air like a fine mist. Ron had run out of canned answers.

The agent dispensed with subtleties. "Did you have anything to do with her ex-husband's bombing?"

Ron smiled weakly and folded his arms across his chest, forming a protective wall. "I'm really not a hunter. I had the gun because I was involved with outfitting. These guys who go deer hunting in deer season . . . I beg off that . . . I'm telling you I'm . . . not a violent person. I had no reason to blow up anybody. I would've loved to kill my kid a few times . . ." His laugh, which came in a sudden burst, startled the agents.

O'Connor frowned. "Aspen's a small town. Pam's a very pretty girl with a lot of baggage. She hates her ex-husband. She's broke but she likes to live the lifestyle of the rich. She likes the toys, the cars, the men, the rich, rich types. She's the quintessential damsel in distress. Her ex refuses to pay her child support but she's not worried. She knows about his $2 million insurance policy. Now she has two million reasons to kill him. Or at least make him disappear."

He let his theory spin. Ron's eye twitched. He played with his handcuffs, tore at the paper label on his empty water bottle.

"Can I pee?"

"She meets a gentleman who's a . . . businessman . . . let's leave it at that. He's willing to do a lot of stuff for her 'cause she's pretty, a pretty thing, and very socially connected. The businessman is basically on the run because of whatever, I don't know. Yeah, I know you explained the business deal to me, and that could be bullshit . . . or it could be legitimate . . ."

"There was a warrant for my arrest."

"Yeah, I know; you told us that already," O'Connor snapped, unwilling to give him air. "The idea might have entered into somebody's head, especially somebody who's on the run who now has no means of making money, *legitimate* money, money that might help him leave the country, hire good legal representation, or whatever. Could be an easy windfall. Your vehicle's recovered within three days of the bombing with information inside that corroborates your trip to Tucson. There's no threats, not a note, not a knife . . ."

"Can I have a drink? Throat's kind of dry."

"Fine." O'Connor paused as his partner brought Ron another bottle of water.

"I don't know why I'm so thirsty. Sugar diabetes thing." *Or nerves,* O'Connor thought. Ron's face flushed. His hand trailed along the column of his throat, and O'Connor noted Ron's fingernails had a bluish tint to them, as if all the blood had drained out of them. The fan continued to click overhead, reminding O'Connor of the heat, even in November. His partner returned with more water and O'Connor pressed on.

"We have a task force not only with Pima County but with the IRS . . . [W]hen you have a bombing investigation, a high-profile case—hell, it made national news—there aren't many stones left unturned. It becomes a financial investigation. We look at sources of income that you've had, you know, like, did you get any of that $2 million?"

Ron tilted the bottle to his mouth.

"Any money that's derived from fraud, you know, is money laundering, okay?" O'Connor emphasized. Ron nodded, clearly nonplussed.

"Did she ever ask you to do it?"

Ron froze. "Absolutely not." O'Connor waited for the follow-up, the inevitable explanation, and Ron didn't disappoint. "Let me editorialize and add I can't envision Pam even *thinking* like that, let alone ever asking someone to kill him. She doesn't associate with those kinds of dirt-bag people. She'd excise herself from that, just her natural instincts. She's a real motherly type."

O'Connor suppressed a smirk; it would be unlike Ron to shift the blame. He would want the credit. The agent had had enough experience with con men to know they took pride in their ability to dupe others, to scam the innocent and live among them completely undetected.

"She's in the jet-setting scene and now she's gone broke."

"She had a best friend named Joy . . . married to a man so rich, it's beyond belief. Oddly enough, she was the one girlfriend of Pam's who actually thought I was a great guy . . . even though I didn't have any money."

"That's a real sticking point with you, isn't it: that you had no money, could not compete," O'Connor interjected.

"Pam got a lot of help from Joy." Ron described equestrian lessons, private-school tuition, and camping trips.

"She's accepting handouts . . . that's pretty devastating to the pride, don't you think? She's got to keep up with the Joneses; that's the way Aspen is, you know?"

Ron appreciated how the agent might misinterpret the pressure Pam felt to compete; but, he offered, Pam did work. She had returned to real estate. She had resources available to her. The agent wondered whether Ron's loyalty to Pam was inspired by love or more darkly motivated.

"There are no secrets when two people know; you know that, right? When two people know what happened, there's no secrets." He let the veiled threat hang between them for a few moments and then he reminded Ron, "You're a fugitive in possession of a firearm. There are federal penalties."

Ron's face contorted. He looked like a teakettle about to whistle. "I didn't exactly plan my life and work my ass off for all these years . . . twenty-two years of maximum stress, successful . . . German and Italian businesses . . .

[I]f anybody was bitter, it was me, you know . . . I haven't had dates since I've lived in Florida. Dates meaning [going] out to dinner and money and stuff . . . I can't get a job, because with a job you have to show a Social Security number . . . I can't do anything [that] requires a driver's license, so I'm a consultant . . ."

"Do you have a storefront?"

"No. I have a post office box."

O'Connor nodded. "I figured."

"To make myself look important," Ron qualified.

"Of course. Makes sense to me."

"Would you be willing to take a polygraph?" Coes interjected.

"You know, I don't like that whole idea." Ron shook his head. "Since I don't date, I read far too many detective and spy novels. I'm not being facetious, but I read about tons of gadgets and ideas and concepts and methodology."

He paused and then quickly turned the tables. "Can I ask *you* guys a couple of questions?"

"Sure."

"Did *you* do it?" Ron's confident mask tore. "I'm sorry, not time to be funny." Sweat moistened his upper lip. His face looked shiny, as if his whole body were slowly filling with water. "I saw a lot of guys out there pointing guns at me today with different T-shirts on . . . I don't know what I did, but I guess somebody thought I was a dangerous person or something."

Gamber hailed a taxi from the Fort Lauderdale airport to the Bureau of Alcohol, Tobacco, Firearms and Explosives field office and barely remembered the ride afterward. His heart slammed in his chest. Dark clouds threatened rain. The humidity wilted his hair. Adrenaline had replaced food. He had been going since early that morning, pumped up only with caffeine and airline cornflakes.

He flew into the interview room. "What do we have?"

"Colorado warrant for fraud and a federal charge, fugitive in possession of a firearm."

"We're transporting him to the hospital now," Coes advised.

"The hospital?"

"His blood pressure's a bit elevated."

I'll bet it is, Gamber thought, but he doubted it had anything to do with high cholesterol.

CHAPTER TWENTY-ONE:
THE DEBRIS

Soon after Ron's discharge from the hospital he consented to the search of his Beach Comber Hotel room, storage locker, Fort Lauderdale residence, and vehicle. He insisted he had nothing to hide and the "sooner they realized that, the sooner they'd release him." Ron's arrogance saved authorities countless hours drafting search warrants and swearing to facts before a neutral magistrate.

With Ron's blessing, police combed through Ron's belongings, searching for any documents that confirmed his intimate relationship with Pam Phillips. They seized phone records, FedEx shipment receipts, plastic bags containing electronic equipment, Sony laptop computers, hundreds of DVDs and CDs, cell phone bills, bank statements, over eleven thousand e-mail printouts, iPods, binders of documents, a Rolodex, notepads, and a journal Ron stashed underneath his hotel bed. Among the papers seized was correspondence concerning Pam's partnership interest in Potrero and her astrology business, Star Babies. Authorities seized a long brown gun case; tucked inside they found photographs of Pam posing with her children, Lois and Trevor, on the slopes of Aspen; a Texas driver's license in the name of "Ronald Kelly"; an FAA pilot's license; a passport; several credit reports; Visa cards in Brady Young's name; two American Express cards belonging to Kelly Young; and fifteen pages of documents listing various account numbers and passwords.

The evidence arrived in the Miami field office: boxes and boxes of paperwork, online banking documents, e-mails, recordings, and handwritten notes contained inside a journal. The ATF solicited the help of the United States Secret Service, specifically the identity theft credit card squad, in an effort to establish a criminal profile. But at first the documents revealed nothing extraordinary: Ron preyed on prospective business partners for the express purpose of stealing their financial lines of credit. He had a reference manual, *How to Stay Hidden*, and recorded his conversations and money transfers for six and a half years. Some of his discussions involved his adult children, who clearly knew of Ron's whereabouts but nonetheless suborned his deception. The federal agents considered pursuing criminal charges against them and alerted the United States Attorney's Office to their findings.

But then they discovered an odd pattern of behavior: although Ron used multiple credit cards in other people's names, he *paid off* most of the balances. With only $7,000 outstanding, the United States Attorney's Office elected not to prosecute. The losses did not satisfy even the minimum statutory requirement, $50,000.*

Once again, the agents had little evidence with which to incriminate Ron with murder.

"Keep digging," supervisors ordered. *There had to be something in the mountains of paperwork, in the thousands of digital recordings. No one could be as meticulous as Ron, as much of a pack rat, and not have saved one thing related to Gary's bombing. It just wasn't possible.*

Hours after the financial records search began, Special

---

* No formal charges were ever filed against Ron for identity theft.

Agent Aucoin with the Secret Service came across hand-written notes that "looked extremely odd" and contained possible references to a murder. He alerted the ATF, and when his expedited package arrived at the ATF field office, Aucoin received cryptic orders to "cease working" on the fraud investigation. Instead he was to compile "binders and binders" containing Ron's financial records and relinquish them to the custody of the ATF.

And while federal agents researched possible murder charges against Ron, photos of Pam sharing cocktails with a transient on her newly remodeled impressive deck appeared in the "Aspen Sojourner" midsummer edition of *Mountain Homestyle*. Years later, the editor would again feature Pam in a four-part "Scandal Aspen" series on "black widows."

November 2005

Interrogation requires a certain amount of psychological manipulation. Gamber had learned to exploit weaknesses in human nature, play on personal conflict and tension. The whole "good cop/bad cop" routine developed out of a belief that people cracked under pressure when confronted with contrasting extremes like dominance and submission, control and dependence. Still, the detective felt nostalgic for a time when police tactics weren't always so complex or civil. In the early 1900s, physical abuse—deprivation of food, water, bright lights, periods of long isolation, mild torture, rubber-hose beatings that left no marks—was a common (if not legal) method of coercing a confession. Such "investigative tools" were admissible in court, provided the suspect signed a waiver attesting that his statements were "voluntary." But by the 1930s police tactics had changed: people were presumed innocent until proven guilty and killers were treated with respect. *Miranda v. Arizona* in 1966 didn't help matters.

Gamber regarded his suspect with morbid fascination. The overweight, elderly man with flat brown eyes dressed in loose jail clothes hardly *looked* the part of a cold-blooded killer. But that's what made him so dangerous: the fact that he was so unassuming. He was unexpected, an awkward giant who actually repelled people's natural curiosity; ugliness evoked discomfort in most, a guarded respect, even for freaks. "Civilized" people learned not to stare, not to be impolite, no matter how disgusted their reaction. Maybe that was the attraction of sideshows: at least onstage, in a cage, beneath a tent, people at last had permission to reject what they could not understand, what they could not accept, what left them empty, without explanation. Ron roamed undetected on the outside.

"So, what kind of contact do you still have with Pam?" Detective Gamber hoped he sounded casual, nonthreatening. The idea behind his calm demeanor was to disarm Ron, put him at ease, and convince him that he was there as a friend, there to offer him solutions.

Gamber sat across from Ron in an airless room that smelled of wet stone. A whiteboard hung from a corner wall. Two dry-erase markers rested on the lip of the tray in case Gamber felt compelled to outline his theories in bold red caps. Studies confirmed that visual displays left a greater impact on a suspect's focus. Two-way glass allowed the detective's colleagues to critique his performance if they wished, armchair his interrogation, observe body language he might miss: a facial tic, an upturned lip, pools of sweat, or the way an inmate slumped like punched clay.

"Occasionally, I talk to her. We're friends." Ron shrugged, eager to please, eager to dispel the "silly notion" that he could possibly belong in shackles.

"Do *friends* tape-record their conversations?"

"I've done that for a while." He stretched, moving his neck from side to side until it cracked.

"Why with Pam?"

"I tape everyone."

"What are we going to find on these little microcassette recordings?

"She had problems with this and that, the kids . . ."

"Gary?"

"Yes."

"Are we going to find anything about Gary Triano's death?" The question buzzed in the air like a jolt of electricity.

"I don't think so."

"What does that *mean*?"

"Well . . . considering I had a gun in my car and I have federal charges . . ."

"You're in a real tenuous position. What spin is Pam going to put on this? If you were sent down to Tucson to investigate Gary's assets . . ."

"He died in '96, right?"

"November 1, 1996," Gamber supplied, dreading Ron's tedious groping for information.

"I was there in 1998."

Gamber forged ahead despite Ron's lie. He already had rental car and hotel receipts that placed Ron in Tucson before the murder.

"The van . . ."

"What van?"

"*Your* van was recovered in California in '96. That puts you in Tucson [in] late October."

"The van was recovered in California." Ron pinched the bridge of his nose, squeezing his eyes shut as if staving off the beginnings of a headache.

"Right."

"It was illegally parked. What does that have to do with anything?" he sputtered again.

"Well—"

"Tucson in October?" he cut him off.

"The van was recovered in late October."

"I'm not following."

Ron was like an animal cornered chasing his tail for relief, trying to solidify which lie made the most sense, which story made him most credible. Gamber relished Ron's internal struggle, his apparent mental anguish, as doubt creased his forehead and a bright rash colored his neck.

Gamber applied more pressure. "When did you leave Aspen?"

"March or April 1996." Ron wiped moisture from his cheeks with the back of his hand.

"So the van sat around for five months?"

The words tumbled out of him. "Like I told you guys . . ." He vacillated between casual banter and marked irritation.

"Look," Gamber said, losing patience. "We can put you in Tucson in 1996. By your calculations it was May. If we put you there later than May, that's closer in time to when the bomb goes off."

"I knew nothing about a life insurance policy!" Ron exploded. Gamber stared at him incredulously, looked into his chillingly blank eyes that reflected nothing.

"I know *now* . . . about one," he recovered, his voice like a flame lit and then suddenly extinguished.

"I'm not convinced that you didn't know about it before." Gamber reviewed with him Pam's fraud claim with the Aspen Police Department, her sudden and inexplicable decision to drop further investigation, the apparent connection between the pair. "It certainly looks like you did a lot of work for her." The detective gave him a moment to absorb that.

"I helped her."

"I'm sure she was appreciative." Ron smothered a smile, and the expression hit the detective like a blast of cold wind. He could not afford to lose this match. He had come too far, invested too much.

"So you know nothing about Gary Triano's death?"

"Right."

"I don't believe you."

The detective *wished* he could dismiss Ron as crazy: it would be easier to process what Gamber knew but could not prove, that Ron was not only a killer but really quite sane. Cunningly cruel, he fit into a category apart. Ron understood exactly what Pam needed; they were two sides of a tarnished coin, both propelled by want, need, and more want. Gamber had his own theories why Ron had recorded Pam, why he had *helped* her with her business affairs, why he had likely killed for her: blackmail, control, and sheer arrogance. But so far none of that translated into a confession. Gamber needed Ron to slip.

Gamber painted the picture for him: "She knows you're on the run. *You* know you're on the run. You just want to disappear."

"Actually, what exactly is the definition of a fugitive?"

"Help me to understand something," Gamber said, redirecting Ron. "You left behind a list, one item of which included a sawed-off shotgun. You claim you left Aspen in April 1996, and yet, *after* you disappeared, Pam asked you to investigate Gary's hidden assets?"

"Yes." Ron's breathing was labored. He bristled at Gamber's questions, suddenly unsure how to play him. He prided himself on verbal jousting, keeping his opponent off balance.

"You had no knowledge that Gary Triano was going to die?"

"No," Ron said, his response, short, direct, like a bullet fired at close range.

"Bullshit."

Ron shrugged.

"Never heard anybody talk about it? Never heard anybody threaten harm to him?"

"No."

The detective felt heat on his cheeks. "Conspiracy to commit first-degree murder carries the same penalty in

Arizona as first-degree murder—you understand that, right? It's as if you pulled the trigger." He was practically shouting. "Twenty-five to life."

Ron stared at him, and Gamber knew that appealing to emotion would have no effect on such an antisocial personality. Ron was a survivor; he gathered shape and energy in the ashes of his own failures. He accepted no blame for his acts and therefore could not evolve or change. He had no *reason* to change. Guilt fell away from him like ice in a warm rain. Gamber knew that if he was not vigilant, if he did not press on and find some creative way to turn the interview around, Ron would fly free, victorious again.

"You're not a young man. You're not a healthy man." Gamber struggled.

"No."

"Twenty-five to life is a long time."

"An eternity."

"Think about that."

"I will." And he sounded sincere, but Gamber knew Ron wouldn't. Couldn't. Ron believed he was innocent.

CHAPTER TWENTY-TWO:
LUCKY BREAK

Federal Detention Center, Miami, Florida
June 2006

Gamber's national manhunt for a suspected sensational bomber resulted in Ron's federal detention for eighteen months on the charge of being a fugitive in possession of a firearm.* Authorities also investigated possible allegations of interstate fraud. *Not murder. Not even close.* The detective's frustration mounted. The Triano case had already absorbed his life, peppered his hair gray, mottled his skin, and formed permanent bruises beneath his eyes. He resisted sleep, the deep REM state that allowed dreams to invade. The bombing replayed over and over in his mind's eye until it became part of the fabric of his life. Pressure pulsed at his temples. *He had had years and the most resources available to any detective, and still he had produced only leads, hunches.* He worried like a dog in search of his favorite bone, unable to accept that the bone might be buried too deep, might never be found.

As the summer of his tenth year approached, he was no closer to solving what the *Tucson Citizen* had dubbed the

---

* He was later extradited to Aspen to face felony fraud charges.

"worst homicide in Tucson's history." And while others in his office powered down at the end of the day, Gamber stayed, slumped at his desk, there when everyone arrived in the morning, there when everyone left in the evening. He owned identical outfits: black slacks, Rockport shoes, button-down shirts in similar shades of white, off-white, cream, ivory—it didn't matter, it was still the same color. Like Tucson's weather, with its varying degrees of heat and sun. He thought of people who lived in rainy climates like Seattle, with its drizzle, torrential downpours, and gunmetal skies. Too much sameness, no matter the temperature, could produce natural depression. He never understood weather people in Arizona, with nothing new to report, the same temperatures, the same blazing sun, the same radiant smile on the anchorperson, the same gold highlighted hair. Monotony was not the same as boredom: the latter implied laziness and inaction. But a worn path, if traveled long enough, eventually morphed into something unexpected, something deeper: a trench.

He stretched, moving to the window, away from his cubicle and noise. He had absorbed the same view every day for years: in the distance, giant saguaros dotted majestic Mount Lemmon and the Catalinas like razor stubble. Ghost towns bordered the desolate beauty. Stark white pillars of gutted buildings punched the wind. Hummingbirds beat frantically against dry cactus husks, flapping their wings so fast that it was as if they stood still. Dangerous summer heat, with temperatures sizzling at 120 degrees in the shade, forced airplanes to circle until the runways cooled.

But then one morning Gamber's phone shrilled. An agent from the Bureau of Alcohol, Tobacco, Firearms and Explosives reported a verified tip from career criminal, Andre Mims, a lifer serving thirty-four years for armed robberies in various federal detention facilities in Miami.

"It might lead nowhere," the disembodied voice cautioned. "But he *claims* he has information concerning a Tucson murder."

How often had Gamber heard that before?

Still, it was worth investigating. And the following morning Gamber and Keith St. John* flew to Miami to interview Mims at the federal detention facility. Mims advised the detectives that he was a "true professional," a "legal beagle," and that what he had to reveal "weighed heavy on his conscience." *Was he serious?* Nonetheless, Mims insisted that the police could not record his interview but he would agree to author an affidavit. He settled into his chair, adjusted his glasses, and, satisfied that *he* controlled the situation, recounted his story.

Mims propped his legs on the metal desk littered with papers and law books. Sunlight filtered through cracks in the ceiling on the eleventh floor's satellite library in the Florida detention center, where he had been moved temporarily from Edgefield, South Carolina, to await his evidentiary hearing on his habeas petition. He had a fine view of the stone yard where inmates exercised for brief respites during the day, shuffled beneath him in their stripes and chains, and bargained secrets for cigarettes. Guards with automatic rifles towered over the barbed-wire fences. Oddly, he felt *safe* from the outside world.

Mims rolled his pen filler between his fingers. Ink creased his dark skin. It was the closest he would ever get to a writing utensil. Deputies considered them contraband,

---

*   Sergeant Keith St. John officially retired from the Pima County Sheriff's Department in 1998 and began employment with the Pima County Attorney's Office's criminal investigations division. He returned temporarily to the Pima County Sheriff's Department cold case homicide unit in order to assist with the continuing investigation into the death of Gary Triano.

potential shanks. But Mims enjoyed privileged status. He was one of the few trustee inmates in the prison. With his habeas appeal process nearly over, he looked forward to endless similar days poring over antiquated statutes, writing summaries of case law, and offering inmates his considerable legal advice. One drizzly morning Ron Young approached him. He rolled his cuffs and sleeves, wiped excess sweat from his palms on his uniform, and extended his hand.

"I didn't like him at first," Mims confessed during his police interview. "He reminded me of a rabbit, a very *tall* rabbit. What do you call those . . . hares?" He snapped his fingers. "He wanted my help. I didn't just take anyone's case, you know. I built relationships of trust with my clients."

Ron straddled a chair next to Mims. "They call you the 'legal beagle'?"

Mims stared at him, removed his glasses, and wiped them on a shirtsleeve. "I can't help you," he said a little too quickly, and returned to his paperwork.

Ron leaned in close. Drool slipped from the corners of his mouth. His breath smelled like sour cabbage. He smothered a smile and whispered, "I could pay you."

Now, *that* caught Mims' attention. Prison policies dictated that no inmate could receive compensation from a fellow inmate, especially not in exchange for services rendered.

"We could work out a deal," Ron said sotto voce. "No one has to know."

Silence rippled between them. Mims considered Ron's proposal. *What did he have to lose, after all? He still had thirty-four years to go for his armed robberies. They could take away his legal privileges. That would hurt.* His reputation in the system depended on his ability to research. He rubbed his bare wrists. It had been years since he wore handcuffs.

Still, "Ron spoke my language," Mims said. He relented. "I won't lie. As a businessman, I appreciated capital in exchange for services." The two agreed to "work something out."

Ron enlisted his daughter, Kelly, whom he had hardly spoken to since his arrest. He needed cash, and quickly.

He dialed her number from the prison. "Hello, baby girl."

"Hi, baby dad." She sounded weary, drained by her father's intrusion into her life. Despite his incarceration, he insisted the stories about him were "barefaced lies" and that worse than "spending time in prison" was the idea that his family thought he was guilty. Kelly offered no opinion on the subject. Instead she spoke of ski slopes and carefree living.

"Did I ever tell you I used to work on a worm farm?"

Kelly laughed uneasily. "No."

"It was a turning point in my life. It's what got me into sailing. I couldn't be an astronaut, so . . ."

"What a strange man you are," Kelly cut him off. "A real weirdo. Worm farm?"

"You sent the money, right?" Ron had tired of the chit-chat and now focused on the real reason for his call.

Kelly sighed. "Yes."

"Look, I'm not a fucking mass murderer," he snapped.

Kelly dutifully deposited cash into Mims's prison account, in amounts ranging from $55 to $325, all traceable sums. Meanwhile, Ron devised a plan to prove his innocence.

"But you pled guilty," Kelly reminded him.

"Because I was boxed in and intimidated and my public defender never bothered to tell me that I *wasn't* a fugitive. This has all been a horrifying miscarriage of justice."

"Didn't you plead to fugitive in possession?"

" 'Fugitive' means 'fled to avoid prosecution,' " Ron pointed out. "The warrant was issued for my arrest *five months* after I left Aspen."

"But didn't you have a warrant *because* no one could find you?"

"That's a mere technicality."

"So, what's your plan?"

"My plan is to get the charge dismissed. It's like an appeal. If I can prove that I was never a fugitive, that my lawyer was a fucking disaster, and this thing gets overturned, then I just have to deal with Aspen and the fraud charge. Unfortunately, Colorado is vigilant; that state will fly all over the country just to pick up fugitives . . . [S]ee, my big beef with all of this is having a felony. I just can't stand the idea of being a *felon*. I almost wanted to kill myself. I would have started shooting people if I'd had a gun. Not a positive thing for my criminal career."

"So you need proof of what, exactly?" Kelly said wearily.

"That I *lived* in Aspen and legitimately left Aspen. I didn't *flee*." He sighed as though Kelly were being obtuse in order to exasperate him.

In his next phone call from prison, Ron solicited affidavits from his children—fill-in-the-blank forms from a template his ex-wife, who worked as a paralegal, produced—corroborating his stance that he *legitimately* left Aspen in April 1996 and relocated to Florida. But no records confirmed that Ron had ever lived at Snowbunny Lane. Any water, gas, electricity, or phone bills had a post office box address.

"That's useless," Ron spat. "Somebody has to *find* that faggot landlord, get him to draft an affidavit stating that he terminated my lease."

"But you didn't . . . terminate it, did you?" Kelly hedged.

"Mail him a template and see if you can get him to sign it anyway. Make up a story. Tell him I'm ill and you're trying to prepare my tax records and you need to establish I lived in Aspen on Snowbunny Lane."

"I'll try."

"Don't *try*." Ron breathed heavily, evenly, like someone sleeping, though he was fully awake.

"He's disappeared," Kelly said.

"What do you mean, 'disappeared'?"

"I can't find him. The last number I have for him just goes straight to voice mail. He's not returning my calls."

"Did you search for his neighbors, relatives of his, on the Internet?" Irritation laced Ron's voice.

"I didn't think of it. I must be retarded. I just don't think like you." Kelly sounded genuinely distraught.

"It's not that difficult. Ask yourself this question: If there was a million dollars cash waiting for you if only you could find it, you'd find it, right?"

"That's not fair."

"It's reality."

"I must be dumb or something."

"Okay," Ron condescended. "The guy won't answer his phone. I'm sure he's there. Have you ever considered maybe just renting a car and driving to his last known address to track him down in person?"

"Well, how far away is he from Aspen, do you think?"

"This is a fucking waste of time!" Ron exploded. "Find his address or his relatives' address, tell them it's an emergency and you need to get a hold of whatever the fucking asshole's name is . . ."

"I'm not like you. I'm nothing remotely like you," Kelly said almost under her breath, and hung up the phone.

Several days later, she gave Ron an update. "Okay, I talked to the landlord finally . . . he won't sign anything. He said you're going to have to subpoena him," Kelly announced triumphantly during their next phone call.

"Did he say why?" Ron sounded incredulous.

"Yes. He said you were toxic."

"That *I'm* toxic?"

"That his whole experience with you was full of negative energy."

Ron absorbed that description, clearly agitated. "I left

specific instructions for Brady on how to talk to this asshole if he refused to sign the affidavit. It's a preprinted piece of paper, for Christ's sake. All he has to do is sign it, lick the envelope, and mail it back to me."

"I explained all that to him," Kelly said patiently.

"Call him back." Ron was emphatic. "Tell him you called my attorney, my *real* lawyer. Make up a fucking name if you have to; tell him this is a federal case and he doesn't have a choice whether he participates or not. Tell him if he's subpoenaed he'll have to travel, and it could be Denver, Florida, wherever." Tension crackled over the line. Then Ron said quietly, almost desperately, "Can you please just ask him again if he'll sign the paper so we can avoid court? I just need to establish a history of residency, the last place I lived."

"I'll try," Kelly said.

"Tell him it doesn't have to be notarized. He just has to sign the document. Takes two minutes. That's it."

"I'll try."

"It's critical. He's got to help me out here." He sounded desperate.

A few days later Ron called his daughter again. She could hear the prerecorded message from the prison.

"This call is from the federal funhouse," he mimicked the recording.

"What's the story, morning glory?" Kelly asked brightly. Ron dispensed with small talk. He had limited time, five minutes remaining, on his prison calling card. What could he really share with his daughter about his days, anyway? They blended into one monotonous film clip.

"What do the Aspen papers report about me?"

"I can send them to you."

"I don't need to *see* them," Ron snapped. "I just need to know what they *say* . . . you know, just in case you move to Moscow or something."

"I was actually considering a quaint city in Russia," Kelly joked.

"I hear Chernobyl's nice," Ron said coolly, and then after a moment: "I'm suing *America's Most Wanted* for slander, you know."

"Yeah, you mentioned that." Kelly sounded distracted.

"Did you order the tape, the November 19 segment? I'd hate for them to delete that. I might miss out on a potential fortune."

"I tried. There's no place to request it. I could call . . ."

"Jesus, if you do that, you'll have to give them a credit card, your name, and then they'll know who you are."

"So?"

"So then they'll know you're my daughter. They'll know *I'm* the one requesting the tape . . ."

"I suppose you have a point."

"What are you doing now?" he asked, changing the subject abruptly.

"Hiking with Brady in the mountains."

"Gee, I hope you don't get killed."

As the days turned into weeks and Ron badgered his children for proof of his residency, Brady boarded a plane to Thailand. He never sent his affidavit. He never solicited affidavits from his personal friends in Aspen, and he never could produce a list of Ron's friends who could vouch for his whereabouts in April 1996.

"Hard to understand why he wouldn't do it," Ron reflected, sounding genuinely surprised. "Maybe he wants me to stay in here for some reason."

"That's ridiculous," Kelly soothed.

"Is it?"

Meanwhile, Ron wrote letters to his mother, confident his "nightmare [would] end soon." He encouraged Kelly, "his favorite daughter," his "super good-looking gal," his "Kelser," to call his mother regularly, to send her flowers on Mother's Day, to make sure she knew Ron was innocent.

"I'll try," she always assured him.

"You'll *try*?"

"I'm busy, Dad."

"Well, how does she sound when you try?" Ron pressed.

"Like an old person."

"Does she mention me?"

"She cries."

"Do *you* mention me to her?"

"I tell her you're innocent." Kelly's voice hitched. Ron detected a slight hesitation, but before he could pursue the thought, the call ended.

His family's perception of him mattered. He needed his children to believe in his innocence; needed his mom to understand that his arrest was a travesty. Kelly provided his only link to the outside; Brady had already distanced himself from him. Perhaps he saw his own reflection in Ron and the image repulsed him. Ron focused on Kelly; he sensed he made her uncomfortable and he used her unease to his advantage. She would be too afraid to turn on him, to disobey him. He hadn't meant to actually steal her identity. At first he only borrowed her name, "Kelly," and it seemed fairly natural. After all, it *was* his middle name as well. But then one thing led to another and it felt effortless to just *be* her. She had perfect credit and an accessible bank account. He hadn't considered she might report the multiple charges to the police.

"This is getting alarming," Ron's ex-wife, Linda, hissed at him the next day. "You stole Kelly's identity?"

"Now, let's not be hasty. Let's think this through," Ron counseled, trying to keep his composure.

"Think *what* through? She's already reported identity theft."

"But she hasn't told them it's me, right?" Ron stammered.

"I don't see how she can't. If she doesn't give you up,

her credit's ruined; she's responsible for thousands of dollars charged to her credit card and for all of these items sent to your address in Pompano, Florida."

"I don't see how giving me up helps Kelly. She still has ruined credit," Ron reasoned.

"How could you do this to her?" his ex-wife screamed at him. *"She's your* daughter!"

"Look, if you mention my name, they'll indict me in here for identity theft. They'll never release me: even if my charge is dismissed, I'll be stuck in here. Is that what you want?"

"She can't even sell her car. The motor vehicle department insists no one named Kelly Young ever registered, licensed, or insured the vehicle. They have no information on her at all. They punch in the Social, the name, and nothing."

"That's strange."

"It *is* strange, isn't it, considering you went with her to register her car. She doesn't exist, Ron."

"You know, it's not unheard-of for [the department of] motor vehicles to transpose a few numbers on a Social; happens all the time. It's probably a mix-up."

"Of disastrous proportions," his ex-wife snapped. "Like the credit card charges. I'm not letting Kelly go down for this. You sent her fraudulent checks, which she deposited into her bank account. If she doesn't say she knows you, *she* takes the fall for this."

"Well, but think carefully whether you want to give me up in this."

"I have. I have thought carefully."

And while Ron worried whether his ex-wife would reveal his identity, Mims researched Ron's claims for post-conviction relief in exchange for fish, "prepackaged salmon, mackerel, and tuna," that Ron purchased from the commissary. Mims's arrangement with Ron was not without risk; inmates could not accept payment for services. For his own protection, Mims cooked meals for Ron.

"My motives weren't pure," he explained. "I figured if Ron ate the proceeds with me, he was less likely to rat me out. Hey, I'm not antisocial, just anti-nonsense. Ron loved my salmon patties, said he once owned a restaurant in the Bahamas and he had never tasted fish like mine. Come on, now, the *Bahamas*. Bullshit."

Nevertheless, they formed a close friendship over the next sixth months, though Mims insisted for him it "was always about the fish." Ron wanted to withdraw from his plea, complained that he received ineffective assistance of counsel, urged Mims to challenge Ron's fugitive status.

"I didn't give a fuck about his claims," Mims said. "I cared about his money."

But then one night Mims broke his own rules. He revealed personal regret. Stretched out on his cot amid his scattered legal papers, he crossed his hands behind his head and reflected on his former abusive relationship. He revealed grisly details—hospital visits and broken bones—and complained that his old lady had no self-respect, and so *he* had none for her.

"I continued the abuse. I'm not proud of that," he said simply.

Ron loomed in the entrance to Mims's cell.

"It's my old lady's birthday today," Mims sighed, and Ron broke spontaneously into song: *"Happy Birthday to her, Happy Birthday to her . . ."*

"She'd be offended," Mims laughed, and suddenly his mood grew dark. Ron, maybe sensing Mims's need for conversation, sat on the edge of Mims's cot.

"I was involved with a woman once," Ron shared suddenly. "Pamela Phillips."

Ron explained how incensed he became over Pam's abuse. He listened intently to Pam's stories of relentless beatings by Gary and couldn't understand how she tolerated him for so long.

"I told her *I* could solve her little problem," Ron bragged. He was a *fixer*.

"Yeah, well, we're all heroes." Mims shrugged. Ron grinned, interlocked his fingers, leaned forward on the cot, and looked Mims straight in the face, his expression like a cold winter blast.

"She told me about a life insurance policy worth $2 million." He paused for effect, licked his lower lip, and exclaimed, "I blew that fucker up."*

* Ron, according to Mims, allegedly also took credit for murdering Steven Grabow, a "rival drug dealer," in 1985, in a similar car bombing. Grabow, the "drug-ring master-mind," had just finished playing a round of tennis at the Aspen Club when a pipe bomb planted beneath the seat of his Jeep exploded. His murder came one month before he was to stand trial in U.S. District Court in Denver for allegedly heading a drug ring that brought $35 million worth of cocaine to Aspen annually, according to news reports. Grabow's murder remains unsolved. Police have not been able to make any definitive links between Young and Grabow's murder.

CHAPTER TWENTY-THREE:
ROAD'S END

"When the day comes, there's going to be a knock on my door; let me know so I can check out . . ."
                                    —Pam Phillips to Ron Young

September 6, 2006

Beneath a chill gray sky, Pima County detectives Gamber and St. John, and Aspen Police detectives Crowley and Crehan, paced outside Pam's Meadowood mansion. A uniformed Aspen Police patrol sergeant stood nearby. An entourage of federal agents, Pima County sheriff's detectives, and Aspen detectives gathered at a staging area, waiting for additional information. The group had arrived the night before, quietly and under cover of darkness. Aspen boasted a safe community, one seemingly free of crime and killers. The sheriff urged discretion: his residents enjoyed certain expectations; he had a veneer to protect, revenue to consider. The presence of law enforcement in his town, and in such sheer numbers, dirtied his pretty landscape and perhaps threatened the commerce. Reluctantly, he signed the two-hundred-page search warrant affidavit requesting the seizure of documents relating to a Seaboard Life Insurance policy; all financial records and correspondence; Dean Witter, Morgan Stanley, and Merrill Lynch accounts; telephone records and Federal Express shipments from April

15, 1996, to the present; computers, electronic media storage devices, disks, Palm Pilots, BlackBerrys, etc. . . .

The sheriff did not appreciate lights and sirens and grand announcements. The subtext to the sheriff's warning: *the rich deserve respect, better treatment, discretion, even for suspected killers.*

The idea of "protect and serve" should have been indiscriminate, but Gamber knew better. The wealthy did enjoy a certain deference, faster response times, genuine concern, a campaign of support. Gamber had worked Tucson's south side for years; crime occurred daily in the barrios. Sometimes uniforms never showed up at all, or if they did, their disdain and apathy were palpable. The elite, however, reported an entirely different experience. Gary Triano's death sparked a national media manhunt, enlisted a multi-agency task force, and inspired countless years of investigation. Had Gary not been rich or famous, would he have received the same attention?

Adrenaline coursed through Gamber as he knocked on Pam's door. White vapor blew from his mouth. *Ten years* rushed at him like a moving car speeding through the night, headlights swishing in the darkness. *This is why you became a cop.* His world fell away and only this moment mattered. The intercom crackled to life.

"Hello?" Pam's voice sounded grainy, distant.

"Detective Jim Gamber. We have some questions for you." His heart slammed in his throat. He imagined this was how an archaeologist felt when he finally unearthed the missing leg bone of an earlier dinosaur discovery.

Silence followed. "I'm not dressed."

Gamber glanced at his partner and smothered a smile. Not the response he expected. He shook his head incredulously and said, "We'll wait."

Normally, he would have rammed the door, dispensing with further pleasantries. But the door seemed to take up an entire wall, and was like that of a fortress, with black studded bolts, crisscrossing iron bars, and decorative brass knobs.

Pam emerged moments later and cracked open the door. She stared blankly at the officers, her face pale like a corpse's. She wore a sleek blue pantsuit that accentuated her curves. Diamond studs lined the cuffs. Her blond hair curled recklessly at her shoulders. She held eyeglasses in one hand.

"May we come inside and talk?" the detective asked. Through the sliver of light he saw a spacious loft with high ceilings and tall windows, unabated by blinds.

"I have an appointment," she said, and shut the door.

Gamber had expected nerves—hysteria, maybe—something other than Pam's strange calm, as if she had just rejected solicitors trying to sell her soap. Police did not fit into her neatly defined world.

He cleared his throat and tried again: "Ma'am, we've spoken to Ron Young. We have phone call recordings between the two of you."

Pam opened the door and peered through the crack again. "I'd like to call someone."

Gamber registered the beginning of panic in her voice, the cold dawning that precedes imminent capture.

"We have a search warrant," Detective Gamber said.

Pam nodded and shut the door.

Gamber contacted the other members of his SWAT team and instructed them to approach. Fortunately, the Aspen police knew the layout of Pam's home. They had responded multiple times to alarm calls at the residence in response to Pam's purported fears of intruders and thieves. They knew she always kept one back door unlocked.

Pam hung up the phone just as the agents scurried across her hardwood floors. They barely acknowledged her presence as she slumped into a puffy leather chair and watched helplessly as scene photographs were taken, hard drives were removed, files confiscated, desk drawers emptied. She would later describe the invasion to a friend as a strange unreality: not an out-of-body experience, exactly, but more like a television show Pam that had switched on halfway through and didn't fully follow. She fixated on her walls, decorated with eclectic pieces of sculpture from her travels; artifacts that defined her world in wood and bone. Years of renovations, and thousands of dollars in loans and personal funds, left her in a perpetual winter.

Gamber could have lived like the wealthy; he appreciated nice things, good clothes, upscale restaurants, but he was unimpressed by opulence. He had the education, the degree, the upbringing, and yet he chose to chase ghosts. Some in his department ridiculed his academic background, called his formal education a waste. But Gamber didn't measure success like that: a cop always gave more than he ever received; service wasn't about income, it was about effort. Police work required a different skill set: courage, a quirky focus, and a heightened sense of awareness. Maybe "intuition" was more accurate? He *knew* people, noticed details the way a writer recorded nuances, evolved style, white, stark rooms that echoed. He knew about secrets that lived inside a person.

He absorbed the way Pam's hand shook as she inhaled a cigarette, and then mashed the butt into an ashtray; the way her voice clinked like ice in an empty glass. She looked worn, frayed, like fabric that had been washed too much.

"My lawyer's on her way over." Pam's remark wasn't uttered as a threat, just to provide information. She stood, paced, her square shoulders slicing through white space; she was in full flight-or-fight response as she processed the wreck that her life had the potential to become. The fact that Pam even *had* a criminal lawyer in the wings *in case of emergencies* was not surprising—not for the rich; it was just unrealistic. Pam no doubt believed her lawyer would clear up this mess, *fix this mistake*, and remove the unpleasant police from her mansion.

Dreaded resignation skittered across Pam's face; she slipped into gray space, dropped the line that connected her to conscience. *She's going to bolt,* Gamber thought. *But she'll wait until her lawyer arrives. She'll want to seem reasonable, civilized, not like a common criminal.* It was part of the play, the overall script. Criminals exhibited regret, remorse, even recrimination, but only on threat of capture. Victims, like Heather, however, felt the impact of murder instantly; aftershocks continued for years. Heather lived in a perpetual fog, as if the day before her father's death never existed and the days after had morphed into one long scream. Some victims experienced an unbearable emptiness, as if permanency itself was just an illusion, particles breaking up and forming alternative shapes. They described the need to *do something* even if it meant calling the same detective repeatedly just to hear his voice, to know he still cared, to know he still hunted for the perpetrator. Heather couldn't accept ambiguity. *Neither could he.*

An attractive woman dressed in a striped brown suit, sensible chunky heels, and an oversize briefcase charged into Pam's foyer like an electric bolt.

"My client invokes her *Miranda* rights," Pamela Mackey announced. She had represented Kobe Bryant in his rape trial.

Gamber smirked. "I haven't gotten to that part yet."

"She's not talking," Mackey repeated.

"It doesn't work that way. You don't get to invoke your client's rights." Gamber shook his head and glanced at Detective Crowley. "Do you believe this?"

"Listen, I didn't want you to think my client was being rude . . . ," Mackey started over.

Meanwhile, Pam patted her lips with fresh gloss, applied powder, snatched her purse, and breezed out the front door.

"I have to go." She waved good-bye to her defense lawyer and left in her Mini Cooper.

Gamber watched helplessly as his prime suspect rounded a curve in the road and disappeared. He had no legal cause to detain her, no formal charges, nothing but potential evi-

dence and, he wagered, several laborious months of interpretation. Meanwhile, Pam had sufficient warning, an
unexpected reprieve, and Gamber had no doubt she would
leverage that to her full advantage. Mackey shrugged, gave
him a sly smile, and followed her client.

While detectives spent the next several months poring over
the voluminous records they had seized from Pam, searching for a reason to arrest her for murder, Pam quietly drove
to the airport in the middle of the night and boarded a plane
to London. From there she caught a connecting flight to
Milan, Italy. She lied to acquaintances that she had relatives
abroad. She journeyed to Lugano, Switzerland, where she
luxuriated for several months in a $5,000-a-night hotel suite.
Meanwhile, her Meadowood home slipped into foreclosure.
Pam owed Wells Fargo $4 million and had defaulted on her
$21,700-a-month mortgage payments.

But at least for now she was free.

December 4, 2006

Ron, meanwhile, had been transferred from the federal detention facility in Florida to the Pitkin County Jail in Aspen.
Gamber and St. John thought it time to reveal information
they had seized from Ron's computer files, evidence they
hoped might force a confession. But as they walked the
pristine halls of the Pitkin County Jail, they had some
doubt Ron would cooperate. The facility itself promoted an
environment of "direct supervision," a revolutionary new
concept designed to transform the former "socially abnor-
mal" large cage located in the basement of the courthouse.
The notion that environment might induce cooperation was
not new or revolutionary: therapists' offices piped in sounds
of waterfalls; the interiors of jails were painted pink; inmates
in some states wore muted stripes. Gamber didn't have much

patience for methodology; he needed a desperate criminal, someone willing to strike a deal, to do anything—maybe even confess—in order to be released.

But what might have worked in Pima County with its rank, dark jail cells likely had no influence in Aspen, where the facility boasted tall cathedral windows that filtered bright sunlight over plush carpets. Staff hoped to "reduce the noise level" so inmates could concentrate. They looked too comfortable, too poised with their porcelain toilet fixtures. Prisoners roamed freely on the premises from early morning until lockdown, alternating between the "dayroom" and the "multipurpose room," where they watched television reruns, played cards, and even casually interacted with detention officers. The inmates had direct access to collect phone calls, mail service, regular exercise, and visits. Prisoners were supplied with clothing, bedding, personal hygiene utensils, and even daily laundry service through the Aspen Valley Hospital.

And the food, a guard gushed, "was balanced, hot, varied, and dietician approved."

"Sounds like a fucking resort." Gamber rolled his eyes. But he knew no matter how pretty the package, the place was still an institution and inmates had rules and regulations. They could not control their time or space; they were not "free," and that fact still made Ron vulnerable. The detectives arranged for Ron to be transported to an interview room in the Pitkin County Sheriff's Department.

"Good to see you again." Ron extended his hand to the detectives as if they were old business associates. Dressed in a baggy beige jumpsuit, Ron resembled a large smudge. A smile cut across his face like a gap in a Halloween mask. His hand felt clammy and fake. Still, Gamber nodded, smiled slightly at Ron's exaggerated congeniality, and took a seat across from him at the table. St. John sat in profile. Both conscious about positioning, neither eager to alarm Ron into silence.

"We're hoping you can help us out," Gamber said, playing dumb. He needed Ron's expertise. He had heard Ron was a "technology genius" of sorts, and Gamber could not make "heads or tails" out of the digital media he recovered from Ron's computer.

Ron straddled the back of a chair, rubbed his chin thoughtfully, and stuttered, "Should I have my lawyer here?"

"That's entirely your choice. We don't plan on asking you any questions," Gamber lied. He actually hoped to rattle Ron, get him talking again at warp speed, offering up nuggets of information he hadn't intended to reveal. Maybe he'd even let it slip that he killed Gary. But Ron's lips thinned. His eyes narrowed. His body telegraphed resistance, like a stone wall.

"We just want to give you a chance to see what we have." St. John shrugged, hoping he conveyed nonchalance. Meanwhile, he squared off like a hunter approaching his prey, shotgun lowered at his side, finger to his lips, no sudden movement. He didn't want to spook the animal.

"Okay." Ron blew out a breath and took the bait.

"We have a couple of phone calls," St. John said, downplaying the thousands of recordings his department had seized. "You probably already know about those, but we thought we'd give you a chance to listen to them and maybe give us some explanation."

Ron shrugged as the detective pressed "Play" and Pam's voice filtered through the space. Snippets of conversation floated around them and startled the smugness off Ron's face. *"If I'm being fucked over by you . . . hundreds of calls from you and me to you, spanning six months prior to the event . . . blackmail. If [I] ever found out you compromised me for your benefit . . . you're a fried duck . . ."*

St. John fast-forwarded the tape and played another section. Gamber chewed the cap of his pen and watched with fascination as Ron paled. A muscle in Ron's jaw twitched. His brown eyes watered slightly. He crossed and uncrossed his arms. He shifted, fixated on a nick in the table. St. John adjusted the volume, rewound the tape, and played it again, insisting that the first few words sounded muffled: "Maybe Ron couldn't quite hear them." Ron flinched as more threats bit through the room. He stared at the ceiling pretending to search the cracks in the paint for justification, denial or excuse. *It wasn't his voice. He had no clue about blackmail. It was all nuance and innuendo.*

"Pam's not sticking up for you." Gamber replaced the cap on the pen. St. John clicked off the tape, leaned back in his seat, and nodded. "We served a search warrant on her house back in September. We've gone through all her computers and all her records and we've talked to her." *All lies.* But Ron didn't know that. Police interrogation was about technique and manipulation.

"We're offering you the choice to tell us what's going on. I mean, we flagged some stuff, some records from your computer, the spreadsheet of the payments, Gary's life insurance policy, and your proportionate share. It's going to come down to . . . blackmail. She's hanging it on you. She's not in jail. She's willing to talk and we're offering you an opportunity to not make the hole any deeper than it already is."

"I think I should talk to my lawyer," Ron said.

"That's fine. You have every right to do that. I've highlighted some of the stuff we thought was most interesting. But I mean, this is probably a fiftieth of what we got out of your laptop. We're still digging stuff out of Pam's computers. Just understand this: the focus is now entirely on you. We're here ten years later and we're not going to go away."

"Well, I would hope not; that would be terribly disappointing if you did,"* Ron laughed.

---

* Ron only spent two months in the Pitkin County Jail. All charges against him were dismissed. The judge ruled that District Attorney Gail Nichols's case was based on hearsay and lacked sufficient evidence to proceed to trial.

* * *

But it would not be so simple. Ron had *not* confessed to murder. His voice on the tapes, while suspicious, did not connect him to Gary's bombing. Still, the recordings provided a necessary crack in a vast wall of silence. Now Gamber had only to convince the Pima County Attorney's Office that Ron's case merited prosecution. He needed a deputy county attorney (DCA) with guts and tenacity, someone unafraid of the political tempest Ron's case might inspire. Most DCAs in the homicide division paid their dues in the trenches, working their way up from misdemeanor prosecutions to tougher felonies, where they finally enjoyed brief notoriety.

Deputy County Attorney William McCollum was no exception. But he was less than enthusiastic to indict Ron for murder. He wanted more: a well-defined scent that in the end would lead to blood. Sleek and striking, the DCA had a reputation for navigating murky waters like a shark on the hunt. He considered law a calling, not a job, as he thrashed in the courtroom and spent long hours on task. Utterly consumed by his cases, sometimes his extreme focus was mistaken for arrogance as he levied personal attacks on his opponents, had frequent emotional outbursts, and stood indignant in the face of what he considered to be "morally offensive" crimes like Ron's.

McCollum despised pretense and people who wore masks.

But he could not afford to lose Ron's case. Gary Triano was too large a public figure, and the fallout for failure would be career-ending. Ron's was no slam dunk; He had reason to worry. He had recently lost a case that had languished for thirty years. The judge accused McCollum of "hibernating" while evidence "dissipated."

"It was not "sufficient," the judge admonished, for the state to say it made some mistakes."

McCollum could not afford to look foolish again. He

had to be sure *this time* he had the right man. It would take another two years before McCollum finally had the courage to indict Ron *and* Pam for murder.

On a crisp October morning in 2008, Gamber and Keith St. John traveled from Tucson to Yorba Linda, California, where surveillance teams from the Pima County Sheriff's Department had already confirmed "Ron sightings" in the Los Angeles area. The Brea Police Department, the agency provider for Yorba Linda, had recovered Ron's van in 1996 and gladly offered to assist with his capture. After a brief review between departments, the Brea police initiated a traffic stop of Ron's car as he left his mother's residence.

Gamber talked with Ron later that evening in an interview room at the Brea Police Department. Ron immediately recognized the detective. His face flushed red. He wanted a lawyer and a bathroom. He felt nauseous. Gamber advised that he had an arrest warrant and Ron's face visibly relaxed.

"For Pam?"

Gamber shook his head. Ron asked for water: "Throat's dry," he rasped. He gulped the liquid, stalling for time. He agreed to waive extradition "of course" and return to Tucson.

"This was such a mistake" and he "wanted to help clear things up quickly." By 10:30, officers transported Ron to the Orange County Jail in Santa Ana, California, where a judge ordered his extradition.

The following morning, Ron arrived in Tucson and Gamber booked him into the Pima County Jail. The judge ordered a $5 million bond.

CHAPTER TWENTY-FOUR:
RECKONING

The trial began on February 23, 2010, in the case of *State of Arizona v. Ronald Kelly Young.* Judge Christopher Browning's courtroom filled with spectators, Gary's family members, local television and news reporters, law students, and Detectives Gamber and St. John, who stood leaning against the far wall, audience to their own road play. No one came to support Ron.

Computers hummed in the courtroom and in the jury box; they cast the players in a bluish haze. Television screens remained darkened, the corners, waiting to crackle to life with exhibits. Ron Young towered over his two public defense lawyers, Walt Palser and Joel Feinman. With readers balanced on the bridge of his nose and dressed in a smart beige shirt, navy tie, and chunky leg brace, he hardly looked the part of a cold-blooded killer. Dark shadows smudged his lower lids. His once brown shoulder-length hair was cropped short in a shock of white. In a few days he would celebrate his sixty-eighth birthday, alone, in his jail cell. He seemed unaware of Gary's family, their glowering scrutiny, and unaffected by the court's cool warning to the media that Ron was not to be filmed in shackles.

Judge Christopher Browning was a man of great dignity

and experience: a graduate of the University of Arizona, he had served on the bench for nearly twenty-nine years, handling mostly civil litigation and wrongful-death lawsuits. Ron stood, expressionless, as the charges against him were read to the jury: count one, first-degree murder; count two, conspiracy to commit first-degree murder.

"He has pled not guilty," the judge advised.

Initially, Ron's defense team moved for change of venue, insisting that Ron could not possibly receive a fair trial, given the blitz of publicity, numerous articles, Web posts, and newscasts dating as far back as 1996. Media had dubbed the bombing the "most notorious crime in Tucson's history" and repeatedly aired clips of Sheriff Dupnik calling Ron a "son of a bitch."

"His comments are tainting the jury pool," Ron's lawyer argued.

The judge remained unconvinced. Epithets did not warrant transferring the case to another county or city. In the final analysis, the jury would have to weigh and consider the evidence against Ron; their verdict would have little to do with personal opinion. In fact, the judge would instruct them as much.

Customarily, the case agent occupies a seat next to the prosecutor and assists with details and witness cross-examination, but Deputy Pima County Attorney William McCollum expressly excluded the stars of the investigation from the courtroom.

"I felt like Helen Keller," Gamber remarked later. "I did this great job and no one heard me." He recalled with mixed emotions the annual awards ceremony he attended in 2009 sponsored by the Pima County Sheriff's Department where he hoped to be acknowledged for his superior efforts in the capture and apprehension of "fugitive" Ron Young. Pima County Deputy Attorney William McCollum also expected to be honored as "prosecutor of the year" for his (as yet to be determined) *conviction* of the killer.*

"I'm not going," Gamber announced to his superiors.

"I'm ordering you to go," his captain admonished.

"I don't accept it," Gamber repeated.

"I'm ordering you to *behave*." Then, as an added incentive, his captain winked at him. "I'll buy the alcohol."

Gamber settled at a separate table and picked at his bloody steak. He recalled his initial briefing with McCollum at the Pima County Attorney's Office in early January 2007. He had eagerly anticipated presenting his eleven-year investigation and had prepared an extensive PowerPoint presentation, a virtual "connect-the-dots" that detailed Ron's six-and-a-half-year paper trail, highlighting his thousands of incriminating conversations with Pam and his numerous FedEx receipts and his elaborate scheme to transfer and receive payments from Pam. But as McCollum sat at the helm of the large conference table, he became increasingly agitated. Gamber's laser bounced from slide to slide over the expansive timeline he'd created dating as far back as 1994, when Ron's relationship began with his coconspirator. The detective synthesized for McCollum more than seventy thousand pages of discovery that spanned five states including federal jurisdictions.

McCollum's features contorted. His cheeks bloomed pink even in the dim lights. He tapped his pen on the edge of the table. Finally he stood, burst into a high-pitched rant, and dismissed the detective's presentation as "amateurish." His department would have to hire a

---

*   The annual awards banquet held in 2009 also honored Keith
        St. John (retired from the Pima County Sheriff's Depart-
        ment and now employed as a Pima County attorney investi-
        gator), FBI forensic accountant Kelly Goldsmith, and ATF
        special agent Jeffrey Bell for the Gary Triano Cold Case
        Investigation Public Service Achievement Award.

"professional"* if he hoped to prosecute a case "like this."
He complained the task was "daunting," and in response to
Gamber's protests he hollered at the detective, ordered
him to "relax, take three months off."

"It was like a scene out of *The Caine Mutiny*," Gamber
reported later to his supervisor. "Suddenly I was talking to
the crazy ship's captain, Francis Queeg."

"Apparently you upset him." His supervisor frowned.

"*Justice* upsets him."

But as both collected their awards, Pam remained in an
Austrian jail cell, her extradition delayed indefinitely. Austrian authorities had arrested her for committing fraud in
Liechtenstein. Pam's limousine driver filed a criminal complaint, alleging failure to pay back wages. Pam also had
outstanding drunk-driving charges.

Each time Gamber had broached the subject of extradition with McCollum, the prosecutor dissolved into what
Gamber described as an "emotional seizure." The Pima
County Attorney's Office "did not negotiate with criminals."
Apparently plea bargains fell into a separate category. Austrian authorities despised the death penalty; their country's
treaty prohibited them from releasing a prisoner to the
United States to face possible execution. Authorities in Arizona knew for years that Pam had left the country, but they
could not bring her home. Legal ramifications and bureau-
cratic red tape had allowed her to remain a free woman.

"Why can't she just be extradited?" Heather, Gary's
daughter, pressed.

"It's not that simple," Gamber replied. "She can challenge the process. She can demand a trial and force the
United States to produce thousands of documents, recordings, and digital media that prove her guilt."

_____

* The Pima County Attorney's Office paid a "professional"
   forensic accountant a reported $41,000 to present the same
   material.

"And if she loses?"

"She can appeal."

"And continue to appeal?" Heather fumed.

"Yes." Gamber relented.

"Until . . ."

"She exhausts her resources." He felt deflated, like a punctured balloon.

"So she can just delay, delay, delay until . . ."

"Yes." The detective sighed. *It's part of the game. Part of the process.*

"So she wins?"

No. *It might look that way, feel that way, but no.* His patience with the process had worn thin. He rejected the notion that his years of sacrifice might all be in vain, that he, too, might become a casualty of the "system." He lost sleep mulling over alternatives, reviewing the legal jousting. On the rare occasions he did dream, he saw his coworkers cemented to their desks, large chains circling their ankles. The message lights on their phones blinked like angry red eyes. Some had wives, kids, and pets they had not seen in weeks. Most, including himself, preferred to chew a ham sandwich alone at his desk than relish a home-cooked meal with family. Guilt gnawed at his insides. He could not enjoy simple pleasures; his victims never would. Body parts swirled in his head, missing pieces of missing people whose cases remained unsolved.

Gamber could not accept the excuse of "insufficient evidence" to prosecute. He could not accept that two purported killers had literally escaped murder. He had night sweats and visions of Heather fading into the dark recesses of the cold-case unit. He worried that his own inexperience might have hampered the investigation. He reviewed his multiple interviews with Pam and Ron for errors, hiccups, revelations, clues he might have missed, anything that would turn the case and propel the prosecutor to action.

But he found nothing. Then, in November 2007, he approached Heather with an idea, something guaranteed to motivate the Pima County Attorney's Office to issue arrest warrants for his two murder suspects. He encouraged Heather, Brian, and Robin Gardner's daughter, Elliott, to file a civil lawsuit under the homicide survivor's and racketeering statutes against Pam and Ron in Pima County Superior Court.* Their civil lawyers puzzled publicly. They could not fathom why no criminal charges had yet been filed. But with only circumstantial evidence, no confession, and no definitive forensic link between the bomb and the killer, the government hesitated. Civil litigation required a lesser standard of proof, a mere preponderance of the evidence; and although both proceedings would rely on the same recordings and financial records, it would take the Pima County Attorney's Office another two years before they would commit to indicting Ron and Pam on first-degree murder.

Ron's defense team would later use the government's pre-indictment delay as grounds to dismiss the case. Counsel argued that it should not have taken *twelve years* to prosecute Ron. *Everyone* knew Ron's whereabouts. He had family in Colorado and parents in California, and he was in federal custody on supervised release for at least two years.

"Nonsense," McCollum retorted. He insisted the defense was clouding the issue, oversimplifying the problem, and creating "red herrings" to confuse and delay the process. McCollum emphasized that it wasn't Ron's *whereabouts* that troubled his office, it was the proof against him. As resources dwindled, the cold-case unit bogged down with alarming demands and deadlines. Experts, laboring to interpret and analyze coded documents and conversations, could not help but stall the prosecution as they struggled

---

* In November 2009, a judge awarded the children $10 million in damages.

with a way to manage the volume of information and present Ron's "well-orchestrated plan." All high-profile murders added pressure on the prosecution; it would have been career suicide for McCollum to prematurely indict Ron and Pam for Gary's murder. But his methodical approach to justice had an unintended consequence: Pam's departure for Europe.

CHAPTER TWENTY-FIVE:
THE CASE FOR MURDER

Jury selection had its intense moments as prospective members disclosed their criminal history, their knowledge of the bombing, their relatives and acquaintances with careers in law enforcement and the law. There were jurists who simply could not sit for weeks; some were teachers and contract workers, and although it was illegal for their bosses to fire them for jury service, they worried "in this economy" about job stability and what the anticipated length of the trial would do to their commitments. The defense worried about prejudice. Ron's lawyers insisted on a questionnaire in addition to oral responses. Jurors could expound on their answers, elaborate on their reservations (if they had any), and detail their media exposure. The questionnaire provided both sides with useful insights into the final twelve jurors who would decide Ron's fate.

And as they filed into the courtroom, they sobered for opening statements. A hush fell over the courtroom, and there was a sense of time rushing forward. Gary's family members waited to exhale. The prosecutor, William McCollum, struggled to find a way to make money sexy. He needed to engage a jury, guide them through the land mines and maze of characters. This was his chance to summarize the facts, to preview what the state's case would prove. He needed no notes. The crime stained his memory. He looked polished and sleek in his black suit, ready to deliver a sobering truth: Ron Young was a killer.

He began dramatically. The courtroom morphed into a kind of crime scene. Metaphoric yellow caution tape surrounded the jury box. McCollum treaded lightly on sympathy, did not appeal to emotion, and resisted the urge to inflame the panel's passions. He did not flinch at photos of Gary's family, their sunny smiles tearing at the glossy finish. He could not fail. He could not disappoint the reporters salivating in the back of the courtroom like hyenas. It was time. Gary's family had waited twelve years for justice.

McCollum opened with what he described as an "overture." Ron's own words supplied the dark, percussive theme. An ominous recording of Ron's threat to his coconspirator, Pam,* drifted eerily over the jury. Pam would find herself "in a women's prison for murder" if she failed to honor her six-and-a-half-year agreement with Ron. Ron sat stone-faced as McCollum recounted the "devastating task" he and his cocounsel, Shawn Jensvold, tackled in the cold-case division of the Pima County Attorney's Office. The prosecution had waded through over 152,989 e-mails and countless digital recordings of conversations between the coconspirators; they solicited experts to decipher the codes Ron used to conceal not only his identities but his computer files, Federal Express tracking numbers, and even the murder plot itself. The lawyers reviewed an estimated 78,000 pages of discovery, 931 spreadsheets of financial information memorializing the defendants' payment schedule, and tedious detailed reports concerning the bomb debris.

"This was a real whodunit of magnitude proportions with a cast of thousands," McCollum expounded. It involved a daunting list of potential killers and bomb fragments,

---

* Len Holiday, Pam's attorney, confirmed during Ron's trial that she was in prison in Austria, awaiting extradition.

with detectives sifting through Gary's ashes following his cremation "just to retrieve metal chips"; an expansive crime scene at a public, swanky resort; and a timeline that spanned a decade. His calm voice belied the violence he described, blowing over the jurors like a cold draft.

The jurors sat transfixed during his presentation. Eventually they stopped taking notes. There was too much to absorb. Most of them had led uneventful lives in which murder-for-hire plots and explosions never figured. They listened as McCollum assured them that, despite the circumstantial evidence, Ron Young had activated the switch that ignited the bomb.

He had motive, McCollum said simply: money.

The prosecutor highlighted the recording he'd just played for them and alluded to the multiple others the panel would hear during the course of the trial. He offered them definitions, Ron Young's codes for money that investigators had learned to decipher, that incriminated Ron and demonstrated his participation in the conspiracy to murder Gary: "stuff," "things," "information," "obligation." But more than cash, McCollum promised jurors they would hear Ron plot with Pam about murder, discussing and referring to the killing as an "event." McCollum previewed the conversations, the financial spreadsheets, the evidence Ron had left behind in his own home, in his van, in storage lockers, and in his hotel room in Florida. And he suggested to the jurors the one damning conversation Ron had with Pam at the Caribou Club in Aspen, the plot that put the plan into motion.

In the end, McCollum left the jurors with a portrait of Ron as a diabolical manipulator who for ten years literally "got away with murder."

"Don't you let him get away again," McCollum ended.

Ordinarily defense counsel reserved its opening statement for its portion of the case, but Joel Feinman seized the opportunity to expound on the state's "whodunit" theory. He took a prudent course to bolster his client's credibility. He *agreed* with the facts as stated, but he promised jurors an entirely different interpretation. He asked the panel to consider how an extraordinarily large man like Ron could possibly have escaped detection. He offered a plausible reason: Ron wasn't there. According to Ron's lawyer-CPA friend, Ron had visited him in California the day of the murder; his alibi placed Ron nearly 471 miles from Tucson. Forensic evidence confirmed that *whoever* detonated the device had to have stood within four hundred feet of the bomb.

Feinman stayed with the crime scene, deliberately highlighting the weak spots in the prosecutor's case, suggesting that the chaos and confusion of the bomb impaired witnesses' ability to recall. He alluded to possible evidence tampering by the sheriff's department, the conflicting descriptions witnesses gave police of cars that sped from the scene, the unguarded second parking lot, and the dark tunnel. With more than 150 witnesses at the scene, how could the state be sure Ron had planted the bomb?

No one had placed him at the crime scene. Other facts didn't add up. Did it make any sense, for instance, that Ron, a "master bomber," would leave his computer behind in Aspen or park his rental van full of his personal effects in his parents' neighborhood? Feinman assured the jurors they would hear plausible explanations for Ron's actions. His client had composed letters to the rental car company negotiating with them for the release and/or safekeeping of his property. Would a killer on the run have risked such exposure? Would a killer have left behind a shotgun and ammunition, hollow-point bullets and shell casings? Did a skeet gun make Ron a bomber? He suggested the gun was a "red herring," an irrelevant piece of evidence offered to make jurors think Ron was a bad person. Maybe he was just a hunter. Jurors would never know Feinman's battle to preclude the shotgun. Once the judge deemed it admissible, Feinman used it to his advantage.

What of the documents in Ron's van, the dissolution paperwork and the map of Tucson? Feinman supplied a plausible explanation: Ron worked for Pam. She had asked him to investigate Gary's hidden assets. Amateur sleuthing did not make Ron a killer. Methodically, Feinman gutted the state's case, leaving the jury to contemplate how, after ten years of investigation, the prosecution had more puzzle than answer, *more reasonable doubt than solid proof.* But what of the "mountains" of recordings the jury would hear, of Ron's cutting voice warning Pam she might sit in a women's prison for murder? Every case had its "bad facts," and Feinman tackled them head-on. His strategy was to deflect the jury's focus from murder and conspiracy to something equally plausible. He injected cacophony into the prosecutor's "seamless symphony," conceding that Ron *was* involved but not as a murderer, not as a coconspirator, but as an extortionist. And as unflattering as that sounded, Feinman assured that the state's case was a dead ringer for blackmail, curiously a charge for which Ron was never indicted.

With the battle lines drawn, each side put on their armor. But unlike war, there would be no ambush, no surrender. Only strategic shots fired, wounded soldiers, and a bloody field. The jury would be left to clear the debris and make sense of what remained. Both sides knew the other's theories well; each expected to be undermined and ridiculed. Each expected the other to spin the same facts into his own calculated tale.

The prosecution provided the foundation.

The defense exposed the gaps, the "reasonable doubt."

CHAPTER TWENTY-SIX:
BLOWN AWAY

The crime scene witnesses testified first, detailing days and days of nearly identical stories. Each corroborated the surreal quality of the blast, the "shock and awe" factor, the frenetic chaos that followed. They described various cars that "fled" the scene—a white, maroon, tan Isuzu. They highlighted the glaring failure of resort security to guard the underground tunnels used in daylight to allow easy passage of golf carts. Jurors heard about Gary's "habits," his preference for leaving his keys in his car "so thieves wouldn't damage [his] steering column," his regular golf days, lunch dates, and easy style with waiters, bellhops, and security personnel. Gary was "likeable," "gregarious," and "perpetually in debt." Some witnesses speculated that the victim might have been depressed, paranoid, and even suicidal in the weeks before his murder. But at the scene, tunnel vision. Mayhem clouded reason. Nobody saw anything or anyone suspicious and "the killer got away, literally disappeared."

At that, Ron shook his head slightly and scribbled frantically to his lawyer on his legal pad. On cross-examination, Ron's cocounsel treaded delicately. The packed courtroom breathed against his neck. None of the witnesses who testified had any motive to lie; some offered help, CPR, even though Gary had no face. Walt Palser, the lead defense counsel, asked about perception amidst chaos and confusion. It was hard to really know who saw what. Lamps and headlights illuminated mass pandemonium. Federal agents worked alongside local law enforcement, focusing on the bomb chips; so much to compile and analyze. But no one ever identified Ron at the scene, did they? No. Defense counsel hammered at the state's foundation, leaving giant cracks.

And soon the attacks turned personal. McCollum and Palser were full-blown adversaries.

"He's using my first name," defense counsel objected, arguing at the bench that he found the casual form of address demeaning and arrogant.

The judge ordered the two to "stop the sideshow" and focus on the facts.

Gary's family members paraded to the stand one by one, each glowering at Ron as they did so. Joy Bancroft, looking regal and elegant in her early fifties, tactfully skirted discussion of the "turkey caper," an "unfortunate incident" the defense successfully managed to preclude from the state's presentation. The jury would never hear that Joy's husband demanded Ron return the stolen carcass; the jury was never privy to the husband's outrage that money his wife had funneled to Pam for the children might actually have funded Ron's advance.

Instead, Joy recounted more pleasant memories of her friendship with Pam, earnest conversations they shared in the meadow, confidences about finances, lifestyle, and men. They had been "very close," she said. Pam "constantly worried" about money; Joy cared for Pam's children. She was their godmother, after all. She felt responsible for the children's financial security. She helped when she could. Then, after Gary's murder, she stayed in touch with Pam. But curiously, Pam never mentioned Ron's name and certainly never revealed that she was romantically involved with him.

Privately, in the conference room reserved for witnesses, Joy expressed "terrible disappointment" at Pam's choices and guilt at having to now betray her friend's trust.

"Tell us about the life insurance policy," McCollum prompted.

Joy explained that the payments had become prohibitive for Pam. She agreed to help "for the children's sakes" but, she said, looking sheepish, sometimes the payments were delinquent. She never told Pam. When asked about October's missed payment, Joy pursed her lips nervously and glanced at the defense table. Her voice wavered, her response so soft, it was difficult to evaluate her emotions. She had been preoccupied with the birth of her son. She had forgotten.

"And what was Pam's reaction when she learned the policy might have lapsed?" McCollum pressed.

Joy described Pam's distraught state. Her friend was inconsolable, not about Gary's death, but about the potential loss of his money.

Defense counsel sat poised at their table, Ron sandwiched between them. So far nothing the state had presented incriminated *him*. The witnesses simply recounted the impact Gary's loss had on their lives. But as the days wore on, Heather testified. As she raised her hand to be sworn in, she shook. She faced the jury, her chiseled features, once vibrant and flush, had an ashen sheen. She wore a stylish suit that accented her long legs. She looked weary, almost resentful at having to testify at all. *We all know who did it,* her expression implied. *Why go through the charade?* It seemed an unnecessary spotlight on a killer who relished attention for his efforts. She fixed Ron with a steely gaze.

Guided by McCollum, Heather talked about her father, the memories clearly causing her deep distress. She described the day of Gary's surprise birthday party like it was a stain in her past she could not blot out. She stayed late at the car dealership where she worked to type up Gary's favorite poem, "If" by Rudyard Kipling. She emphasized that her father was broke at the time of his death, having filed for bankruptcy in 1995. None of the children benefited from his murder. She was made executor of his estate, his life reduced to paper and finances. Heather's voice dropped to a near whisper as she described the aftermath of her father's murder. She became a drifter, moving to New York City for seven years, until the terrorist attacks. She was ready for change, ready to heal. She accepted Pam's invitation to help her rejuvenate Star Babies, a business Gary had started. They became friends; Pam referred to her as her "houseguest." Pam left her daily reminders on sticky notes. And then, one bright spring afternoon, Heather stumbled across something she was certain she wasn't meant to see.

"It was a sticky note from Pam to Ron," she testified.

"What did it say?" McCollum prompted, showing her an exhibit.

" 'You have no idea how betrayed and angry I am,' " Heather's voice cracked as she recited Pam's rant about the money Ron had defrauded from her bank accounts. " 'I'm getting calls from a Detective Crowley. I don't claim to be communicating with you. I would like to say I have gotten some of my money back. I think the apparent connection between us is best kept at a minimum. . . . I'm feeling pretty helpless and not real healthy . . . [E]verything feels like quicksand lately.' "

"Tell us about Basalt." McCollum faced the jury. He watched their incredulous faces. He was a mercurial man who wore his emotions in his face and posture.

"It's tiny, two grocery stores, two lights, very windy roads. It's about forty-five minutes from Aspen."

"Does Aspen have a Federal Express facility?"

"Yes. Federal Express picked up at the house. There was no reason to travel to Basalt."

Ron gave nothing away in his facial expression. He looked cool and confident as he adjusted his reading glasses. The trial highlighted *Pam*, not him. Some of the jurors watched

William McCollum. Others stared down at their laps. Only a few looked at Heather, as if they thought it somehow rude to stare. She had suffered such a terrible loss, endured such a brutal end.

McCollum asked the question he knew defense counsel wanted answered.

"Did you ever suspect Pam?"

"She was my friend. I trusted her," Heather said tearfully, as if she still had not come to terms with her stepmother's depravity. Her responses came as if she had been holding her breath.

Palser, did not relish the cross-examination of Heather. She was a sympathetic witness, and if he came down too harshly on her, the jury would discount his arguments. They would berate him for his coldness; they would liken him to his client. But if he treaded too softly, he might miss an important opportunity. Thankfully, he didn't need much from Heather, just confirmation that Pam had never mentioned Ron to her.

The prosecution now needed to explain to the jury the "apparent connection" between the two and why Pam had made so many trips to Basalt. His case was not about the human debris left in the wake of Gary's murder, it was about the money.

Kevin Childress, an employee with Federal Express, explained in detail the life of a package dropped off at a facility.

"If a document is dropped off March 27 and sent from zip code 81621, a tracking number is assigned to that customer, that package, that day. The number cannot be reused."

"That's the Basalt zip code?"

"Yes. Aspen's is 81611."

"So it's possible for something to be shipped in March but billed in April?"

"They're air bills. Three pieces of paper handwritten

preprinted with information, address, and account number. Example, sender: Richard Perez, Business Services, Inc., 1126 South Federal Highway, Suite 254, zip 33326."

"The recipient address is the same."

"Yes."

"What would be the reason for that?"

"Billing or inability to trace."

McCollum shifted to the murder script that put the death plan in motion that compelled Ron to perform. He called forensic accountant Robert Semple to the stand. The expert testified for two full days regarding the complicated money transfers, cash conversions, spreadsheets, and codes Ron and Pam used to memorialize their payment schedule. He read chunks of e-mails verbatim between the two until the defense finally objected to the "tedious" nature of the state's presentation. Jurors heard reference upon reference to Pam's "800-pound monster" and the "Gary problem" Ron had agreed to fix. They heard snippets of recordings where the two bickered over balances and interest like an old married couple. But equally compelling was what jurors *didn't* hear: any definitive dialogue about murder.

Semple reviewed Pam's exhausting routine, her twice, sometimes thrice weekly withdrawals in cash increments of $1,400, $1,600, and $1,800 from four different banks: Wells Fargo,* Alpine, Vectra, *and* Morgan Stanley. Caution was paramount: banks reported cash deposits that exceeded $10,000 to the United States Treasury. They also scrutinized multiple successive transactions—"$6,000 today, $7,000 tomorrow"—as evidence of possible fraudulent activity.

Pam worried about tax implications and spending money she never *earned*. Moving funds back and forth between banks "bothered her." The constant arguments over "stuff," "pieces," and "things" made Pam "not right in her head,"

---

* Previously Norwest Bank.

setting her "house of cards crumbling." Semple simplified the codes for the jury: "18" meant $1,800, "14" meant $1,400, and so forth. He highlighted oddities in the spread-sheet, one lump sum payment of $25,000 six months *before* the murder; several larger payments years later.

"Ron's world was small," he explained. "Alternating between home and hotel, he collected his Federal Express package from the post office, traveled to his nearby 7-Eleven, where he converted the cash into money orders, and then visited his Bank of America, where he deposited the checks into an account he established in his son, Brady's, name."

But Palser on cross-examination still played out his "whodunit" theory, getting Semple to admit the money was no proof that *Ron* manufactured a bomb, much less committed murder.

As if anticipating the defense's questions, the prosecution presented Special Agent Anthony May of the Bureau of Alcohol, Tobacco, Firearms and Explosives. His specialty lay in the manufacture of homemade grenades, pipe bombs, remote-controlled devices, chemical weapons, and nuclear explosions. Constructing a pipe bomb, he assured jurors, was "easy" and "inexpensive." Components, like the nipple and end caps, could be purchased at common hardware outlets and other circuitry at electronic stores such as Radio Shack or hobby shops. Explosive powders, including smokeless powders could be purchased readily at gun shops, no questions asked. Red Dot, also known as Hercules powder, worked as a propellant.

"If I lay out a line of powder across this desk and light one end, it will burn down the column of material to the other at a uniform rate. That's called a particle burn. Now, if I take that same length of powder and I combine it into a pile and I put a match to it, instead of a uniform burn, now we have a small explosion. It will have a puff of smoke, a flash of light, possibly even a sound. The only thing I've done different is I have changed the configuration." The prosecution offered a video of a pipe bomb explosion as demonstrative evidence.

"Maybe they'd like to introduce a mock model bomb as well?" defense counsel objected.

That came next. Despite May's assurances that his reconstruction was "completely inert," jurors nonetheless flinched at the mini-explosion. They watched transfixed as they witnessed in slow motion the devastating effects of a pipe bomb. May narrated the demonstration and explained that "friction is a problem" and sometimes bombers regrettably "blew themselves up" when putting the pipes together.

"What about lubricants?" a juror scribbled in a note to the judge. "Could something be used to screw the end caps on to avoid that friction?"

"Yes," May replied, smiling, pleased that the panel had followed his technical explanation. "A person could use almost anything to reduce friction: paste, Vasoline."

"Toothpaste?" McCollum prompted.

"Sure."

McCollum reminded the jury later of Ron's one fear: killing himself.

CHAPTER TWENTY-SEVEN: SCORE ONE FOR THE DEFENSE

One week into the trial, Andre Mims, the prosecution's star witness, shuffled to the stand. Dressed in prison stripes and shackles, he adjusted his large glasses on his nose and swiveled to face the jury. McCollum wasted no time with pleasantries. He went for the jugular, hoping to defuse the defense's anticipated attempt to discredit Mims.

"Why are you dressed like that?"

"I'm a felon." Mims shrugged unapologetically.

"Have I made you any deals in exchange for your testimony today?"

"No, sir."

"Are you familiar with Ron Young?"

"I was his lawyer."

"His *lawyer*?" McCollum barely disguised his sarcasm.

"Well, not his *real* lawyer." Mims shifted uncomfortably.

"Explain." McCollum stood and crossed his arms as Mims smiled and spoke directly to the jury.

"I'm what they call a 'legal beagle.'"

"A jailhouse lawyer?"

"Yes."

"You were housed in the same facility as Mr. Young?"

"Yes."

"Tell us about that relationship."

"We liked the same fish."

McCollum's lip twitched. He tried a more direct question. "Did Mr. Young ever tell you about Gary Triano?"

Mims fixed the jurors with a hard stare, as if he held the winning card in a game of legal poker. "He told me, 'I blew that fucker up.'"

"That's not what he *said*." Walt Palser shot up from his chair like a crazed jack-in-the-box and approached the bench for a sidebar conference. "'He got what he deserved'—that's what Mims *said* Ron said." He waved Mim's affidavit at the judge and moved for a mistrial. The judge excused the panel, motioned for the deputy to remove Andre Mims from the courtroom, and met the attorneys in his chambers.

McCollum dismissed Palser's wordplay—"blew him up," "got what he deserved"—as mere semantics. But in fact there *was* a problem with Mims's statement.

Mims had told the detectives that Ron bragged to him about his drug escapades, insisting he flew cargo from the Bahamas to Aspen during the period 1985–86. And when a rival drug dealer muscled in on his business, Ron "blew the fucker up." *Which fucker?* Detective Gamber pressed. Mims clarified. He learned of Ron's involvement in a Tucson bombing after Ron disclosed his relationship with a woman named Pamela Phillips. Ron told Mims he and Pam agreed to live apart prior to her ex-husband's murder with assurances that Ron could "kill two birds with one stone": end her reported domestic abuse and cash in on her husband's life insurance proceeds. But when Mims submitted to a subsequent polygraph, his results indicated deception, specifically a "problem" with the polygrapher's question "Did Ron Young confess to you that he killed Gary Triano?"

The lawyers asked to approach the bench. In hushed tones they argued over semantics. McCollum agreed that Mims's initial statement "I got it done" was inadmissible.

"That's because Mims retracted it. I specifically asked him I don't know how many times in how many ways whether Ron ever confessed to him. This is the first time he says anything about blowing anyone up."

McCollum feigned shock and replied sarcastically, "What did you think was going to happen here? That Mims was going to waltz into this courtroom and drop roses on the floor?" He reminded the court that Mims's statements wouldn't mark the "first time a felon decided to change his story" during a trial. "He's a criminal: Impeach him."

The judge dismissed the jury.

"I agree, you were surprised." He turned to Palser. "I previously ruled the statement 'That motherfucker got what he deserved' would be admissible."

"But that's not what he just *said*," Palser insisted. "We're splitting hairs."

McCollum teetered in a precarious position; no lawyer could knowingly offer a witness that he *knew* would lie without violating an ethical canon. He insisted Mims could be impeached with the statements in his affidavit. Mims was a "key" witness for the state, the "missing link" between Ron and the bombing. The jury would decide whether *any* of Mims's statements were credible. The judge compromised. He placed restrictions on Mims's testimony. As the felon shuffled back to the witness stand, the judge handed Mims his affidavit with yellow highlighting: "areas to avoid" when testifying.

"Do you understand the rules?" the judge asked before he summoned the jurors.

"Yes, sir."

The panel returned and defense counsel began his cross-examination,

"Ever hear of attorney-client privilege?

Mims smiled. "Of course."

"A lawyer doesn't testify against his client?"

"Yeah."

"Mr. Legal Beagle sure as heck didn't follow that one, right?"

"No, sir."

As the trial labored through the weeks, jurors heard from the computer forensic analyst who explained the elaborate coding systems Ron had installed on both his compact laptop seized from his Florida hotel room in 2005 and the computer authorities removed from his Aspen residence on April 26, 1996. The software allowed Ron to communicate with "off-site" terminals, receive and send faxes, "speak" to fax services, and convert incoming documents to digital format. Ron created mirror images of hard drives and zip discs, had folders for voice mails, spreadsheets of accounts, various backup systems and backups of *those* systems. Ron used fifteen separate e-mail addresses that were completely unrecognizable; Pam, on the other hand, was less savvy. She had only five and used her true name, location, and business in the address.

In characteristic fashion, Ron drafted "notes" to Pam in outline form, breaking down his points into categories, "a., b., c.," often lamenting that it "made him crazy" when Pam questioned "his integrity" or "implied that he was some sort of cheat." He considered himself Pam's "most trusted friend," and it "pained" him each and every time she chose to "screw around" with the accounting. He labored over his "advice" to Pam about her personal affairs and her business practices—writings that took him "hours and hours" to craft, and hundreds more for law enforcement to decipher and interpret.

Even if Ron chose not to testify, his voice and opinions were now familiar to the jury. They listened to countless dark threats on recordings but none would ever place him at the scene of the crime. Still, they heard from Richard Cummings, the consummate insurance man, about the money trail. He gave the jury a crash course in life insurance and underwriting. It was his company, now Industrial Alliance Pacific (formerly Seaboard Life), that issued the

policy to Gary in 1992. It was a term life, annually renew-
able, with an increasing premium.

In October 1995, Pam requested a change of ownership
from Pamela Triano to Pamela Phillips, with Joy Bancroft
assuming the payments. The premiums were designed to
increase each year, and at the time of Gary's death they
hovered at $500 per month.

The jury learned that, following the bombing, Seaboard
Life paid Pam over $2 million plus interest on Gary's death
claim. The company had delayed the final payout: they had
yet to fully investigate Gary's manner of death. Pam's lawyer drafted a letter to Seaboard Life disclosing several
newspaper articles about the incident and suggested police
reports might offer a better description. Pam, meanwhile,
drafted a letter to her insurance agent imploring him to keep
any distribution of monies "strictly confidential." Discretion was imperative, she urged, given Gary's debtors and
the exposure his murder would likely produce. She and her
children might be in danger; money could signal an easy
target.

Mention of the policy itself did not alarm the defense
and did not prove Ron's culpability in Gary's murder. Neither, necessarily, did the figures, although the state had
illuminated the "apparent connection" between Ron and
Pam. The life insurance proceeds and Ron's regularly
shipped installments were now closely aligned. Spreadsheets confirmed Ron's payments stemmed directly from
Pam's life insurance money. Recordings and e-mails revealed that Ron had badgered Pam about interest, amounts,
and methods. Six and a half years after the life insurance
proceeds were distributed, Ron insisted that Pam was "only
halfway there" toward fulfilling her "obligation." Still, the
defense parried, none of it proved Ron's involvement in
murder.

The state pressed forward, producing more paper, such

as hotel receipts from the Ramada Inn placing Ron in Tucson for eighteen days in July 1996. The defense countered on cross-examination that the receipts showed *Phillip Desmond* paid cash and signed in and out each day. The state responded by producing Phillip Desmond's credit card receipt from the Caribou Club in Aspen. Authorities had seized it from Ron's rental van. The real Phillip Desmond testified that he and Ron were distant business associates. He had never given Ron permission to use his credit card. And he had never been to the Caribou Club in Aspen.

The state produced no recorded conversations of Ron's alleged dinner with Pam. But it produced plenty of messages on answering machines and e-mails afterward that suggested the two were there and had plotted Gary's murder. The absence of recorded details fit Ron's profile, McCollum argued later, indicating to the jury that the exchange between the two that night had to be very clear: no codes, no misunderstandings. They had to reach a mutual agreement that would forever bind them in conspiracy. The state produced more receipts recovered from Ron's van, including an American Express airline charge for Pam to fly to Denver in May, and a handwritten list, which analysts testified matched Ron's script, for gunsmiths and electronic circuitry and toothpaste.

McCollum presented a carefully sequenced case with a flowing timeline so the jury could follow the intricate threads that connected Ron to Gary's murder. Jurors could absorb the evidence and testimony and weigh the significance of each detail. Experts followed experts to explain the money trail and documents that led to more evidence. The jurors had to believe beyond a reasonable doubt that Ron killed Gary.

After five weeks of testimony, the prosecution wound down and rested its case. And as it did so, it left the jury to wonder about Ron's intent. Had Ron plotted a diabolical murder for insurance proceeds, or, consistent with Ron's criminal charges out of Aspen, had Ron simply seized an opportunity to defraud a woman with whom he had once shared intimate relations?

The defense had already dropped several hints about its theory, blackmail, and in an unusual twist the state's strongest points were also the defense's aces. Each side had simply spun the details differently. The money, recordings, and receipts, according to the state, proved Ron's conspiracy to commit murder. The defense insisted through its cross-examination that they proved something else entirely. If Ron worried about the strengths of his case, he never showed signs of wear to his lawyers. Instead he sat, unflappable, at the defense table, barely blinking as each state witness expounded on his meticulous record keeping, the money he received from Pam over the years, and his elaborate payment arrangement. If he was guilty of anything, it was of saving too much.

Andre Mims, the state's star witness, who had been escorted to the stand by deputies, had nearly inspired a mistrial. But the damage his testimony caused resonated through the jury, leaving them to wonder: *Had Mims told them the truth after all, that Ron "blew that fucker up"? Had he waffled from nerves or some other motive? Had he really been offered a federal deal?*

Either way, his testimony offered the jury Ron's *only* confession to the murder. And as the jury filed out for a break, the lawyers huddled with Ron. They worried Ron might make it worse if he elaborated on Mims's statement. Too much emphasis might encourage debate among the jurors. Ron, his lawyers surmised, had no ability to see himself as others did. If he testified, he could cause irreparable damage.

A defendant's decision to testify remained the defense's one surprise for the prosecution. The media salivated in the back of the courtroom, waiting with bated breath to see if they could report on the 5:00 news that Ron had taken the stand in his own defense. It was never wise to expose a defendant to state scrutiny. Still, it was necessary for a defense attorney to establish a decent rapport with his client, to make him at least *think* he controlled the playing field, make him believe it was *his* desire to remain silent. And sometimes psychology just didn't matter.

Palser and Feinman risked a tantrum. Ron would not testify.

It would be several more days before summations began; meanwhile, the lawyers and judge reviewed jury instructions. In the now nearly empty courtroom, there was a sense of impending loss. No matter the outcome, they had all endured an ordeal and it would be difficult to erase the images, the voices, from their minds once the jury had deliberated. As with any long and arduous trial, the victims left an imprint in the courtroom, a cold presence that reminded everyone that justice hung in the balance. For five weeks jurors and witnesses had focused on a tragic and horrific moment that irrevocably changed the lives of many. Jurors had listened to disembodied voices, cold and meticulous and devoid of compassion. Their own routines had been disrupted as they entered the dimly lit courtroom and prepared to take notes day after day, breaking only to eat and urinate. Jurors formed a strange silent family, unable to discuss the most disturbing details of a crime for weeks on end. Their conversations resembled commercials: mundane, repetitive, superficial discussions about the weather and clothing styles. Only during deliberation could they reveal their concerns, revelations, and opinions. Soon the twelve would disband, take their secrets with them, and reconnect with their newly formed friends in other venues and circumstances.

Soon they would be asked to decide the fate of a man they had never met.

Meanwhile, the lawyers prepared for the grande finale. No matter how many felony jury trials each had successfully conducted, nothing compared to this. Neither side could afford to slow down or relax. McCollum worried about gaps in his case, vital details he might have overlooked or emphasized too little. He had two chances to tie up loose ends, his opening and rebuttal closing argument, two chances to convince the jury beyond any reasonable doubt that Ron was a killer. McCollum did what any great prosecutor would: he prepared a strong *defense*. He already knew *his* case well. What he needed now was to see it through the lens of his opponents.

CHAPTER TWENTY-EIGHT: WHODUNIT

The courtroom filled with Gary's relatives, reporters, and other lawyers. Television crews and journalists clustered against the wall. Gary's mother and sister took the front seats. Gary's children, with the exception of Lois and Trevor, crowded toward the middle. They had become fixtures, afraid that if they missed even a single day, they might jeopardize the case or, worse, leave the jury with the mistaken impression that they did not support the prosecution. Time did not exist inside the courtroom with its yellow tinge and dim lights. It didn't matter that spring loomed just around the corner or that the days were gorgeous and crisp. Ugliness permeated the inside walls.

Jurors filtered in, on time, and took their seats as Ron shuffled toward the defense table.

The judge addressed the panel and it was as if the final curtain opened on the third act of a disturbing play. "The lawyers' arguments are not evidence," he warned. "You must rely on your memories of what each witness said." And in the ensuing hush, William McCollum approached the podium. He telegraphed no emotion. His short-cropped blond hair lay perfectly flat on his head; his pressed navy suit and bold tie conveyed his serious mood.

The tension in the courtroom was palpable. Jurors, so

solemn, so absorbed, so buried in technical information, waited for a stunning revelation, a road map to conviction. McCollum thanked them for their patience and attention. He complimented their "uncanny insight" as reflected in the questions they posed to each witness. They "got it." He beamed. "They had actually listened." And now McCollum needed them to deliver.

"Do the right thing," he implored them. "Find Ron Young guilty of murder and conspiracy to commit murder."

The courtroom fell silent as McCollum spoke, his staccato voice mimicking Ron's cold, methodical plotting. The information, now condensed into sixty minutes, packed an even greater punch as the prosecutor synthesized Ron's motive: greed, greed, greed. He had no regard for another human being, no interest in Gary's life. Ron operated like a machine; he acted, he took, "and took, and took," before and well after the "event" occurred. During the long weeks jurors heard the recordings, Ron's voice nagging, stuttering, instructing, and erupting into anger. His words had taken on a surreal quality, almost too impossible to believe.

"Gary's bombing," McCollum analogized, was "Tucson's version of the Kennedy assassination or 9/11"—a comparison defense counsel Walt Palser found repugnant. He argued later to the jury that the state's characterization was an "emotional appeal that had no basis in reality," considering nearly "three thousand people lost their lives in 9/11 . . . And *everyone* remembered where [they were] after Kennedy was shot."

"Frankly," defense counsel would address the jurors later, "*I* don't remember where I was when Triano was murdered."

The prosecutor reminded the jurors who Gary was in life. He displayed a photograph, hoping jurors would find the contrast between Gary's striking good looks and the grim bomb fragments offensive. He thanked the jurors for remembering that his death marked Ron's descent into evil: Count one, for his murder; count two, for his conspiracy.

"Did Ron *intend* to kill?" McCollum asked rhetorically, pointing to the makeshift bomb on the evidence table. "This was not some child's toy, not a Fourth of July fire-cracker."

The prosecutor summarized the meticulous planning that followed Ron's expensive meal with Pam at the Caribou Club, courtesy of someone else's credit card, then Ron's sudden departure from Aspen to dispense with his old self and welcome a revised version. If jurors believed the state thus far, they accepted that Ron *premeditated* Gary's murder *months* before he blew him up. His death was not impulsive. It was cold, calculated, and planned.

But the more difficult legal concept for the jury was the conspiracy itself; the legislature deemed actual killing and plotting to kill to be two separate crimes. Thus, even if Ron *hadn't* flipped the switch that ignited the bomb—and the state conceded no such alternative—he could *still* be found guilty of premeditated murder. The concept, the prosecutor explained, mirrored "vicarious liability" and accounted for multiple criminal actors. The law required a "meeting of the minds," an "overt act," before jurors could find conspiracy. In a murder-for-hire case—which, the prosecutor submitted, fit these circumstances—there had to be more than conversation or fantasy. The Caribou Club provided the foundation for the murder plot; Ron's actions afterward solidified his role as a coconspirator. He accepted "serious money" from Pam: "Twenty-five thousand dollars is not lunch change, not hotel money, not McDonald's money. It's a good-faith advance you'll take to your grave."

McCollum emphasized to the jury that neither player, neither Ron nor Pam, ever "withdrew" from the plan. Instead, the evidence confirmed that Ron had forged ahead, accepting, after his lump-sum earnest money, smaller installments for *years* afterward. And he concealed the blood money through elaborate payment schedules, cash conversions, and FedEx accounts; he "walked around as dead people" and borrowed different identities. But for his own arrogance, Ron might have truly committed the perfect murder.

Ron couldn't let his perfect crime escape proper credit. McCollum reminded jurors of Ron's meticulous record-keeping, his admissions of guilt through recordings, bank deposits, and precious computer files. He *wanted* someone to know of his brilliance. He wanted someone to know of his control. He left his computer behind in Aspen, piles of evidence in his van, "visions coming into focus," his apparent connection to Pam. Ron solicited his children from jail, knowing his calls were monitored. He blabbed to Mims about how he had done it, how Gary "got what he deserved."

"No person has ever saved more, created more, or intended more evidence in a first-degree murder case than Ron Young."

It wasn't stupidity or carelessness McCollum theorized; it was ego.

"Recall in March 1996 when Judge Maxwell found Pam in contempt, described her as petty and cruel, Pam had exhausted her resources, the court system, Gary, nowhere to turn and money was running out. She's been ordered to deliver the children to Gary. Enter Ron to the rescue. He puts together a spreadsheet to show her money is running out. She might have to forgo nights at the Caribou Club, evenings with the Trumps, or, worse, she might be forced to leave Aspen. She needed Ron's help. And Ron found a way to stay important in Pam's life."

Theirs was a symbiotic relationship. Pam needed money. Ron needed *Pam's* money. And Pam needed Ron to secure her cash flow. If any one of them failed to deliver, the result would be the same: no money.

"He *says* he knew nothing about a life insurance policy," McCollum noted, anticipating the defense. "Yet, he quarrels with Pam over interest she's earned on the proceeds.

He wants his fair share. 'That wasn't the agreement,' she retorts." McCollum reminded jurors that by the end of 1997, Pam had paid Ron nearly $68,000. By 2002, she lamented she "was only halfway there," and by 2004, Ron had received $248,000. "The defense will insist Ron's guilty of blackmail," which McCollum defined as "extortion for money, [the] threat of exposure of something criminal." He posed a rhetorical question to the jury: in a case without fiber, fingerprints, blood evidence, or DNA, where the only thing left is money, the jury should ask themselves: *Who* had the most to gain, who masterminded the plot to kill, who encouraged and spent and deposited blood money week after week for six and a half years? Who warned who about "honoring agreements," about becoming a "fried duck"? They should ask themselves: Who *was* Ron Young? Would he have taken a backseat to murder?

The tapes, the e-mails, the files, all revealed Ron remained front-row center.

"No one saw the killer at the scene"—McCollum paused for effect—"but he was there. I'd bet my lunch money he was there."

Walt Palser stood at the low railing surrounding the jury box. He was fairly certain no one envied his position. In his experience, most jurors confused his role, regarding him as an extension of his client, rather than a conduit for upholding the Constitution. He had been asked often how he could represent hopelessly evil sociopaths and still sleep peacefully, and his response was always the same: How could he *not*? Justice wore many cloaks and he was never more proud to unearth the truth, no matter the consequences. Palser reminded the jury of their charge, to find "guilt beyond a reasonable doubt," a standard that differed from finding Ron "innocent." No one would ever know for certain Ron's "innocence," but there was a great chance, Palser argued, that Ron was *not* guilty of murder.

Despite the recordings and e-mails, Ron's lawyer insisted that Gary Triano's murder was still "unsolved" and that his client could not possibly show remorse for a crime he did not commit. "He's guilty of blackmail," the attorney offered in a plausible explanation for Ron's participation. "He's not proud of it, but that's what he did." Ron was the "spider" Pam referenced, lurking "in an entangled web," "waiting to catch what he could." And at the end of the day, Palser challenged jurors, "what has the state really proven to y'all? That Ron Young is a master bomb builder because he uses toothpaste?"

Palser hadn't meant to be insulting, but he did wish to emphasize the absurd lengths to which the state might go to prove Ron's guilt. He focused on the prosecution's "weakest link": nothing connected Ron to the bombing.

"They're searching for the proverbial one-armed man. This case is about could have, would have, should have." He paused for dramatic effect and then emphasized his point: "I could sprout wings and fly . . . and Lee Harvey Oswald could have been brought back to life and hit the transmitter or something. It's a logical fallacy, the proverbial 'Anybody could have, would have, or should have done it.' If anybody could have done it, *Ron* must have done it, right? Anybody who does not appear obviously crazy can walk into any Wal-Mart, hand over his money and take his Red Dot powder home. Anybody could do it. *I* could have bought it. Does that make me guilty?"

He reminded jurors that federal agents spent "weeks" scouring Radio Shacks and hobby stores trying to match end caps, pieces of pipe, and receipts to Ron.

"They came up with nothing."

Palser held up four fingers. One by one he folded them and repeated for jurors the critical numbers they should consider: zero for the amount of evidence the prosecution presented, four hundred feet for the range required to detonate the bomb, five to eight seconds for the time it took police to arrive at the scene, and three to four days since anyone had last seen Ron in California. He threw up his hands and shook his head: Did it make any sense that Ron Young, a giant of a man "wearing his country club camouflage," just wandered over to the Westin La Paloma, an exclusive, members-only golf resort, and walked "through the parking lot with a bag [slung] over his shoulder" undetected?"

He laughed, not meaning to be cruel to his client, but to stress again the absurdity of the state's theory: "A man *this size* does not have much ability to lurk in a public place like that."

Ron smiled slightly at the barb, happy that the jury giggled too. Did it make sense that Ron could construct the device without being seen, that he could virtually become invisible, had a great plan to recoup life insurance proceeds, and yet never ensured that the policy had even been paid? Any connection, Palser insisted, between Ron and the bomb was "mythical," "magical," and entirely fabricated by the prosecutor.

Palser tossed out another plausible theory that he insisted "made just as much sense as the state's"—namely, that the bomb *could have been* Gary's. An audible hiss resounded through the courtroom. Palser moved on, even—possibly seriously—suggesting that Sheriff Dupnik was engaged in suspicious activity at the scene of the crime.

"Show me a *CSI* program," defense counsel challenged, "where the sheriff demands a deputy's flashlight, then ducks beneath the crime tape and proceeds to rummage through the crime scene without protective gloves, dislodging items and generally tainting the debris. How many bomb guys did we hear from that stressed the importance of being meticulous, of documenting the location of every little piece of the bigger puzzle?"

Palser recalled the testimony of a defense witness, former Department of Public Safety officer Karl Jensen, who bravely testified that he had "major concerns" about what he observed at the crime scene and in fact "was afraid to author a report." His tone had implied relief that finally the truth would surface after fourteen years.

"Sheriff Dupnik was in that car," Jensen said. As the first responder, he arrived at 5:38 that evening. He controlled the scene, entered a building to interview potential witnesses, and returned to the parking lot two hours later. "It was at least 7:38 p.m.," he said.

"Did you learn why he was there?

"He told Deputy Blair it was to identify the body.

"Did that make any sense to you?

"No. Everyone knew the victim was Gary Triano."

"And they knew it almost instantly," Palser emphasized. "By the time Sheriff Dupnik arrived, Gary Triano had been in the parking lot for *two hours*. Within minutes of the explosion, a cardiologist administered first aid. Witnesses told him the victim was Gary Triano. Joy Bancroft said by 7:00 pm, in Aspen, was already hysterical about the murder. Ruben Lopez, Gary's golfing buddy, muttered under his breath minutes following the explosion, "Those bastards killed Gary." The bombing was all over the evening news *before* 7:38. Channel 4 knew. Channel 9 knew. Channel 13 knew. Stations in Aspen, Colorado, knew. Ruben Lopez knew. Dr. Samuel Butman, the University of Arizona cardiologist, knew. Everybody in the parking lot knew who was in that car at 7:38 pm, everyone except Sheriff Dupnik." He let the insinuation of cover-up hang over the jury. *Sheriffs* did not routinely identify the dead at crime scenes. *So why was he there? Why had he made a special trip to see Gary? What did he hope to find inside the car?*

Palser undermined the investigation itself as a ploy to deflect the panel's attention away from the mountain of damning evidence against his client. If counsel convinced jurors that Ron was nowhere near the crime scene, nowhere near Tucson, and entirely too tremendous a person to have escaped detection, then all that remained was the money.

"How many recordings did y'all listen to?" He categorized the back-and-forth dialogue, labeled the recordings "Upset Pam" and "Happy Pam" to emphasize their bickering, not plotting. And when he came to the clincher, the so-called smoking gun, counsel analyzed Pam's response to Ron's warning that she might "sit in a women's prison for murder." "The very next phrase Pam utters is not 'Guess what, jerk, you're going with me. You're going to be in your own prison.' She does not say 'What do you mean? I didn't do anything wrong. I'm a socialite with a conscience.' She *says*, 'I'll be back at four.' No denial."

Ron defrauded Pam, had a warrant for his arrest, and served jail time for his indiscretions. He stole from people; he didn't kill them. Even McCollum, in his closing, had failed to mention the state's "star 'legal beagle' witness," Andre Mims, career criminal, liar, and opportunist. "He got no deal for his testimony," Palser mocked. "Now, y'all, I went to law school. I don't have one of those 'legal beagle' degrees. But I know a liar when I see one. I want to give you a *real* lesson in the law, not the 'legal beagle' kind. The state of Arizona does not have any hold over Andre Mims. This is a state court. Neither of these gentlemen"—he waved his hand at the prosecutor's table—"has the authority to make a deal in a federal case. Of course they didn't promise Andre anything. They can't. They just put him on the stand to see what would happen. They *played* with you and your intelligence. They *knew* he lied but they put him on the stand anyway. Their witness, y'all, blew up on *them*."

And as if that irony were not bad enough, Ron's lawyer reminded jurors of the state's numerous other suspects, all of whom had been mysteriously—and, he suggested, miraculously—cleared so that the focus could once again return to Ron. Distasteful as it was to disparage the murder victim, Palser would have been ineffective had he not underscored Gary's questionable activities, his business ventures that even his closest friends found "financially risky" and "too rich for [their] blood." Counsel stressed that Gary Triano had a long list of enemies, most of whom had motive and opportunity to have exacted revenge. He left a trail of scorned girlfriends, too, one of whom carried his child. She knew his routine. She "hounded" him for money. She even commiserated with Pam. But she, too, was "miraculously" cleared. So why Ron? Palser was caustic: "Because the State wants you to believe it's all here, the evidence against Ron is all here." Counsel picked up a "fancy clippy thing" and walked to the box that contained the evidence from the van,

"Let's take a look." He paused to read the Post-it on the box that read "It's all here." He shoved his hand inside and pretended to rummage around. "Somebody want to show me a license plate or a shotgun? *Because it's all here.*" He frowned, allowed silence to deafen the room, and twisted lines from Shakespeare's *Macbeth*: "He saved things, therefore he's guilty." He studied the jurors' faces, hoping for a slight nod, a flicker in their eyes, something that indicated that his arguments had been persuasive. But the panel gave him nothing.

"It's *not* all here, now, is it?" he said simply, folding his arms across his chest. "The van's not a time capsule, it's a time *machine* that has transported the shotgun to another space and time." He pointed a finger in the air and ended with a flare:

"Somewhere the real killer is laughing."

The prosecutor stood for rebuttal close, his final chance to win over the jury. He focused on his weakest link, hoping to convince the panel that Ron *was* the real killer. He was at the scene of the murder. McCollum connected the dots for the jury: "There *is* a link between Ron and the bomb, a very important link. The sawed-off shotgun found in Ron's van was a skeet-type weapon. French's [gun shop] in Denver sold Red Dot powder. Red Dot powder is used to reload skeet guns. It's also the main component of a bomb."

His delivery rattled Ron, and he visibly paled. McCollum struck like a snake, hitting the nerve, potent, raw, and deadly.

CHAPTER TWENTY-NINE:
FLOWERS ON A GRAVE

With the evidence in, the arguments over, Judge Browning chose two alternate jurors, and as he read the randomly selected names, an audible sigh resounded in the courtroom. Jurors chosen had to leave immediately; they could not deliberate with the others, could not even discuss the case with loved ones, until a verdict had been reached. Alternates were necessary in long trials in case of illness, unanticipated absences, or misconduct. No one wanted a mistrial.

Browning instructed the panel to choose a foreperson, typically the member with the strongest opinion. The jurors filed out of the courtroom to begin what would become two days of deliberations. The longer a jury stayed out, the more nerve-racking for the prosecution. It meant that the panel was weighing and reweighing the evidence, perhaps listening again to recordings, debating the merits of both sides' theories. In a circumstantial case, there were no guarantees. No one could guess the one fact that might sway the jury most to convict or acquit. No one would ever know because the province of the jury was sacred. Courts discouraged jurors from speaking afterward to lawyers because of the potential chilling effect those discussions might have on later panels. Evidence the judge precluded based on sound legal reasoning might be disclosed, and jurors who had waffled might unduly agonize over their decision.

Waiting for a verdict could, at times, be more stressful than the trial itself. Family members wandered aimlessly through the halls of the courthouse, wondering whether it was wise to return to work, to eat, to entertain a conversation on a mundane topic. Time filled like white space. Some compared the waiting to being on call, anticipating the action to start, unable to commit completely to anything else, suspended on pause. Only the present existed. No one wanted to think the worst, but as the hours ticked by, the possibility of conviction dimmed. It was almost impossible to think it, but if the jury acquitted, Ron would have committed the perfect murder and would be released into the world to strike again without warning.

The very possibility made Detective Gamber shudder.

Gary's daughter, Heather, could not fathom the delay. Since she had heard the recordings and listened to the testimony, she felt that the case against Ron was open-and-shut, and nothing that had happened in the five weeks of testimony had changed her mind. She just wanted it to be over and for Ron to be sent to prison, where he belonged. She alternated between nausea and panic, her body hollow with grief. And though Gamber tried to reassure her that the jury would "do its job," he knew his was an empty promise. The truth was he could not second-guess the jury's musings. He could not begrudge them time, either. It had taken him ten years to compile enough evidence against Ron; if it took the jury ten days or ten weeks to convict, he could live with that. But as with most ordeals that ended, his emotions were mixed. Responsibility weighed heavily on his shoulders as he absorbed the family's pain. They had attended every day of the trial diligently, and the case had worn them down. Their faces, masks of grim resolve, telegraphed their true feelings.

No matter what the ending, there never really would be

an end. The specter of Pam's trial loomed in the near future. Closure was a pretty package, but the package, all too often, was just another empty box. The real damage—the death of a loved one—could never be repaired. Each time Gamber did a death notification and stared into the stricken faces of the victim's loved ones, he knew they knew it was already over, the victim's killer, already in his box, lowered into the ground and shoveled over with dirt.

Finally, on March 31, 2010, after two long days of deliberation, the bailiff appeared in the entrance to the tiny conference room where Heather and her family paced.

"They have a verdict," he announced, and he may as well have used a megaphone. The words buzzed excitement and sent a shiver through Heather. She walked solemnly into the jam-packed courtroom with the other spectators. The press, their microphones, cameras, notebooks, court staff all crowded into the back. Gary's family—his mother, sister, and children—and several attorneys from other cases filled the seats. Even strangers dropped in to watch the spectacle. The prosecution and defense milled about in front, waiting expectantly for the conclusion.

Ron shuffled in and took his seat between his counsel. He watched intently as the jury filed in. They didn't look at him. No one knew how to interpret the distance: good or bad? Once the last juror was seated, the foreman passed a folded slip of paper to the bailiff, who handed it to the judge. The courtroom was like a giant breath waiting to be released. Judge Browning opened the paper, read the verdict silently, and motioned to his clerk. His face remained poker straight.

"All right, ladies and gentlemen, according to your foreman, you have reached a verdict."*

---

* Ron was also convicted of building and installing the seventeen-inch bomb.

The clerk stood and in a clear voice announced: "We the jury, duly impaneled and sworn in the above-entitled action, upon our oaths do find the defendant, on the charge of first-degree murder on November 1, 1996, as a result of the death of Gary Triano, *guilty*." The pronouncement vibrated through the courtroom. "Count two, conspiracy to commit murder . . . *guilty*."

Heather's knees buckled. She thought she might collapse, dissolve right into the seat. She struggled to breathe, couldn't talk, grabbed Detective Gamber's shoulders for support. Her mom paled, started to shake. The hopelessness that gave way to rage over the years manifested into an asthma attack. Gary's mother wept inconsolably, great heaving sobs that sounded as if she were choking. Ron's head fogged and the room buzzed around him. He heard nothing after *"Guilty."* Jurors' faces glazed over, forming one unified wall. They glowered at him. He floated above the scene, watched it from a safe perch in the ceiling fan. The judge set sentencing for another day, but as far as Ron was concerned, the punishment had already been determined. After court was adjourned, Ron whispered to his lawyer and was led away in handcuffs.

"We're going to appeal," his lawyer told the court. "This has been a double tragedy."

At his sentencing one month later, Ron showed no remorse. Juror No. 3, the panel's elected foreperson and the most outspoken of the group, sat quietly in the gallery. Ron could not anticipate the disturbance this juror's presence would cause or the motion for a new trial his lawyers would file weeks after his sentence, alleging that Juror No. 3 had a sordid criminal history and had lied on his questionnaire. Felons were not permitted to serve on jury duty. But Ron had small hope his conviction would be overturned. Motions for a new trial were often formalities, precursors to appeals. Criminal appeals could take months if not years.

And meanwhile Ron, now sixty-eight, would continue to age and weaken and rot.

Heather had not yet appeared for sentencing, and McCollum begged the court's indulgence; her "tardiness" was highly unusual, and he was certain she wanted to be heard. The judge nodded and turned to the remaining victims. Several advocates and civil lawyers flanked them on either side.

"Are you *all* going to speak?"

"Elliott needs representation: she's only twelve." The child's civil lawyer stepped up, prepared to give a speech on how Gary's murder had left Robin's daughter hollow. Robin Gardner could not attend, although she had mailed the judge her sentiments. Her child would grow up without a father; she would not be educated in the manner that Gary's children were accustomed to.

"My life, the life of my daughter, has been shattered by this man's brutality. We will have to live with his acts. Make *him* live the rest of his life guilty and guilt-racked with what he's done."

Gary's oldest son, Brian, shook at the podium. He had prepared a written speech but then at the last moment improvised. He echoed Elliott's lawyer's sentiments: the worst possible outcome had come to pass. Gary's other children, Elliott, Lois, and Trevor, now had no parents left. Their father brutally murdered; their mother indicted for his murder and facing a life sentence. Brian could not imagine a more ominous future. He spoke of Gary's love for his children: "He would have made a wonderful grandparent." Brian's own child had questions Brian could never answer. His father's death haunted him, left his entire family empty. His own life had been derailed as he worried for years whether Gary's killer would terrorize him. But what he found most appalling "was to learn that my father's murderer was someone I loved and trusted."

Brian's words rippled through the courtroom. The judge

listened as one by one the victims spoke passionately about the man who "stole their peace," and when Heather approached the podium he struggled to maintain his composure. Detective Gamber watched quietly from the back of the courtroom. Gary's death investigation marked the end of his law enforcement career. He had officially announced his retirement from the Pima County Sheriff's Department. But even as he absorbed Heather's heartfelt condemnation of the man who had given *her* a life sentence, Gamber knew he would forever remain her friend.

Browning turned to the lawyers. "Any legal cause why sentence should not now be imposed?" he asked. Palser pointed out misperceptions in the presentence report, phrases that might have been taken out of context. The exchange between probation officer and client, Palser advised, was meant to be "light," even "joking," and the court should not misconstrue that "any serious discussion was going on." Counsel's insight was not well-taken. The idea that any part of Gary's murder would invoke a humorous reaction from his killer sounded repulsive. Sentencing was delayed thirty days to present mitigation, letters of support for Ron, cracks in his past that warranted leniency. But no letters came. The judge instead received several condemnatory statements from the victim's family, asking that he impose the maximum sentence allowed under the law. The tone implied that Ron was somehow impelled by animal instincts and should spend the rest of his days caged.

Ron did not address the judge. The best his lawyer could do for mitigation was offer Ron's unremarkable life of drug experimentation. Ron drank at the age of thirteen, smoked marijuana habitually, snorted powder cocaine daily until the age of thirty, tried LSD and mushrooms at twenty-three, ingested Ecstasy at twenty-seven, and never sought drug treatment. He insisted he had no drug problem "until he ran out of coke." Perhaps his statement was another attempt at humor. His father—who might have been a cop—died when he was eighteen. Ron married, divorced, and had two children. He had become famous not for the life he lived but for the life he took.

Browning addressed Ron, staring into his flat dull eyes, and said that in all his years of experience he had never presided over a case whose killer was as "cold, calculated, and cruel" as Ron. He called Ron's unbridled greed "obscene," with consequences "beyond quantification."

"The court struggles to comprehend how a rational human being could choose to commit such a heinous crime." He then pronounced consecutive natural life sentences.

Ron's face flushed red, the only physical sign that he thought the terms unjust. He searched his counsels for reprieve, some mistake. Surely they could do something.

"Excuse me, sir," Palser said, clearing his throat. "I believe you just gave Mr. Young an illegal sentence. The statutory range is twenty-five to life."

"I'm not sure that it is." The judge glared at him, unwilling to concede error in a courtroom full of spectators.

"Just pointing out for you, not trying to argue." Palser recognized his awkward position. No lawyer publicly relished educating the judge in the law, but Palser, as any effective defense attorney understood, had an obligation to preserve all objections on the record for appellate purposes. While consecutive natural life sentences might have *sounded* harsh, practically the result was nonsensical. The judge was obligated to pronounce a range, twenty-five years stacked for a total of fifty, or thirty-five for a term of seventy years. Ultimately the legal interpretations seemed mere semantics for Ron who was already sixty-eight years old: even one day in prison meant a lifetime.

"I understand."

"Not trying to waste your time."

"Not wasting my time at all, sir. And not changing my mind," he said implacably, and with that, the judge slammed down his gavel and announced that court was adjourned.

Two consecutive life sentences might have communicated the resentment and rage Heather carried for Ron and the community's outcry for his senseless crime, but Heather knew there would be appeals and more delays, more restless sleep as she anticipated the higher courts' denials. And there would be another trial: her stepmother's. As she watched Ron shuffle out of the courtroom, she felt nothing but numbness. He had taken everything from her and yet he still breathed, still had a family he could call and badger. They could still visit him in prison. She could only visit her father's grave.

CHAPTER THIRTY:
CRAZY LIKE A FOX

Pam Phillips entered the United States from Austria in the custody of United States marshals. She served seven months in a Vienna jail before being heavily sedated and placed on a flight home to Tucson International Airport to face a murder indictment. Austrian authorities arrested her initially on money laundering charges out of the country of Liechtenstein, located between Switzerland and Austria. When Austrian police detained Pam, they learned from the International Criminal Police Organization, Interpol,* that she had a "red notice," similar to an international "wanted" poster seeking the provisional arrest of a fugitive.

After much negotiation and surrender, Austrian authorities arranged for her extradition. The marshals delivered Pam to the Pima County Jail, where she awaited her initial appearance. Broke and despondent, Pam shuffled into the crowded tank next to other inmates waiting to be arraigned. She wore black stripes, no makeup, and a haunted expression. In the wake of her $10 million civil judgment, Pam's assets had all been frozen. She had no money, no financial

---

* Interpol has no authority to compel a subject's arrest.

resources. Still, Judge Roger Duncan* deemed it appropriate that she pay $400 toward her legal representation. Pam addressed the judge via closed-circuit television; her attorney complained that it was "unfair" that she be seen in shackles like a common criminal.

"My client, Pam Young," defense counsel slipped. "Excuse me, Pam *Phillips* . . ." Pam narrowed her eyes, her dirty-blond hair knotted below her shoulders. At fifty-two, Gary's age when he died, she looked beaten down. She barely registered her counsel's arguments for reduced bond; $5 million was "outrageous," her attorney insisted.

"She's a flight risk," Heather countered, faithfully present with her entourage of family support. "Pam lived as a fugitive for two years in Lugano, Switzerland's version of Monte Carlo and it took months to extradite her from Europe."

"She pleads not guilty."

The judge affirmed the bond.

And Pam spent the next three weeks in solitary confinement, surrounded by the smell of wet stone and bright, penetrating lights. The walls absorbed the screams of other inmates, their wails resounding like wounded pups. She shuffled from corner to corner to pass the monotony and wrote to her former lover, Seppi, "They air me out for forty-five minutes a day. I'm shackled and cuffed." She counted the cracks in the floor, the number of steps to the fetid toilet. She thanked her "little public defender" for trying to help. She lost all sense of time. A terrifying loneliness gripped her. Occasionally, vents in the walls blew cold air over her skin and she shuddered. *It wasn't supposed to end like this.* Her mind played

† Defense counsel argued for a change of judge; prosecutor William McCollum insisted the case should stay with Judge Christopher Browning, who had heard Ron Young's trial. McCollum lost and the case was reassigned to Judge Charles Sabalos.

tricks on her and she imagined different coping scenarios. She had been placed in this cell "for observation" only; someone would rescue her soon. Panic clogged her throat. She tucked her thin blanket around her ankles and closed her eyes, willing her body to sleep.

The nightmare is in your head, she repeated over and over.

And just when she couldn't stand it any longer, her "little public defender" had her moved.

She shared a cell with eight women, taught them yoga and kabbalah, and studied the Bible "just to breathe." Her world was concrete, glass, and steel. She meditated, absorbed the writings of Edgar Cayce, and agitated over her "fading good looks." She complained about the substandard amenities, the jail's failure to provide makeup, cream, or hair color; there was no healthy food at all.

"It's very stressful. I'm getting fat." She wrote to Seppi as she fondly recalled Vienna's civilized jail, with its ready supply of "real silverware," organic food, and cosmetics. At least there she could purchase fruits and vegetables, unlike the "junk" available in the Pima County Jail.

"Here they just want you to look as bad as possible," she lamented to Seppi. Her letters to Seppi had a familiar theme: bad food, bad conditions, bad hair.

She never spoke of her children except to ask Seppi, "Do you think my son knows I gave him Potrero?"

Do you think he knows I gave him the only asset I had left?

For her next court appearance, Pam appeared in an orange jumpsuit, flanked on either side by her public defender, Peter Herberg, and his investigator, whose long silver ponytail, chiseled features, and deep tan gave him the flare of a romance hero. Pam laughed easily with him, seemed to enjoy his hands caressing her back. She looked relaxed and comfortable and fat.

Meanwhile, Herberg, wound like a spring, insisted that Pam shouldn't be locked up. It would be prejudicial for cameras to film her wearing jail garb.

"But she's in jail," Judge Charles Sabalos quipped.

"She should be allowed to wear street clothes for pre-trial hearings."

"No."

"There's a very real possibility she didn't do this," her lawyer insisted.

"Give me specifics." Judge Sabalos rubbed his temples, lowering his head as if to stave off a migraine.

"Gary's murder may in fact have been mob inspired."

Prosecutor William McCollum released an exaggerated sigh.

"*Which* mob? Italian, Greek, Russian, Irish, Mexican, Jewish, or Chinese?" the judge condescended, catching defense counsel off guard.

The attorney straightened his suit jacket and said, "Well, that's just it: there were over a thousand suspects investigated and 'cleared,' but possibly LCN, La Cosa Nostra."

"I know who LCN is."

"Even Sheriff Dupnik advised police that this had all the appearances of a professional hit. The state produced a thirteen-page list of suspects, one thousand names over fourteen years. We're requesting discovery on those people."

The prosecutor looked incredulous. The tips of his ears reddened. He stood and shook his head emphatically. "We have no authority to tell the DEA or their counsel in Chicago to participate in interviews or disclose documents of potential suspects. I've had multiple conversations with the U.S. Attorney's Office and they won't produce anything."

"Have you asked?" Herberg arched a brow at him.

"You want me to ask them for names of people in the parking lot, average Jameses and Joes?"

"And Janes."

The prosecutor bristled. "I'm not submitting names of golf players to the United States Department of Justice to investigate."

"Your Honor, we've been advised that any specialized units targeting the Mafia have 'expunged,' 'destroyed,' or 'will not provide' any evidence." Herberg threw up his hands.

"I can't ask them," McCollum said.

"You Honor, if the prosecutor relied on the feds for so many aspects of this case and now counsel says he can't or won't ask the feds for information or jurisdiction doesn't extend, then he has a problem. The FBI, U.S. Marshals, ATF, DEA, *were* all involved in prosecuting and investigating this case. Now counsel insists he can't get their cooperation?"

The question hung in the air for several seconds until Herberg offered a reasonable solution. "One option is to dismiss the case."

The judge smothered a smile. "Did the feds ever prosecute? I mean, *whose* case is this?"

McCollum blurted out, "It's Pima County's. The feds never gave us a commitment."

"Judge, they won't give us any names."

"This is disclosure harassment." McCollum put his hands on his hips. "Counsel has ordered us to investigate the court clerk, for goodness sakes. Maybe we should investigate *counsel's* investigator!"

"I'm not picking names out of a hat." Herberg shrugged.

The judge did not intervene. He seemed to enjoy the verbal Ping-Pong.

Then Herberg smiled. "The prosecutor admitted that his office pays dues to the ECIU, a private intelligence organization, a 'gathering network.' Its 'red squads' monitor social activities using illegal methods."

McCollum looked flustered and then sputtered, "Objection."

"What's the objection?" Sabalos laughed.

"Your Honor," Herberg continued, "this organization allegedly requires secrecy and oath and uses black-bag tactics, illegal wiretaps, two police agencies have already been removed for breaching rules. The ECIU is outside the scope of FOIA [the Freedom of Information Act] because it's a 'private' entity. We're not going on a fishing expedition here. From 1996 to 2005, this was a *federal* investigation. They were following bankruptcy fraud, real estate fraud, and drug smuggling. Gary was a suspect under investigation by the DEA and FBI way before his death."

McCollum stood. He had had enough of the charade.

"Counsel has given us a potpourri of possible defenses. He's just throwing ideas at the wall. What does he *want*?"

"We're asking for names . . . and, while we're at it, a competency hearing."

The prosecutor's face flushed. He looked ready to explode. Rule 11, the provision in Arizona that governed competency proceedings, could only be considered if probable cause existed to believe that a defendant could not assist his or her lawyer, suffered hallucinations or auditory feedback or possibly had previous diagnoses of mental illness. It was risky for any judge to discount "crazy"; if he was wrong and the defendant really did have problems, the case would be reversed on post-conviction or appeal.

Herberg argued that Pam arrived from the Austrian authorities "heavily medicated" and remained in a mental health ward until her arraignment.

McCollum seethed and held up a binder containing more than eleven thousand e-mails written between Pam and Ron that "proved she wasn't crazy." And, as if that demonstration weren't enough, he powered on his computer and soon the courtroom echoed with Pam's voice:

"The food at the county is just terrible. I must eat 3700 to 4000 calories a day. I haven't received my boxes. My house in Meadowood was foreclosed, no representation, no notice. How can they do that?"

"I object to this." Herberg reached across the table to shut off the computer. "I *object*."

"Clearly that's not the sound of a crazy woman." McCollum slapped counsel's hand away.

"Your Honor, the prosecutor is pretending to be a doctor," Herberg said, insinuating that McCollum believed he was somehow qualified to diagnose mental illness.

"Well, he *does* have a juris doctorate," the judge said, tongue in cheek.

"She's conveniently acquired a mental illness," McCollum said, unable to mask the sarcasm in his voice.

"There's documentation . . ."

"By all means, let's see it. If it's 'in limbo' at the Austrian jail . . . the defense has noticed insanity. They have three days to produce this stuff."

"We've offered every defense known to the legal system," Pam's lawyer replied.

"So she's *not* insane?" The judge arched a brow at him and suppressed a smile.

"Five of us have observed thought processes that appear to be delusional, indicative of problems with reasoning, understanding reality. The opinion of counsel should have some value."

"I always give the opinions of counsel value," the judge quipped. "But I do need specifics."

"When she arrived from Austria, she was so medicated she couldn't speak. The medications were similar to those prescribed for mental health issues. They expressed concerns to the jail. The Austrian authorities gave her a diagnosis, but it's in German. We need to get it translated," Pam's lawyer offered.

"Can't you guess what it might be?" The judge ran his fingers through his hair.

"It's been years since my high school German." Palser said, adding "Contents taken from her purse indicate mental health concerns."

"I'm going to order a preliminary screening," the judge said.

Pam smiled slightly, the skin around her eyes cutting grooves into her face. The expression telegraphed her arrogance; even if she was "lucky" enough to escape prison, life in a mental ward exposed to drafty rooms, wails, and hours enveloped between white walls, that was hardly the consolation prize Pam expected. But the practical result of her "little public defender's" plea did not concern her yet . . . she *could* be crazy. She could be anything her lawyer wanted her to be, as long as he ensured she would not serve one day in prison.

But her reprieve from prosecution was brief. On March 8, 2011, just three months after her lawyers insisted she had severe mental health issues that precluded her ability to assist in her defense, the judge deemed her competent to stand trial and scheduled the case to begin in January 2012. Her lawyers had less than a year to prepare her defense . . . and to convince a jury that Pam had nothing to do with her ex-husband's bombing—that she was just a convenient scapegoat.

If her attorneys failed, Pam planned to appeal. Typically, the process dragged on for months if not years; she would join the many convicted murderers who complained about mistakes made during their trials, errors in the court's rulings, attorney misconduct. And if she was unsuccessful at the appellate level, she planned to pursue post-conviction relief, accuse her public defenders of ineffective assistance of counsel, allege newly discovered evidence—and if there weren't any, she'd find some. She would search for some shred of redemption. She could not—would not—spend the rest of her days labeled a *murderer*. That, after all, would be a sentence worse than death.

ACKNOWLEDGMENTS

As with any massive project, there are multiple people to thank. I could not have written this book without the important contributions of the Pima County Sheriff's Department, specifically Sean Holguin, Kathleen Gale, and the delightful staff who assisted me in processing my myriad requests for documents, transcripts, and recordings. Your professionalism and grace were impressive and rare. A special thank you to former detective James Gamber, whose tireless investigation, wonderful sense of humor, and patience with my questions helped me enormously in putting together this book and adding to the details and impressions. I hope I have paid him sufficient tribute and that *this* honor will not share the same fate as the award he received from his own department.

Thank you to photographer extraordinaire David Bean for your stories and insights and of course your wonderful photographs! Thank you to reporter Lupita Murillo of KVOA/News 4 in Tucson. I will treasure your hospitality (and wonderful homemade quiche!) and appreciate the tour of your station. A special nod goes to Rayner Ramirez of *Dateline NBC* for your valuable contacts! Thank you to the Pima County Attorney's Office, to the Pima County Superior Court and Court of Appeals, and to those individuals (who shall remain anonymous) for your assistance and opinions in reconstructing many of the hearings in this book.

Thank you to my faithful critique partners, Carol Webb, Kim Watters, Linda Andrews, and Starr Cochran for your support, kind words (being steeped in the world of sociopaths was not easy), and encouragement. Gary's family members and friends had several opportunities to interview with me but chose to rely instead on their earlier statements to police. I respect their positions and hope this book allows others to know their grief, to know they are not alone, to know that people do care.

Thank you to my husband, homicide detective Sergei Droban, whose patience and gentle correction with all things technical—shotguns, bullets, bombs—was surely appreciated. Thank you to my mother, Elizabeth Ticknor, who was kind enough to trudge through several drafts and offer constructive criticism. My agent, Jill Marsal of the Marsal Lyon Literary Agency, has been one of my strongest advocates, my first reader, and my compass. Lastly, a heartfelt thank you to my editor, Rob Kirkpatrick, who has guided me on many a journey and has never steered me wrong.